Affirmative Action Around the World
An Empirical Study

Affirmative Action Around the World

An Empirical Study

THOMAS SOWELL

YALE UNIVERSITY PRESS   NEW HAVEN & LONDON

Designed by James J. Johnson and
set in Baskerville type by Keystone Typesetting, Inc.
Printed in the United States of America by R. R. Donnelley & Sons.

Library of Congress Cataloging-in-Publication Data

Sowell, Thomas, 1930–

Affirmative action around the world : an empirical study / Thomas Sowell.

p. cm.

Includes bibliographical references and index.

ISBN 0-300-10199-6 (cloth : alk. paper)

1. Affirmative action programs — Cross-cultural studies. 2. Discrimination
in employment — Cross-cultural studies. 3. Discrimination in
education — Cross-cultural studies. I. Title.

HF5549.5.A34S685 2003
331.13′3 — dc21   2004
2003014024

A catalogue record for this book is available from the British Library.

The paper in this book meets the guidelines for permanence and durability
of the Committee on Production Guidelines for Book Longevity
of the Council on Library Resources.

10 9 8 7 6 5 4 3

Facts are stubborn things, and whatever may be our wishes,

our inclinations, or the dictates of our passions,

they cannot alter the state of facts and evidence.

—JOHN ADAMS

Contents

Preface

Many — if not most — people who are for or against affirmative action are for or against the *theory* of affirmative action. The factual question of what actually happens as a result of affirmative action policies receives remarkably little attention. Assumptions, beliefs and rationales dominate controversies on this issue in countries around the world. This book addresses the empirical question of just what does and does not happen under affirmative action — and to whose benefit and whose detriment.

Even an observer highly sympathetic to affirmative action in Malaysia noted in passing, "new policies were often put forth without considering what the success or failure of past policies boded for their own prospects."[1] This was not unique to Malaysia. It has been the rule, rather than the exception, in many countries with affirmative action policies, as well as with other policies. The purpose of this book is to consider the actual consequences of affirmative action.

The experience of more than 30 years of researching and analyzing affirmative action policies in the United States has gone into this book. A considerable part of that period has also included the study of similar policies in other countries. An international perspective on group preferences and quotas enables us to examine the arguments on both sides of this issue with a much larger and more varied sample of evidence.

There are few policies more in need of evidence with which to weigh the heated assertions and counter-assertions of advocates and critics. Merely cutting through the jungle of semantics which surrounds controversies over preferential policies in many countries is a formidable challenge. If this book can contribute to clarity on that issue alone, it will have achieved one of its main goals.

In the course of gathering material for the study of affirmative action policies, under the many different names that these policies have in different countries, I have incurred many debts to scholars, officials, librarians and others in many lands—too many people to mention here by name. But I am grateful to them all. My greatest debt, however, is to the Hoover Institution at Stanford University, which paid for lengthy and costly international trips to gather the information presented here. As with my other writings over the past 15 years, my research assistant Na Liu has contributed not only dedicated efforts but also many insights.

THOMAS SOWELL
The Hoover Institution
Stanford University

Affirmative Action Around the World
An Empirical Study

CHAPTER 1

———————◆•◆———————

An International Perspective

W hile controversies rage over "affirmative action" policies in the United States, few Americans seem to no-
tice the existence or relevance of similar policies in
other countries around the world. Instead, the arguments pro
and con both tend to invoke history and traditions that are
distinctively American. Yet group preferences and quotas have
existed in other countries with wholly different histories and
traditions — and, in some countries, such policies have existed
much longer than in the United States.

What can the experiences of these other countries tell us?
Are there common patterns, common rationales, common results? Or is the American situation unique?

Ironically, a claim or assumption of national uniqueness is
one of the most common patterns found in numerous countries where group preferences and quotas have existed under a
variety of names. The special situation of the Maoris in New
Zealand, based on the 1840 treaty of Waitangi, is invoked as
passionately in defense of preferential treatment there as the
unique position of untouchables in India or of blacks in the
United States.

Highly disparate rationales have been used in different societies for programs which share very similar features and often

lead to very similar results. Some group preferences have existed for minorities, some for majorities, some for the less fortunate and some for the more fortunate who feel entitled to maintain their existing advantages over other members of the same society. Today, it is programs for the less fortunate which are called affirmative action in the United States or by such other names as "positive discrimination" in Britain and in India, "standardization" in Sri Lanka, "reflecting the federal character of the country" in Nigeria, and "sons of the soil" preferences in Malaysia and Indonesia, as well as in some states in India. Group preferences and quotas have also existed in Israel, China, Australia, Brazil, Fiji, Canada, Pakistan, New Zealand and the Soviet Union and its successor states.[1]

Despite how widespread affirmative action programs have become, even the promoters of such programs have seldom been bold enough to proclaim preferences and quotas to be desirable on principle or as permanent features of society. On the contrary, considerable effort has been made to depict such policies as "temporary," even when in fact these preferences turn out not only to persist but to grow.

Official affirmative action or group preference policies must be distinguished from whatever purely subjective preferences or prejudices may exist among individuals and groups. These subjective feelings may of course influence policies, but the primary focus here is on concrete government policies and their empirical consequences — not on their rationales, hopes, or promises, though these latter considerations will not be wholly ignored. Fundamentally, however, this is a study of what actually happens, rather than a philosophical exploration of issues that have been amply — if not more than amply — explored elsewhere.

LIMITED AND TRANSIENT PREFERENCES

The resurgence of group preferences in societies committed to the equality of individuals before the law has been accompanied by claims not only that these preferences would be temorary, but also that they would be limited, rather than pervasive. That is, these programs would supposedly be limited not only in time but also in scope, with equal treatment policies prevailing outside the limited domain where members of particular groups would be given special help.

In India, for example, a government minister urging lower university admissions standards for untouchables and members of disadvantaged tribes included the proviso that he was recommending "relaxation for admissions and not for passing or grading."[2] Just as he was for limiting the scope of preferential treatment, so others were for limiting its duration. As an advocate of reserving certain numbers of jobs for members of specified groups in India said: "Even the staunchest supporters of reservation acceded that it is a transitory provision."[3] It was the leaders of the untouchables themselves who proposed a ten-year cutoff for reservations, in order to forestall political opposition and social conflict.[4] That was in 1949 — and the reservations are still in place today.

Similar reasoning was applied in the United States to both employment and admissions to colleges and universities. Initially, it was proposed that there would be special "outreach" efforts to contact minority individuals with information and encouragement to apply for jobs or college admissions in places where they might not have felt welcome before, but with the proviso that they would not be given special preferences throughout the whole subsequent processes of acceptance and advancement. Much the same rationale appeared in Malaysia — and so did the further extension of preferential treatment which developed despite this rationale:

Although grading is supposed to be without reference to ethnicity, all grades must be submitted to an evaluation review committee having heavy Malay representation. Individual faculty members report various instances when grades were unilaterally raised, apparently for purposes of "ethnic balance."[5]

Similar policies and results have also been achieved in less blatant ways. During the era of the Soviet Union, professors were pressured to give preferential grading to Central Asian students[6] and what has been called "affirmative grading" has also occurred in the United States, in order to prevent excessive failure rates among minority students admitted under lower academic standards.[7] In India, such practices have been referred to as "grace marks."[8] Similar results can be achieved indirectly by providing ethnic studies courses that give easy grades and attract disproportionately the members of one ethnic group. This too is not peculiar to the United States. There are Maori studies programs in New Zealand and special studies for Malays in Singapore.

In the job market as well, the belief that special concerns for particular groups could be confined to an initial stage proved untenable in practice. Initially, the term "affirmative action" arose in the United States from an executive order by President John F. Kennedy, who called for "affirmative action to ensure that the applicants are employed, and that employees are treated during employment without regard to race, color, creed, or national origin."[9] In short, there were to be no preferences or quotas at all, just a special concern to make sure that those who had been discriminated against in the past would no longer be discriminated against in the future — and that concrete steps should be taken so that all and sundry would be made aware of this.

However, just as academic preferences initially limited in scope continued to expand, so did the concept of affirmative action in the job market. A later executive order by President

Lyndon Johnson in 1968 contained the fateful expressions "goals and timetables" and "representation." These were not yet full-blown quotas, for the 1968 guidelines referred to "goals and timetables for the prompt achievement of full and equal employment opportunity." Still later, another executive order in 1970, by President Richard Nixon, spoke of "results-oriented procedures" and, finally, in December 1971, yet another Nixon executive order specified that "goals and timetables" were meant to "increase materially the utilization of minorities and women," with "underutilization" being spelled out as "having fewer minorities or women in a particular job classification than would reasonably be expected by their availability." Affirmative action was now a numerical concept, whether called "goals" or "quotas."

In a very different society and governmental system halfway around the world — in Pakistan — attempts to confine affirmative action policies within their initial limits proved equally futile. Here preferential policies began in 1949 as an explicitly "temporary" measure, to be phased out in five to ten years.[10] The principal beneficiaries were to be the very poor Bengalis of East Pakistan who were "under-represented" in business, the professions and the military, while even the administration of East Pakistan was largely in the hands of West Pakistanis.[11] However, the preferential policies continued decades past the initially specified cut-off time by repeated extensions.[12] Even after East Pakistan seceded to become the independent nation of Bangladesh in 1971, the preferential policies in Pakistan had sufficient other political constituencies to continue on after their principal initial intended beneficiaries were gone.

Britain's Lord Scarman expressed a view widely held by those initiating affirmative action in many countries when he said:

> We can and for the present must accept the loading of the law in favour of one group at the expense of others, defending it as

a temporary expedient in the balancing process which has to be undertaken when and where there is social and economic inequality.[13]

This confident pronouncement, however, presupposed a degree of control which has proved illusory in country after country. Moreover, "when and where there is economic inequality" encompasses virtually the entire world and virtually the entire history of the human race. A "temporary" program to eliminate a centuries-old condition is almost a contradiction in terms. Equality of opportunity might be achieved within some feasible span of time, but that is wholly different from eliminating inequalities of results.

Even an approximate equality of "representation" of different groups in different occupations, institutions or income levels has been a very rare — or non-existent — phenomenon, except where such numerical results have been imposed artificially by quotas. As a massive scholarly study of ethnic groups around the world put it, when discussing "proportional representation" of ethnic groups, "few, if any societies have ever approximated this description."[14] Another international study of multi-ethnic societies referred to "the universality of ethnic inequality" and pointed out that these inequalities are multi-dimensional:

> All multi-ethnic societies exhibit a tendency for ethnic groups to engage in different occupations, have different levels (and, often, types) of education, receive different incomes, and occupy a different place in the social hierarchy."[15]

A worldwide study of military forces likewise concluded that "militaries fall far short of mirroring, even roughly, the multi-ethnic societies" from which they come.[16] At one time, nearly half the pilots in the Malaysian air force came from the Chinese minority.[17] In Czarist Russia, 40 percent of the army's high command came from the German ethnic minority that was only 1 percent of the country's population.[18] Similar gross disparities in ethnic representation in occupations, industries and institutions can be found in country after country around the world and in century after century.[19] Often those overrepresented in high-level occupations have been minorities with no power to exclude others, but simply possessing particular skills. Germans, for example, have predominated among those who created the leading beer companies in the United States, as they created China's famous Tsingtao beer and established breweries in Argentina, Australia, Brazil and other countries. Similarly, Jews have predominated in the manufacturing of clothing in medieval Spain, the Ottoman Empire, Argentina, the United States, and other countries.

In short, the even representation of groups that is taken as a norm is difficult or impossible to find anywhere, while the uneven representation that is regarded as a special deviation to be corrected is pervasive across the most disparate societies. People differ — and have for centuries. It is hard to imagine how they could not differ, given the enormous range of differing historical, cultural, geographic, demographic and other factors shaping the particular skills, habits, and attitudes of different groups. Any "temporary" policy whose duration is defined by the goal of achieving something that has never been achieved before, anywhere in the world, could more fittingly be characterized as eternal.

PREFERRED AND NON-PREFERRED GROUPS

Just as we cannot presuppose continuing control over the scope and duration of preferential policies, so we cannot simply assume what will actually happen to those designated as the preferred group or groups. Neither they nor the non-preferred groups are inert blocks of wood to be moved here and there according to someone else's grand design. Both confront laws and policies as incentives and constraints, not as predestination, and react in their own ways. These reactions include redesignating themselves, altering their own efforts and attitudes toward achievement, and altering their attitudes toward members of other groups.

Designation and Redesignation

One of the reactions of members of non-preferred groups has been to get themselves redesignated as members of the preferred group. This can be done either individually or collectively.

Some individuals of mixed ancestry who have been regarded and self-identified as members of group *A* may choose to redesignate themselves as members of group *B*, when group *B* is entitled to preferential treatment and members of group *A* are not. In the United States, during the Jim Crow era, some light-skinnd blacks simply "passed" as white, in order to escape the legal and social disadvantages that went with being designated black. Later, during the era of affirmative action, whites with traces of American Indian or other minority ancestry likewise redesignated themselves, in order to take advantage of preferential policies for disadvantaged groups. These have included blond-haired and blue-eyed individuals with official papers showing some distant ancestor of another race.

The number of individuals identifying themselves as American Indians in the U.S. Census during the affirmative action era rose at a rate exceeding anyone's estimates of the biological growth of this population. Moreover, a breakdown of Census data by age cohort shows that the number of American Indians increased over time *in the same age cohort*—a biological impossibility made possible on paper by redesignations of the same individuals. For example, the number of American Indians who were aged 15–19 in 1960 was just under 50,000. But, twenty years later, when these same individuals would be in the age bracket 35–39 years old, there were more than 80,000

American Indians in that cohort.[20] In other words, more than 30,000 people in the same cohort who had not designated themselves as American Indians in 1960 now did so in 1980, causing more than a 60 percent increase in the number of American Indians in that cohort.

A similar pattern emerged among the aborigines in Australia. A study in that country found that there was "a 42 percent increase in the size of the Aboriginal population between the 1981 and the 1986 censuses"[21] — virtually a demographic impossibility in five years, except by redesignation of the same individuals with different ethnic labels. As an Australian scholar has noted:

> The dramatic increase in numbers has much to do with record keeping, increasing intermarriage and the growing availability of substantial subsidies to people of Aboriginal descent. . . . The definition of 'Aboriginal' includes many persons of predominantly non-Aboriginal descent, who might with equal or greater genetic justification designate themselves as non-Aborigines.[22]

It was much the same story in China, where, in the 1990s, more than 10 million Chinese proclaimed their ethnic minority status, in order to gain preferential treatment, such as college admissions. Even China's draconian restrictions on having more than one child did not apply to ethnic minorities as they did to the majority Han Chinese:

> Article 44 states that, "in accordance with legal stipulations," autonomous areas can work out their own family planning measures. As a result, urban minority couples generally may have two children, while urban Han are restricted to one. Rural minorities may have two, three, four or even more children, depending on their ethnicity and location.[23]

An official of China's State Nationality Affairs Committee commented: "Some people would try all means to change their nationality because they wanted to make themselves eligible to enter a university with lower scores or to stand a better chance than their colleagues when it comes to promotion." As in other countries, people with mixed ancestry had the option of choosing how to designate themselves. Some "traced their ancestry back hundreds of years to prove minority blood" and claim the benefits.[24]

Another individual response to preferential policies has been to use someone genuinely of the qualifying ancestry as a "front" for businesses seeking preferential treatment in the awarding of government contracts or other desired benefits. This practice has been so widespread in both Indonesia and Malaysia that it has acquired a name — "Ali-Baba enterprises," where Ali is the indigenous individual who ostensibly owns the business and is legally entitled to government benefits, while Baba is the non-indigenous person (usually Chinese in these countries) who actually controls the enterprise and essentially pays Ali for the use of his name and ancestry.[25] Similar arrangements have been uncovered in the United States and elsewhere. Anti-Semitic policies in Poland during the years between the two World Wars likewise led some Jewish businesses there to operate behind Gentile front men.[26] Decades later, under preferential policies in Kenya, Africans served as fronts for Asian-owned businesses, as they likewise served as fronts for Lebanese-owned businesses in Sierra Leone.[27]

Members of some non-preferred groups can also get themselves redesignated collectively. The Fourteenth Amendment to India's Constitution, like the Fourteenth Amendment to the Constitution of the United States, provides for equal treatment of individuals but India's Constitution provides explicit exceptions for benefits to the untouchables, disadvantaged tribal groups outside the Hindu caste system and "other backward classes." This last proviso, especially, has created opportunities for many other groups to get themselves collectively designated as being among the "other backward classes." Eventually, this miscellaneous classification provided more individuals with the coveted rights to preferential treatment than were provided to the members of the untouchable and tribal groups for whom the preferences were created. In 1997, organized efforts were also begun to seek preferential treatment for India's 15 million eunuchs,[28] though obviously they were not the descendants of other eunuchs, and so could not inherit historic group disadvantages.

Redesignations of individuals and groups, like the spread of preferences from given groups to other groups, take preferential policies further and further away from the initial rationales on which they were based. No historic sufferings of blacks in the United States can justify preferential benefits to white women or to recently arrived immigrants from Asia or Latin America who happen to be non-white, but whose ancestors obviously never suffered any discrimination in the United States. Similarly, the painful history and continuing oppression of untouchables in India can hardly justify preferential benefits to local majorities in particular states, such as Assam, Maharashtra, and Andhra Pradesh. Yet these local majorities and members of "other backward classes" outnumber the untouchables and are often in a better position to take advantage of the preferences. Thus quotas for government jobs or university admissions have often remained unfilled by untouchables, while this has seldom been the case for members of the "other backward classes."[29]

The spread of benefits from group to group not only dilutes those benefits — especially when more than half the population of the country becomes entitled to them, as in both India and the United States — it can also make the initial beneficiaries worse off after the terms of the competition are altered. For example, in the United States, where hiring and promotions decisions are subject to review by government agencies investigating discrimination, objective criteria may be used increasingly by employers for legal self-protection, even if the relevance of these criteria to the job is questionable. If these criteria are met more often by one of the preferred groups than by another — if white women have college degrees more often than black men, for example — then one preferred group may be no better off, on net balance, than if the preferences did not exist. It is conceivable that they can be worse off.

Such a situation is not peculiar to the United States. An official report in India in 1980 noted that the advancement of one preferred group tended to "push back" another, creating "greater tension between structural neighbors in this hierarchy than between the top level and the bottom level." That continued to be so in the 1990s, with violent clashes in several Indian states being found to be more common among competing poorer groups than between these groups and the more elite castes.[30] In 2001, a rally was held in the state of Rajasthan, protesting the inclusion of new groups among the backward classes and demanding "separate fixed quotas for original backwards" so that "new entrants" would not be able to reduce the existing benefits enjoyed by those for whom the preferences were created.[31] Calls have been made for a "quota within quota" to deal with such situations.[32]

Insofar as affirmative action policies are aimed particularly at offsetting existing economic disadvantages, their rationale is undermined when the benefits of these policies go disproportionately to those individuals within the designated groups who are the least disadvantaged — or perhaps are in more favorable positions than members of the country's general population.

In India's state of Tamil Nadu, for example, the highest of the so-called "backward classes" legally entitled to preferences, constituting 11 percent of the total "backward classes" population in that state, received almost half of all jobs and university admissions set aside for these classes.[33] In Malaysia, where there are preferences for the indigenous "sons of the soil" majority, Malay students whose families were in the top 17 percent of the income distribution received just over half of all scholarships awarded to Malays.[34] In Sri Lanka, preferential university admissions for people from backward regions of the country appear likewise to have benefited primarily students from affluent families in those regions.[35]

This should hardly be surprising, nor is it necessarily a matter of corruption. Preferential access to education or jobs is just one factor in getting the education or the job. Obviously, those people who have more of the other factors required are better able to turn preferential access into actual success. Pre-existing prosperity provides more of those other factors.

Those American minority business owners who participate in the preferential program called business "set-asides" under Section 8(a) of the Small Business Act average a personal net worth that is not only higher than the average net worth of the groups they come from, but also higher than the average personal net worth of Americans in general.[36] A scholarly study of group preferences in India pointed out that preferences that benefit more fortunate members of less fortunate groups "borrow legitimacy from the national commitment to ameliorate the condition of the lowest," while at the same time "they undermine that commitment by broadcasting a picture of unrestrained preference for those who are not distinctly worse off than non-beneficiaries."[37]

Just as specifying the scope and duration of affirmative action policies has proven illusory, so has the designation of the beneficiaries in accordance with the rationales of these policies. Both attempts suffer from assuming far more comprehensive knowledge and control than anyone has been able to exercise, in any of the countries in which preferential programs have been instituted. What has also been over-estimated is the extent to which the attitudes resulting from such programs can be assumed to be beneficial to the groups concerned or to the country at large. These attitudes tend to respond to incentives, rather than to rationales.

Incentives

Both preferred and non-preferred groups have modified their own behavior and attitudes in response to preferential policies and the rationales for such policies. While members of the officially preferred groups who already have the complementary factors needed to take the fullest advantage of preferences can do so, those who lack these factors often feel less incentive to acquire them, now that entitlements are available as substitutes for achievements. The development of job skills, for example, may be de-emphasized. As a leader in a campaign for preferential policies in India's state of Hyderabad put it: "Are we not entitled to jobs just because we are not as qualified?"[38] A Nigerian likewise wrote of "the tyranny of skills."[39] In Malaysia, where group preferences exist for the majority population, "Malay students, who sense that their future is assured, feel less pressure to perform."[40] In the United States, a study of black colleges found that even those of their students who were planning to continue on to postgraduate study showed little concern about needing to be prepared "because they believe that certain rules would simply be set aside for them."[41]

Both preferred and non-preferred groups can slacken their efforts — the former because working to their fullest capacity is unnecessary and the latter because working to their fullest capacity can prove to be futile. After Jamaica gained its independence from British rule, many whites living there no longer bothered to compete for public office because they "felt that the day of the black man had come and questioned why they had to make the effort if the coveted job or the national honor would go to the blacks, despite their qualifications."[42] While affirmative action policies are often thought of, by advocates and critics alike, as a transfer of benefits from one group to another, there can also be net losses of benefits when both groups do less than their best. What might otherwise be a zero-sum game can thus become a negative-sum game.

In some countries, complete physical withdrawal from the country by those in non-preferred groups has occurred in the wake of preferential policies which reduced their prospects. The exodus of Chinese from Malaysia, Indians from Fiji, Russians from Central Asia, Jews from much of prewar Europe, and Huguenots from 17th century France in response to discrimination drained all these countries of much-needed skills and talents. In short, preferential policies represent not simply a transfer of benefits from one group to another, but can also represent a net loss, as both groups respond by contributing less than they could to the society as a whole.

Not all incentives are economic or even tangible. Honors are among the most powerful of incentives in many situations, especially where dangers and death must be faced, and where money is less effective than a sense of honor, as in the military. In less dire circumstances as well, honor and the respect of peers play important roles, not only as rewards for achievements, but also as factors helping to make individual achievements possible in the first place.

The cooperation and collaboration of colleagues can be important in a variety of occupations from scholars to policemen — and that cooperation and collaboration can be compromised by group preferences. For example, minority professors on American campuses have complained that being thought of as "affirmative action" professors by their colleagues has led to less intellectual and research interaction, which in turn reduces the minority faculty's development as scholars.[43] This can be a serious handicap in achieving one's potential. In life and death situations, such as those faced by the police, firefighters, and soldiers, mutual confidence is even more important. Yet black police sergeants promoted in Chicago over white policemen with higher test scores — as a result of a court order — found themselves taunted as "quota sergeants" when they made mistakes.[44]

Intergroup Relations

Even aside from losses to the economy as a whole, because of disincentives created for both preferred and non-preferred groups, there are social losses due to intergroup resentments, which can be even more serious. Nor are these resentments due simply to the transfers of benefits.

When a serious political backlash against affirmative action began in the United States, many in the media were quick to characterize it dismissively as due to "angry white males," resentful of the losses of various benefits to blacks and other minorities — in other words, just an emotional reaction by people irked at losing a few of their many advantages. But this resentment was by no means proportional to intergroup transfers of benefits or it would have been far greater against Asian Americans, who displaced more whites in prestigious universities and in many high-level professions, especially in science and technology. At many of the leading universities in the United States, whites "lost" more places to Asian Americans than to blacks, and yet there was seldom any backlash against Asian Americans. The outstanding academic and other achievements of Asian Americans were widely recognized and widely respected. It was not the intergroup transfer of benefits that was resented, but the basis for those transfers.

Among Americans especially, the idea that some are to be treated as "more equal than others" is galling. It was this feeling in the general population which leaders of the civil rights movement of the 1960s were able to mobilize behind their efforts to destroy the Jim Crow laws of the South, so that a majority of the members in both houses of Congress from both political parties voted for the landmark Civil Rights Act of 1964 and the Voting Rights Act of 1965. It was this same American resentment of special privilege which responded so strongly to the historic words of the Reverend Martin Luther King, Jr., at the Lincoln Memorial in 1963, that his dream was of a country where people would be judged "not by the color of their skin, but by the content of their character."

It was after the civil rights movement itself began to move away from this concept of equal treatment of all individuals and toward the concept of equalized outcomes for groups, that a backlash against affirmative action set in and grew over the years.

There is yet another sense in which resentments against preferences for other groups are not proportional to the benefits transferred. An observer of preferential policies in India noted the disproportionate resentment of places reserved for "scheduled castes," the official euphemism for untouchables:

> . . . we hear innumerable tales of persons being deprived of appointments in favour of people who ranked lower than they did in the relevant examinations. No doubt this does happen, but if all these people were, in fact, paying the price for appointments to Scheduled Castes, there would be many more SC persons appointed than there actually are. To illustrate: supposing that 300 people qualify for ten posts available. The top nine are appointed on merit but the tenth is reserved, so that the authorities go down the list to find an SC applicant. They find one at 140 and he is appointed. Whereupon all 131 between him and the merit list feel aggrieved. He has not taken 131 posts; he has taken one, yet 131 people believe they have paid the price for it. Moreover, the remaining 159 often also resent the situation, believing that their chances were, somehow, lessened by the existence of SC reservations.[45]

In the United States as well, those who resent group preferences may be some multiple of those who have in fact actually lost anything that they would have had in the absence of these preferences. In the 1978 landmark Supreme Court challenge to affirmative action brought by Alan Bakke, a white student denied admission to a University of California medical school, neither side to the dispute could state with confidence that

Bakke would or would not have been admitted in the absence of the affirmative action policies which admitted minority students with lower academic qualifications than his. The admissions process was sufficiently complicated that it was not clear whether some other white or Asian-American student might have been admitted instead of Bakke.

In other words, it was not certain that Bakke had in fact lost anything as a result of affirmative action, and yet his sense of being wronged was sufficient for him to pursue the case all the way up to the highest court in the land. One of the things that prevents affirmative action from being a zero-sum process is that minor transfers of benefits can cause major resentments among far more people than those who have actually lost anything. Moreover, these resentments do not end with political or legal actions.

In India, where preferential policies have a longer history than in the United States, they have also had more bitter consequences. Forty-two people died in riots over places reserved for untouchables in a medical school in the state of Gujarat—just seven places.[46] This was part of a national trend of rising violence against untouchables amid adverse reactions against preferential policies in general.[47] Meanwhile, less than 5 percent of the medical school places reserved for untouchables in Gujarat had actually been filled over a period of years. Studies of university admissions in general, in various parts of India, showed a similar pattern of many places reserved for untouchables going unfilled.[48] Nevertheless, minor transfers of benefits led to major resentments, including resentments erupting repeatedly into lethal violence.

Nowhere has this resentment led to more violence than in India's neighboring nation of Sri Lanka, which has been racked by decades of civil war, in which the non-preferred group—the Tamils—have sought to secede and become an independent nation. This tragic story will be left for Chapter 4. Here it is sufficient to mention it among other examples of intergroup polarization brought on by affirmative action. It is clear that affirmative action in Sri Lanka has not been a zero-sum process. The material, political, economic, and social havoc created by that country's long civil war has undoubtedly left all segments of the population worse off than they would have been in the absence of group preferences and the reactions to which those preferences led.

TRENDS

Even where there are adequate statistical data on the progress of groups that have been given preferential treatment—and often there are not—it remains a challenge to determine how much of that progress was due to preferential policies, rather than to other factors at work at the same time. Simple before-and-after comparisons will not do, as that would be assuming that nothing else had changed, when in fact the very dynamics of establishing affirmative action programs often reflect changes that were already under way before group preferences began. Seldom is there a stationary situation to which a given "change" is added.

Often it was precisely the rise of newly educated and upwardly mobile groups which led to demands for preferential policies. A study in Bombay, for example, found a "marked advancement of the Maharashtrians occurred prior to the stringent policy measures adopted by the state government" to promote preferential hiring of indigenous Maharashtrians.[49] In part this reflected a prior "enormous growth in school enrollments in Maharashtra" and a "rapid expansion in college enrollment"—also prior to preferences.[50] In Malaysia as well, the number of children attending the government's secondary schools increased by 73 percent in just five years immediately preceding the New Economic Policy, which expanded preferences and quotas for Malays.[51] In Sri Lanka likewise, there was a "rapid expansion of educational opportunities in the Sinhalese areas" after independence[52] — and before demands for preferential treatment of the Sinhalese.

A similar growth of an indigenous, newly educated class in Poland, Czechoslovakia, and Lithuania during the years between the two World Wars led to demands for preferential policies in the form of group quotas, in order to relieve them from having to compete on an equal plane with Jews,[53] who were already educated, experienced, and established in the positions to which the newly-educated classes were aspiring. Likewise, in Nigeria, it was the recent growth of an educated class in the north that led to demands for preferential policies to relieve them from having to compete with southern Nigerians, who had predominated in universities and in many desirable occupations.[54] This same pattern of a rising educated class *prior* to the preferential policies that they promoted can also be found in Indonesia, the Quebec province of Canada, and much of sub-Saharan Africa.[55]

In the United States, the proportion of the black population going to college doubled in the two decades preceding the civil rights revolution of the 1960s,[56] and this was reflected in the occupational rise of blacks. While it is an often-cited fact that the proportion of blacks in professional and other high-level occupations rose substantially in the years following passage of the Civil Rights Act of 1964, it is an almost totally ignored fact that the proportion of blacks in such occupations rose even more substantially in the years *preceding* passage of the Civil Rights Act of 1964.[57]

Dramatic progress was also evident during these same decades in the lower socioeconomic levels of the American black population. The percentage of black families with incomes below the official poverty line fell from 87 percent in 1940 to 47 percent by 1960 — all of this before the civil rights legislation of that decade, much less the affirmative action policies of the 1970s. Between 1960 and 1970, the poverty rate among black families dropped an additional 17 percentage points and, after the decade of the 1970s in which affirmative action was established, the poverty rate among blacks fell one additional percentage point.[58]

This striking difference between the political myth and the economic reality has many implications. Among them is that what might otherwise be seen as a remarkable achievement by black Americans is instead seen as an example of government beneficence and largess—and a reason why affirmative action is an absolute necessity for black advancement. The effects of this misperception include white resentments and their questioning why blacks cannot advance themselves like other groups, when in fact that is what most blacks have done. Incidentally, it is an equally ignored fact that the incomes of Asian Americans and Mexican Americans also rose substantially—both absolutely and relative to that of the general population—in the years preceding passage of the Civil Rights Act of 1964 and its evolution into preferential policies.[59]

Any assessment of preferential policies must take account of pre-existing trends, rather than assume a static world to which "change" was added.

SUMMARY AND IMPLICATIONS

Despite the highly varied rationales for official group preferences and quotas in particular countries around the world, the logic of their incentives and constraints tends to produce similar consequences in very disparate societies. Moreover, both the incentives and the consequences tend to get ignored in political discussions of these policies, which focus on their justifications and presumed benefits, while ignoring actual empirical results. In the United States, mythical results—affirmative action as the basis for the economic rise of blacks, for example—have so completely supplanted facts that few who discuss this policy find it necessary to check historical evidence at all.

For some supporters of affirmative action, it is just a matter of being in favor of helping the less fortunate, with the "details" being left for others to consider and work out. However, even a broad-brush look at what affirmative action programs have actually done in various countries reveals that a failure to achieve their goals may be the least of the problems created by these programs. Poisonous intergroup relations and real dangers to the fabric of society have also been produced by affirmative action in some countries. That should become painfully clear when we look at the "details" in the chapters that follow.

CHAPTER 2

Affirmative Action in India

India is the world's largest multi-ethnic society — and the most socially fragmented. A land of well over a hundred languages and hundreds of dialects, where even the most widely spoken language in the country is spoken by less than one-third of the population, India is also cross cut by strong caste, religious, regional and ethnic divisions — expressed in a wide range of ways, from radically different lifestyles to bloodshed in the streets. India has also had affirmative action policies longer than any other nation, beginning in British colonial times, and then provided for in its constitution when it became an independent country in 1947.[1]

The Fourteenth Amendment to India's constitution, like the Fourteenth Amendment to the constitution of the United States, prescribes equal treatment for individuals. Unlike the constitutions of the United States, however, India's equal-rights amendment provides an explicit exception for policies designed to help disadvantaged segments of its population — affirmative action or "positive discrimination" as it is often called there. These provisions were originally set to expire in 20 years, but they have been extended again and again[2] — and expanded.

Today, there are basically two kinds of preferential policies

in India—policies for national minorities deemed less fortunate and policies for various local groups in their respective
states. The minority policies were quite explicitly designed primarily to deal with the severe social disabilities and discrimination faced by India's untouchables. Tribal groups outside
the social mainstream of the country were also included, as in
some ways analogous to untouchables. For others who might
have similar disadvantages, an omnibus category of "other
backward classes" was included in the constitutional exemption from equal treatment provisions. This last mentioned category provided an opening through which numerous other
groups could acquire preferential access to jobs and other
benefits.

Statistically, members of the omnibus category of "other
backward classes" now outnumber the untouchables and tribal
groups combined. The untouchables ("scheduled castes" or
"Dalits") constitute about 16 percent of the country's total
population and members of "backward tribes" another 8 percent. However, these two very poor and historically outcast
groups are greatly outnumbered by members of the "other
backward classes," who constitute 52 percent of all Indians.[3]
Clearly, these "other backward classes" are in practice not
the incidental after-thought that they might have been in the
minds of those who wrote India's constitutional exemption
from equal-treatment requirements.

SCHEDULED CASTES AND SCHEDULED TRIBES

Nationally, preferential policies were meant to raise the socioeconomic levels of the scheduled castes and scheduled tribes
through "positive discrimination" in jobs, university admissions, representation in parliament, and other benefits designed to overcome historic patterns of discrimination and
backwardness. By virtually any definition, discrimination
against India's untouchables ("scheduled castes") has been

among the worst against any group in any society. Although untouchability was officially abolished more than half a century ago, and the term "untouchable" banished from official and polite discourse, the same people have faced continuing discrimination under their new designations as "scheduled castes," "Harijans" (children of God, a name given them by Mahatma Gandhi) or "Dalits" (the downtrodden).

Untouchables have been outcastes in the literal sense of not being one of the four broad categories of castes recognized by the Hindu religion. Because their work, such as working with leather, often goes against the tenets of Hinduism, there have been serious questions whether they could be considered Hindus at all. While they have historically considered themselves Hindus, many have converted to other religions that do not have a caste stigma.

History

Historically, prohibitions against any physical contact with caste Hindus were just some of the restrictions placed on untouchables, backed up by severe punishments for any violation. In some places, untouchables were not even to allow their shadow to fall upon a caste Hindu and had to beat drums upon entering a Hindu community, in order to warn others to keep their distance.[4] They could not draw water from the same well used by caste Hindus — and, in some places, still could not in practice, decades after they had the legal right to do so.

Two incidents involving wells showed the persistence of caste taboos in the late 1970s. In one episode, an untouchable girl who drew water from a well reserved for caste Hindus had her ears cut off.[5] In another incident, in a place where untouchables were allowed to draw water from the same well as caste Hindus, an untouchable woman put her pot on the pot of a caste Hindu woman, setting off a riot in which an untouchable was killed.[6] Similar incidents were reported by the international organization Human Rights Watch in the 1990s[7] and, in 2001, the Indian publication *The Hindu* reported: "Attacks on Dalits (most often orchestrated by collectives representing upper caste interests) and even massacres of men, women and children belonging to the lowest rungs of the social order are indeed a regular feature in most parts of the country."[8]

In 1991, the news magazine *India Today* reported that, in a village about 100 miles from Delhi, "a rural Dalit laborer dared to have a love affair with the daughter of a high-caste landlord" and as a result "the lovers and their Dalit go-between were tortured, publicly hanged, and burnt by agents of the girl's family in the presence of some 500 villagers."[9] The presence of 500 witnesses takes this out of the realm of isolated incidents, since those who did these things obviously did not fear punishment or retribution. This says something about the society, not just about them.

While such behavior is not pervasive across India, neither is it confined to isolated incidents. Government statistics on atrocities against untouchables never fell below 13,000 per year during the decade of the 1980s and reached well over 16,000 in 1984.[10] Far from abating with time, these officially recorded atrocities escalated to more than 20,000 a year in the 1990s.[11]

This escalation of violence has been associated with backlashes against the official preferences given to untouchables and with competition among other recipients of preferences, such as the "other backward classes." Although there was little public criticism of affirmative action in India before the 1970s,[12] such criticisms have grown louder over the years, along with escalating violence. A 1997 study concluded that "the quota system has eliminated whatever goodwill the upper castes had for the lower castes," partly because of a "pervasive overestimation of the amount and effectiveness" of preferential policies—which in fact benefit only an estimated 6 percent of untouchable families.[13]

Despite such horrors, restrictions against untouchables or Dalits have been in an irregular retreat across India for decades—more so in the cities than in the countrysides and more so in public accommodations than in religious temples. As a 1997 study reported: "The social stigma of caste and tribe is absent in day-to-day intercourse in urban centers, but in rural India to be from a scheduled caste or scheduled tribe is still a social burden."[14] Yet in some places untouchable university students are socially accepted as roommates of caste Hindus.[15] In other contexts, according to a Human Rights Watch report in 1999, Dalit women were "raped as a form of retaliation" by upper class men when there were organized movements among the Dalits to seek enforcement of minimum wage laws or other redress.[16] India is a nation of sharp contrasts, in this as in many other things. One sign of these contrasts is the Sixth Annual Report of the Commission for Scheduled Castes and Scheduled Tribes in 2001, which found that three states provided nearly two-thirds of all the thousands of atrocities committed against untouchables, while there were several other states with none.[17]

While the untouchables are, in many places, too economically dependent, powerless, and outnumbered to do much to defend themselves, in other places, where they have been able to respond, that response has been extreme, in both political and physical terms. The state of Bihar has been particularly prime to violence and counter-violence involving the scheduled castes. After two families of untouchables were murdered in 1987, neighboring villages inhabited by members of higher castes were attacked by almost a thousand men, armed with sticks, spears, and guns. Villagers were pulled from their homes, hacked to pieces and thrown into flames by attackers who shouted, "We will take revenge" and "Love live the Maoist

Communist Centre." Although the attackers had guns, they preferred to cut their victims to pieces.[18]

The classical four castes of the Hindu religion are fragmented into literally thousands of local castes or sub-castes, which are what circumscribe people's social life. Back in colonial times, the British had a list or schedule drawn up of those castes which were considered untouchable. This was what led to the phrase "scheduled castes" as a euphemism for "untouchables." The term "untouchable" originated early in the twentieth century and was banished from laws and polite discourse by the late twentieth century.

Whatever the historical origins of this pariah status in particular occupations or ways of life, over the centuries the social stigma acquired a life of its own, and was applied even to those whose occupations and ways of life were very different. For example, Dr. B. R. Ambedkar, destined to become the best known leader of the untouchables, was evicted from a hotel in India when he returned home after receiving a Ph.D. from Columbia University, once his outcaste origins became known.[19]

The caste system also followed Indians to other countries, somewhat attenuated in more distant countries and in more robust form in countries closer to India. In nearby Ceylon, for example, untouchables were not allowed to be seated in buses in the 1930s:

> ... there was the refusal to concede to *harijans* the right to a seat in buses. Eventually it required government intervention to enforce this right, but attempts to enforce it led to outbreaks of violence in 1930–31, and to a strike of bus drivers and conductors. Previously, *harijans* were expected to stand at the back of the bus, or to sit, or squat, on the floor of the bus even though they were required to pay the normal fare. It took decades before *vellalas* accepted this change, and most of them did so with undisguised reluctance. Discrimination against *harijans* extended to restrictions on entry into cafes and "eating houses," access to village amen-

ities like wells and cemeteries, and on the clothes they wore—their right to wear shoes was a frequent point of contention.[20]

Historically, then, the untouchables were clearly an oppressed minority. Many people did not consider untouchables to be Hindus at all[21] because (1) they were not among the four *varnas* designated by the Hindu religion, but were literally outcastes in the sense of being outside—and below—those in the caste system, and (2) some of their occupations involved making products from animals slaughtered in violation of Hindu tenets. Only relatively recently, as history is measured, did a widespread concern for the predicament of the untouchables arise in the early decades of the twentieth century. Nor was this belated concern wholly a matter of humanitarian consideration. During the later colonial era, as Indians were struggling to achieve independence from Britain, the inclusion or exclusion of untouchables from the ranks of Hindus had profound political implications for the political balance of power between Hindus and Moslems in post-independence India. Politics therefore dictated concern for the classification of the untouchables and led Hindus to accept untouchables as fellow Hindus for political purposes, even if they were still kept out of many temples. In this climate of opinion, Dr. B. R. Ambedkar sought to gain whatever concessions he could and Mahatma Gandhi made the fate of untouchables a moral issue.

Even for Gandhi, however, the over-riding concern was that the untouchables remain classified as part of the Hindu electorate. When the British created a special electorate for the untouchables in 1932, Gandhi vowed to fast till death unless this decision was reversed. In the national crisis that this created, a compromise was reached in which there was to be no separate electorate for untouchables, but they would still have seats reserved for them in the legislature. This historic episode has sometimes been depicted as a fast against the principle of untouchability, rather than as what it was—a desperate effort to keep the Hindu vote from being splintered. Nevertheless, the increased attention to the untouchables and their problems growing out of this episode led to various attempts to better their condition. In some states, there were laws passed to grant them equal access to public accommodations, including Hindu temples. There was also preferential access to government jobs for untouchables in some states. In short, preferential policies for untouchables began under British colonial rule and were later expanded after India achieved national independence.

PREFERENCES IN PRACTICE

The census of 1991 showed that the literacy rate was only 37 percent among members of the scheduled castes and 30 percent among members of the scheduled tribes.[22] In higher education, most untouchables or members of backward tribes are unable to use the quotas and preferences to which they are legally entitled, even when the government provides scholarships. A study of scholarships for untouchables pointed out the reason:

> The scholarship money . . . can hardly be expected to induce the really poor to go in for higher education and, if one does go in for it, to continue till he completes the course. Only those who have some other sources to rely on can avail of these scholarships. A few respondents were frank enough to admit that this money provides them with pocket money while their parents bear the major portion of the educational expenditure.[23]

Among the consequences of this situation are that (1) many reserved places go unfilled, (2) those places that have been filled have been filled disproportionately by the more fortunate members of the less fortunate groups and (3) those members of these groups who have gone on to higher education have usually gone to the less demanding institutions, specialized in the easier (and less remunerative) subjects, taken longer to graduate, and dropped out much more often than other students. Unused reservations or quotas have long been common, and especially striking at the university or postgraduate level.[24] Studies in the 1960s and 1970s showed that scheduled caste students filled less than half the places reserved for them in universities in general and in medical and engineering schools in particular.[25] Some institutions did not have a single student from either the scheduled castes or the scheduled tribes.[26] Such patterns have persisted. In 1997, *The Times of India* quoted the chairman of the National Commission for Scheduled Castes and Scheduled Tribes as declaring that none of India's elite universities and engineering institutes had filled its quota for members of scheduled castes.[27] In 2001, the central government asked universities and medical schools "to ensure that the full quota of reserved seats was filled up" and suggested organizing "special coaching" for students from scheduled caste and scheduled tribe backgrounds.[28]

These unfilled quotas in higher education are not a result of strict admissions standards. Explicitly lower cut-off scores for members of the scheduled castes and scheduled tribes have been common among Indian universities and technical institutes.[29] None of the students preferentially admitted to six highly selective engineering schools progressed through these schools on schedule and most did not maintain a high enough grade average to continue in these institutions.[30] For the country as a whole, members of the scheduled castes and scheduled tribes — combined — did not receive as much as 3 percent of the degrees in engineering or medicine,[31] though together they add up to nearly one-fourth of the population of India.

Not only in higher education, but in elementary and secondary education as well, the need for complementary resources, in order to be able to actually make use of preferences and quotas, limits the benefits that members of the scheduled castes and scheduled tribes receive. Even when the government provides primary schooling free of charge, the costs of books and supplies may not be affordable by very poor people. For secondary education, rural students especially may not always find a school nearby, so that those whose parents cannot afford the costs of commuting or relocating—and paying for housing and boarding—have little realistic prospect of attending, regardless of preferential admissions policies. Perhaps the largest cost of sending children to secondary and higher education is their lost labor on farms and their lost income elsewhere, especially among poverty-stricken people struggling to make ends meet.

These educational handicaps can lead to employment handicaps. Patterns of unused quotas have existed in government employment, in part because of difficulties in passing the relevant examinations. According to a 1984 study:

> When the State of Orissa conducted a combined examination for several of its services, 133 candidates were successful—i.e., had test scores high enough to support appointment. Although 18% of the places in each of the two services were reserved for Scheduled Castes, there was just one successful SC candidate, who had scored 105th on the examination.[32]

There were still unfilled job reservations for untouchables in the 1990s.[33] Moreover, the jobs they did fill were concentrated at the bottom. While untouchables were 16 percent of the population, they were in 1994 nearly half of all sweepers but just 10 percent of the Class A government employees.[34] Nor were all the jobs they held necessarily due to quotas, since these totals include those who met the normal job qualifications. In short, the actual net benefit of quotas and preferences on the wellbeing of the scheduled castes and scheduled tribes is problematical, however much such "positive discrimination" may generate bitterness and resentment toward them from other groups.

Government jobs and education are not the only level where preferential benefits often remain unused. The same is true of housing subsidies, health programs, maternity and other benefits which remain unused so frequently that governmental spending on these programs has often been less than the sums authorized to be spent.[35] In all these cases, complementary factors are needed, in order to be able to actually use the preferences and quotas. Sometimes the complementary factor is money, sometimes a good educational background, sometimes job skills and experience, and sometimes just being well informed as to what is available. Given the need for complementary resources, it is hardly surprising that the more prosperous of the scheduled castes have often taken the lion's share of the benefits.[36]

Chamars, for example, began an economic rise during the Second World War when there was a sudden increase in demand for leather goods.[37] In the state of Maharashtra, the Chamars are among the most prosperous of the scheduled castes. A study found that they were 17 percent of the state's population and 35 percent of its medical students.[38] In the state of Haryana, the Chamars received 65 percent of the scholarships for the scheduled castes at the graduate level and 80 percent at the undergraduate level.[39] Meanwhile 18 of the 37 untouchable groups in Haryana failed to get any of the preferential scholarships. In the state of Madhya Pradesh, Chamars were 53 percent of all the scheduled caste students in the schools of that state.[40] In Bihar, just two of the 12 scheduled castes in that state — one being the Chamars — supplied 61 percent of the scheduled class students in school and 74 percent of those in college.[41] In Uttar Pradesh, according to the *Economic and Political Weekly*, the Chamars "have nearly monopolised the dalit quota."[42] In 2001, Uttar Pradesh passed an ordinance splitting the quota for the scheduled castes, so that Chamars were limited in how large a percentage of the government jobs set aside for scheduled castes they could receive.[43] However, in early 2002, the Supreme Court stayed the implementation of that ordinance.[44]

In the state of Tamil Nadu, various less fortunate castes constituted 12 percent of the backward classes in that state, while more fortunate castes constituted 11 percent of the backward classes. Yet, despite their similarities in numbers of people, the more fortunate castes within this group received more than four times as much money per capita in scholarships and they provided 44 percent of the backward classes' students admitted to study engineering, compared to less than 2 percent among the least fortunate castes in this category.[45] Such disparities among preferred groups in their utilization of preferential benefits have been found in other parts of India, for both scheduled tribes and scheduled castes.[46] Similar disparities among the "other backward classes" have led to demands for "quota within quota" policies to prevent the more advanced of the other backward classes—widely known as "the creamy layer"—from taking the lion's share of the quotas, at the expense of what are called the "most backward classes."

When it comes to seats in both the national and state legislatures set aside for untouchables, the pattern once again is one of a disproportionate share of these benefits going to those who were more fortunate to begin with. While members of 65 untouchable sub-castes were eligible for legislative seats in the state of Andhra Pradesh, only 5 of these 65 untouchable sub-castes were actually represented in that state's legislature.[47] People who were not born untouchables held a majority of the seats set aside for untouchables in the state of Rajasthan. At one time, 16 of the 28 legislators holding seats reserved for untouchables in that state had acquired certificates of untouchability by being adopted.[48] Adoption as untouchables has also been used by students as a means to gain admission to medical and engineering schools,[49] among other means of redesignating themselves to take advantage of group preferences and quotas. Although reserved seats in legislatures were scheduled to expire in ten years, they were repeatedly extended as new deadlines for their expiration arrived.[50]

LOCAL PREFERENCES

While the scheduled castes and scheduled tribes are legally entitled to preferences nationwide, there are also local groups entitled to preferences within their own respective states. Here the rationale is not the same as that which was used to create quotas and preferences nationally. Local indigenous status as "sons of the soil" has been taken to confer an entitlement to special consideration,[51] especially in states where outsiders have clearly out-performed the locals in free competition in the marketplace or in examinations for college admissions or government jobs. In the states of Assam, Maharashtra, and Andhra Pradesh, for example, such outsider dominance has sparked both political movements and mob violence.

Where local preference laws have been instituted, "local" has not meant simply people residing in the given state, because some groups — Marwaris and Bengalis in Assam, for example — have resided in that state for generations. What is meant, even if the law does not permit it to be said, is *ethnic* preference. As a committee of the state legislature in Assam put it:

> In the absence of any clear-cut definition of the term "local people," the Committee has had to base its analysis in place of birth in Assam as being the yardstick of local people. This yardstick is palpably inadequate and misleading and a clear understanding should be there in government and all others concerned in the matter as to what is meant by the term "local people."[52]

In the state of Maharashtra, a directive specified not merely "local" persons but also speakers of the Marathi language — that is, people *ethnically* Maharashtrians. In the state of Andhra Pradesh, where 86 percent of the people spoke the same language, and where the group seeking preferences was of the same race, religion and culture as the group whose superior performances they were trying to offset, making the distinction between groups required much ingenuity and sophistry—but it was done.[53]

In all these cases, there was abundant evidence that the less successful indigenous groups simply did not have the skills, experience, or attitudes that had enabled others to come in and surpass them. In Maharashtra, for example, the Maharashtrians themselves preferred to buy from South Indian shopkeepers, rather than from their fellow Maharashtrians. In Andhra Pradesh, even a local leader who was demanding preferences admitted that a rival group had higher qualifications:

> Yes it is true that they are also better qualified for many of the jobs than we are. Maybe they are better qualified but why is merit so important? We can have some inefficiency. That will be necessary if our people are to get jobs. Are we not entitled to jobs just because we are not as qualified?[54]

In the state of Karnataka, a local political leader uncompromisingly advocated local preferences while in office. But, ten years later and out of office, he expressed very different views:

> ... outsiders come in when the local people are lazy and lethargic. If the local people are active and enterprising, outsiders cannot come in. Many Kannadigas do not like to come out of their villages. Especially for particular jobs like nursing, army, sweeping, carpentry, masonry and construction works, Kannadigas did not seem to be interested. They do not like to do the manual jobs, because they feel that such jobs are inferior.[55]

While statistical disparities are often used as showing a need for affirmative action, the *reasons* for these disparities usually get little serious investigation, while much attention is focused on the supposed injustice of it all. The situation described in Karnataka is not unique.

Andhra Pradesh

The state of Andhra Pradesh is the product of one of the internal reorganizations which have occurred at various times after India received its independence. During the era of British colonial rule, the city of Hyderabad was capital of the state of Hyderabad — a state ruled by an Indian prince. Meanwhile, ethnically and culturally very similar people living in the adjoining state of Madras were under the rule of the British. After India became independent and absorbed the princely state of Hyderabad, it was understandable that a territorial reorganization would bring these very similar people together in the newly created state of Andhra Pradesh. But, although these peoples were the same in such things as race, language, and religion, their different histories under two different sets of rulers turned out to create very serious social, economic, and political disparities. As elsewhere on the Indian subcontinent, people living under indigenous rulers tended not to become as educated or as modernized as those living under British rule. For example, 17,000 out of 22,000 villages in the state of Hyderabad lacked a school.[56]

It was already understood on all sides, before the creation of the new state, that the people known as Andhras, who had lived under British rule, had become more advanced — in agriculture, in education, and in modernization in general — than the people called Telanganans, who had lived under princely rule in Hyderabad. Accordingly, various "safeguards" were provided in 1956 to assure the Telanganans of, among other things, numerical representation in government and in educational institutions for a period to end in 1969.[57] However, when time for the end of these preferences and quotas arrived in January 1969, demands were made for their extension and expansion.

What had happened in the intervening years was that the Andhras had surpassed the Telanganans in field after field, wherever they came into competition. The city of Hyderabad, as the capital of the new state of Andhra Pradesh, became a center of competition and confrontation between the Teleganans and the Andhras. Although Hyderabad was located in the Telanganan region, Andhras who had migrated there were more successful in this competition and formed what became known as "Andhra colonies" in the capital. By 1961, one-fourth of Hyderabad's inhabitants were migrants. Although most Indians were, and would remain for decades more, illiterate, most of the Andhra migrants were literate and thousands of them had gotten higher education.

Unskilled migrants in the city were largely from other parts of the Telanganan region, while Andhra migrants held clerical and other white collar or middle-class jobs. Andhra farmers followed a long-standing practice of buying up land from Telanganans and making it more productive. The "green revolution" was put to use by the Andhras, but not by the Telanganans.[58] In short, the Telanganans were bested in many ways on their own turf, despite the preferences and quotas known as "safeguards," and were therefore understandably apprehensive about their future if these safeguards ended on schedule in 1969.

University students began protests that spread to other areas and escalated into mob attacks on railroads and government facilities. State officials promised to replace "outsiders" with local Telanganans in government jobs but the Supreme Court of Andhra Pradesh ruled that they had exceeded their authority. Later India's Supreme Court overruled the state court, allowing local officials to proceed with local preferences. This set off six months of violence by contending forces in Andhra Pradesh.

Telanganans now began to demand their own separate state, which would have given them the uncontested right to establish their own preferences and quotas, but the central government of India saw in this the threat that other states would begin to fragment into innumerable ethnic enclaves seeking their own statehood. Although it was legal for a state to establish preferences and quotas to favor its indigenous people over "outsiders," in this case both contending parties were from within the state. Amid political strife and violence in the streets, a compromise was worked out, even though it required a constitutional amendment. Preferences and quotas for local people were now officially permitted within a region within a state. This gave the Telanganans what they wanted, without the need to fragment the state.

Although the situation in Andhra Pradesh was ultimately resolved without the on-going strife found in other Indian states, this unusual situation highlights the fact that the differences in language and religion which have been so contentious in other states are neither necessary nor sufficient to cause intergroup polarization. What the situation in Andhra Pradesh had in common with intergroup conflict in other states — and nations — was that one group was unable to compete on even terms with another and therefore turned to politics and to violence to get the preferences and quotas they wanted.

Assam

In the state of Assam, the economic development of a modern industrial and commercial sector has been largely the work of outsiders, going all the way back to colonial times in British India. The British imported Chinese laborers from as far away as Singapore, paying them four or five times the wages paid to the local Assamese.[59] Later, in post-colonial India, other migrants continued to earn more than the Assamese.[60] Comments from those employing Assamese workers were largely negative, both from the British in colonial times and from Indian employers during the later era of independence. Marwari businessmen characterized their Assamese employees as lethargic, unreliable, untrustworthy, and unwilling to work long hours,[61] just as the British during the colonial era had complained of the "indolence and incapacity" of the Assamese and to their "utter want of an industrious, enterprising spirit."[62]

Marwaris are an entrepreneurial group that originated in the western state of Rajasthan. Under British rule, they began migrating all over the Indian subcontinent, often beginning as poor traders and later rising to prosperity as merchants, manufacturers, bankers and in other commercial and industrial roles. In the state of Assam, the Marwaris were a major factor in opening the region to trade, becoming in the process the dominant group in that trade. Marwaris remained a separate group in Assam, with their own charities, hospitals, schools, newspapers and other institutions. Their language remained Hindi, rather than Assamese.[63]

Another group whose history in Assam was in sharp contrast with that of the indigenous Assamese has been the Bengalis. They have included both Hindus and Moslems from Bengal, where land was much more scarce than in Assam. Arriving in Assam in colonial times, the Bengalis eagerly seized the abundant idle land now available to them, cleared jungles, and farmed with far more care, energy and success than the Assamese. Bengalis were not only successful in agriculture and in the professions, the British authorities relied on them to fill responsible positions in the colonial bureaucracy. Bengalis also seized upon educational opportunities created by the British, while the Assamese were slow to see a need for education. Unlike many others in India, the Assamese were seldom landless agricultural laborers but were largely peasant farmers with rich, fertile land. What they suffered from was seeing others come in and surpass them in their own region.

Because the Assamese were slower to take advantage of educational opportunities, the Bengalis were far better represented in educational institutions and in government employment. Thus the language of education and government in Assam became Bengali, rather than Assamese. As a result, those

Assamese who eventually began to seek education found a language handicap confronting them. However, as far back as the mid-nineteenth century, the Assamese were able to get the British authorities to change the language of the schools from Bengali to Assamese.[64] Political activity to redress the imbalances created by unequal competition elsewhere became a pattern for the Assamese in the years and generations that followed. In response to their fears and resentments of the Bengalis and others, by 1920 British authorities sought to restrict the inflow of migrants into Assam.[65]

As elsewhere in India, ethnic conflicts were often fought out as language conflicts in Assam. Allowing both Assamese and other languages to be used in state institutions would imply equal opportunity for the various groups in Assam but only an *exclusive* use of the Assamese language could provide the preferential treatment the Assamese were seeking, in order to buttress the preferential treatment they already received in government employment and were seeking in private employment. During the 1960s, Marwari employers were denounced by Assamese politicians and students for not hiring enough Assamese employees. Such complaints were backed up by riots and arson. The Assamese also favored socialism which, in Assam, would mean confiscating businesses owned by the outside groups who dominated the local economy.

By 1972, both the Assamese and the Bengalis were rioting over the unresolved language issues. When Bengali students were allowed to answer questions on university examinations in their own language, widespread riots, arson, and looting broke out in a number of towns in Assam and troops had to be called in to restore order.[66] Once again, in 1983 the Assamese and members of local tribes attacked Bengalis, killing 4,000 of them and making more than a quarter of a million people homeless.[67] Assam has remained so unsettled that no census was possible there in 1981 — or in the decades since then.

Maharashtra

Violence in pursuit of ethnic preference claims have not been confined to Assam. In Maharashtra, a paramilitary movement called Shiv Sena has specialized in intimidation and violence, directed against various "outsiders" who dominated the economy of Bombay (the capital of Maharashtra), as various other outsiders dominated the economy of Assam. This intimidation and violence has likewise been directed against political authorities and private businesses from whom preferential hiring of Maharashtrians was demanded. When presenting such demands to an official of India Oil, for example, these demands were accompanied by the observation: "You are sitting inside the office, but your oil drums are outside."[68]

The background to the pressures for preferential policies in the city of Bombay (now renamed Mumbai) and in the surrounding state of Maharashtra was much the same as in Assam: Indigenous locals were simply no match for outsiders who were much preferred as employees and much more successful as entrepreneurs. Indeed, even advocates of the locals tacitly admitted that they were not equal in performance to outsiders, and used that as an argument for preferential treatment:

> If you have two plants, one with hardy roots and broad leaves and the other with only weak roots and small leaves, they can not drink the water, the soil nutrients or absorb the sun's energy with the same efficiency. The weak plant needs more attention so that it can catch up and one day produce beautiful fruit.[69]

Entrepreneurs from the neighboring state of Gujarat were the largest group of business executives in Bombay in the middle of the twentieth century and were more than half of all managers in companies surveyed then.[70] Maharashtrians were virtually non-existent at these high levels and were also not much in demand as workers, since they were considered to be lacking in both skills and productive attitudes.[71] All this was turned into sources of resentment of "discrimination" against indigenous locals by an ambitious editor named Bal Thackeray, who also founded the Shiv Sena movement to redress these grievances. In 1965, the magazine that Thackeray edited ran a series of stories about the dominance of "outsiders" in high economic positions in Bombay.[72] These exposés not only caused the magazine's circulation to skyrocket, it created the atmosphere in which the Shiv Sena movement could be born and flourish. Operating much like the paramilitary forces which brought Mussolini and Hitler to power, Shiv Sena became a force both in politics and in the streets. It ran candidates for political office, organized boycotts, and has been implicated in violence and murder, principally against "outsiders."[73]

Originating in Bombay, Shiv Sena over the years became a dominant political force in the whole state of Maharashtra and, at the beginning of the twenty-first century, had 15 seats in India's national parliament. Its central issue of hiring preferences and quotas for Maharashtrians expanded to include anti-Moslem agitation, opposition to foreign ownership of Air India, refusal to allow a cricket match between India and Pakistan to take place in Maharashtra—in short, whatever issues would appeal to xenophobia against a growing list of "enemies." Meanwhile, group-identity politics was growing in other states and localities and, nationally, a Hindu extremist party was rising to challenge the Congress Party that had ruled India for 30 consecutive years since independence in 1947. This Bharatiya Janata Party, better known as BJP, whipped up emotions over such things as the fact that Moslems had invaded India in centuries past. BJP formed a political alliance with Shiv Sena and eventually became the ruling party of India.

In the wake of the rise of Shiv Sena, more Maharashtrians began to be hired in greater numbers, and in higher positions, than before. However, as noted in Chapter 1, this rise had been preceded by a huge increase in the number of educated Maharashtrians, antedating the founding of Shiv Sena, so that it is not easy to determine how much of their advancement was due specifically to that organization and the preferential treatment that it fostered. What is more clearly attributable to Shiv Sena is an escalating polarization in Maharashtra between the indigenous people, who are barely a majority, and various other ethnic and religious groups, who began to fight back. A correspondent for the distinguished British magazine *The Economist* reported from Bombay in 1993:

> The murder, looting and arson that began on January 6th soon spread from the Muslim ghetto to the enclaves of the privileged. First the police were called in, then the paramilitary forces, and then, on January 9th, the army—and still the mayhem spread. This week the railroad station was swamped with thousands of families trying to flee the city. At the airport fights broke out as the rich found flights had been curtailed by a pilots' strike.[74]

More, and sometimes worse, intergroup violence was to break out in Bombay in the years ahead. In a series of such outbreaks in 1994, the official death toll was more than a thousand people—and the *Far Eastern Economic Review* reported that unofficial estimates were in the thousands. It added, with quotes from *The Times of India:*

> These statistics convey little of the real horror of hordes "stopping vehicles and setting passengers ablaze"; of "men brought bleeding to hospital who were knifed afresh"; of the autorickshaw driver who "decoyed a Muslim couple into a fatal ambush"; of "neighbors leading long-time friends to gory deaths"; of women driven mad having "seen their children thrown into fires, husbands hacked, daughters molested, sons dragged away," and of the 150,000 people hounded out of the city.[75]

It was not only people who fled the city. More than a million jobs also left, as businesses began to consider Bombay a risky place to be. Whether Maharashtrians gained as many jobs through preferences and quotas as they lost through the exodus of employers is a question that may never be answered — or asked. No such considerations, however, dissuaded Shiv Sena from pushing on with its anti-Moslem rhetoric and symbolism. One such act of symbolism in 1995 was changing the name of Bombay back to a name it once had, centuries earlier, before the British conquests and — more to the point — before the Moslem conquests. Other names of towns and villages were also changed back to what they had been before the Moslems arrived in earlier centuries.

Asiaweek magazine said of Bal Thackeray: "Though he holds no elected office, he is now widely acknowledged to be the most powerful leader in Maharashtra, India's richest state."[76] *Time* magazine said: "Authorities have been so afraid that the Hindu leader's arrest could trigger mass unrest that he wasn't touched even after proclaiming in 1992 that stormtroopers from his Shiv Sena party had demolished the disputed mosque at Ayodhya, setting off nationwide violence."[77]

The turmoil that has been the life's blood of an extremist movement like Shiv Sena has drained away economic resources from Bombay (Mumbai). Despite the city's long predominance as India's pre-eminent commercial and industrial center — 40 percent of all the direct taxes in India were collected there — many foreign companies began choosing Bangalore, Hyderabad, and Madras for their headquarters instead, and domestic businesses have likewise begun to relocate. In 1998, Bombay's excise and customs revenues dropped for the first time.[78]

None of this seems to have dampened Shiv Sena's penchant for symbolic outbursts — for example, "ransacking and throwing cowdung at McDonald's outlets."[79] However, there have been signs that Shiv Sena may be losing support. In 2001, Bal Thackeray was finally arrested for his part in the destruction of a mosque that he had admitted publicly nine years earlier.

However, the political success of local xenophobic movements seeking preferential treatment in various parts of India has promoted xenophobia of other kinds, including anti-

Western xenophobia. The state of Uttar Pradesh, for example, has officially banned Valentine's Day celebrations, and gangs in the state of Orissa have launched attacks on Christians:

> Bibles were burnt, priests and nuns assaulted, churches damaged and chapels set afire. Graham Staines charred to death with his children. Father Christudas paraded naked and humiliated on the streets of Dumka and a nun in Bihar forced to drink human refuse.[80]

Tolerating, condoning, or rewarding lawless xenophobia has only caused it to spread and become more extreme and more ugly. In December 2002, the Hindu extremist Bharatiya Janata Party won a landslide victory in the state of Gujarat.

NON-PREFERRED GROUPS

Despite the relatively small amount of actual realized benefits to the untouchables and poor tribal groups, the whole system of preferences and quotas bears heavily on non-preferred groups, especially those higher-caste individuals who do not have independent sources of income or wealth, and who are therefore more dependent on access to education for professional and government jobs. The progressive extension of preferences and quotas to numerous groups, and especially to "other backward classes" who are in a better position to actually utilize these preferences, means that at least three-quarters of the population of India are members of officially preferred groups. While the remaining minority are generally members of higher castes, that ascribed status does not automatically translate into economic privilige. While brahmins are in general more prosperous than untouchables, there are also poor brahmins and affluent untouchables. Those young people from non-preferred groups who are dependent on gaining an education to earn the kind of living required to maintain their position in society can thus find themselves in a desperate situation and resort to desperate measures. After the national government elected in 1989 expanded quotas, there were violent reactions from the non-preferred groups:

> Students set fire to themselves; others led protest campaigns across the country; trains were derailed and vehicles burnt; the police opened fire and demonstrators were killed.[81]

Much more is involved here than a simple moral melodrama of the rich versus the poor. Most of the truly poor are little affected by the preferences and quotas instituted in their name but going primarily to others. Nor are most of the truly rich likely to be seriously inconvenienced by lessened access to civil service jobs, especially since they can be appointed to much higher positions if they wish. Moreover, the ability of the rich to provide their children with the finest primary and secondary education virtually ensures that their offspring will be able to score high enough on university entrance examinations that they are not likely to be the ones sacrificed to provide places to members of preferred groups.

In short, neither the rich nor the poor are likely to be greatly affected by preferences and quotas. It is those in between who receive either windfall losses or windfall gains, according to which broad-brush category they happen to fall in, and regardless of whether their individual circumstances are more fortunate or less fortunate. As for the genuinely affluent or wealthy, they seem to have done well. As one study concluded:

> The wealthier 25 percent now owned more land than they had a generation earlier, and the level of rural unrest had risen in proportion to the immiseration of scheduled-caste families.[82]

Preferences and quotas are not merely zero-sum games, as the rich-versus-poor image might suggest. There are costs to society as a whole, borne to some extent by all the various groups in it. These include whatever losses of efficiency may follow from putting less qualified people in particular jobs or admitting them to universities for which they do not qualify and from which they are unlikely to graduate. More serious costs include increased intergroup hostility, as well as the violence and deaths to which this often leads.

SUMMARY AND IMPLICATIONS

As the country with the longest history of preferences and quotas for the purpose of advancing poorer and disadvantaged groups, India's experience is particularly relevant to the story of the actual *consequences* of such programs, as distinguished from their hopes or rationales. Much of what happened in India foreshadowed what happened later in other countries that followed in her wake with similar affirmative action policies.

The record is particularly clear in India because of more detailed statistics being available on the country's many subgroups. While statistics in the United States, for example, are kept on such broad-brush categories as blacks, whites, and Hispanics, in India the four broad castes of Hindus are broken down more finely into the many sub-castes that are the living reality in particular localities across the country. Thus it is easier to see how the benefits set aside for untouchables go disproportionately to those groups of untouchables who are more prosperous. While there is evidence that preferences and quotas in the United States — and in Malaysia and Sri Lanka, for that matter — also benefit primarily the more fortunate members of less fortunate groups, American government statistics do not break down the black population by recognizable classes (or ethnic sub-groups like West Indians) to see who gained and who lost.

There is no need to quarrel with the underlying purposes of affirmative action programs to help severely disadvantaged groups. Nor is there the slightest reason to doubt that India has had — and continues to have — some of the poorest and most oppressed groups in the world. But, unless one is content to

simply "do something," without regard to the actual consequences, it is hard to escape the conclusion that affirmative
action in India has produced minimal benefits to those most in
need of them and maximum resentments and hostility toward
them on the part of others. The need for supplementary contributions — whether financial or cultural — from members of the
designated beneficiary groups themselves, in order to make
preferences and quotas effective, has all but ensured that the
benefits would go disproportionately to those individuals and
subgroups who are already most fortunate, rather than those
most in need.

Hard data tell this painful story again and again. Despite an
emphasis on intergroup disparities as the driving force behind
affirmative action policies in India, these policies have themselves shown great disparities in their distribution of benefits.
Nor has this fact been lost on Indians themselves. Opponents
of affirmative action have argued in parliament that "a section
of the backward castes are already wealthy and need no help to
compete."[83] India's Supreme Court in 1992 upheld the exclusion of more fortunate individuals and groups from quotas for
members of "other backward classes." In 1999, the Supreme
Court struck down a quota law in the State of Kerala which
had declared that there was no "creamy layer" among those
granted preferences in that state.

The continuing legal and political controversies in India
over what to do about the skewed distribution of the benefits of
group quotas, which go disproportionately to those already
more fortunate, at least shows a public awareness of this skewness — an awareness that has not yet become widespread in the
United States, where a similar skewness exists.

Despite talk of limited or temporary preferences, these
preferences have persisted and spread until they now apply to
at least three-quarters of the population of India,[84] though Indian courts limit quotas to 50 percent of available places. Moreover, as an exhaustive scholarly study of group preferences in

India concluded, quotas for the "other backward classes" are often not only larger than quotas for untouchables and tribal peoples, "they never go unfilled."[85]

Such facts have been known for decades, but this has not led to any alternative approach to help those at the bottom of the socioeconomic scale. Given the vast amount of intellectual, judicial, and political thinking that has gone into assessments of affirmative action in India, it is hard to believe that there is any readily available solution. Nor does it seem politically possible to end such programs, despite growing demands that they be ended and the rising tide of violence against untouchables as supposed beneficiaries. Nor have members of the "other backward classes" escaped violence. After the state government of Gujarat expanded the size of the quotas for members of the backward classes in 1985 from 10 percent to 28 percent, riots broke out in which "some two hundred and seventy five people died in an orgy of arson and murder."[86]

Neither advocates nor critics of affirmative action seem ready to back down. Where courts or officials have balked at various double standards, those double standards have often gone underground, rather than going away. Objective standards have been offset by an increase in non-objective standards, used clearly as counterweights to produce the same group representation results produced by explicit double standards. For example, applicants to a medical school in Tamil Nadu were allowed to receive 75 out of 275 points for such things as sports, extracurricular activities, "aptitude" and "general abilities" — as determined by interviews *which lasted approximately three minutes* per applicant. Moreover, the ratings of these applicants on the interviews showed what an Indian court called a "disturbing" pattern of discrepancy from their ratings on other criteria.[87]

In short, whatever the appeal of "nuanced" and non-objective criteria, they lend themselves to being used as arbitrary offsets to deficient qualifications by objective criteria. In another case that reached the Indian courts, it was found that many "students whose performance in the University examinations was none too satisfactory nor their past records creditable" nevertheless received "very high marks at the interview" while "a large number of students who had secured very high marks in the University examinations and who had performed well in their earlier classes had secured low marks at the interview."[88]

Although the initial rationale for affirmative action or "positive discrimination" in India was to help the poorest and most discriminated against groups, these preferences and quotas rapidly spread to "other backward classes" and to many local groups — such as those in Assam, Andhra Pradesh, and Maharashtra — whose main problem was their own inadequacy and their resentment of other groups who were more successful in education and in the economy. Neither the scope nor the rationale for group preferences and quotas could be confined to what they were initially.

Within the short run — which is to say, within the time horizon of elected officials — the most politically expedient thing to do is to continue to extend preferences to more groups and more sectors of the society and the economy. That is in fact what is being done. In the longer run, cultural changes within the intended beneficiary groups would be necessary in order for the poorest of them to actually utilize all the benefits theoretically available to them. Yet there is no political mileage to be made by telling people to change themselves. Nor would it be easy for untouchables and others to adjust to changed conditions in ways that would promote their own advance or the advance of their children.

Money for school supplies, transportation to schools that are widely scattered, or living expenses for residential schools or colleges, are not easy to come by for desperately poor people.

Equally difficult to provide are cultural prerequisites — parental literacy, books in the home, or just an appreciation of a need for education great enough to overcome the competing need for the fruits of the children's labor in families living on the edge of subsistence. Uneducated or less educated parents are also less able to provide guidance to their children in their educational choices. Moreover, the apathy born of hoplessness does not evaporate immediately when a new world of opportunities and prerequisites appears. Even a fervent advocate of the untouchables, and of preferential policies for them, has urged untouchable students in medical and engineering schools to abandon their "indifference."[89]

The cumulative effects of these disadvantages are staggering. Moreover, most of the ways of lightening the burden are not politically expedient. In addition to telling disadvantaged groups unpalatable truths, statesmanlike political leaders would have to tell taxpayers the equally unpalatable truth that more money is needed to cover complementary costs that the poorest simply cannot afford — and tell more fortunate individuals and groups that there is no excuse for them to absorb benefits more urgently needed by others. Given the scope of the political task, it can hardly be surprising that it has not been performed.

Even for intellectuals on the sidelines and free of the need to get re-elected, there are challenging tasks. The first challenge is to give up easy indulgence in moral melodrama and look at the actual empirical consequences of affirmative action, rather than its rationales or its vision. It is so much easier to condemn a painful social reality than to determine what can be done in an almost impossible situation to make matters incrementally better without making other things worse. Dealing seriously with such problems means giving up easy "feel-good" gestures like adding points to the scores of less fortunate applicants for university admissions and subtracting points from the scores of the more fortunate — none of which changes the underlying realities or the consequences that will ultimately follow from those realities, including massive failures of students in settings where they are overmatched.

Any serious concern for the success of socially disadvantaged students in higher education must begin years before they reach universities. This means that even the most successful efforts at giving them the educational foundation that they need — and such success is not easy to come by — is unlikely to show results at the university level until perhaps a decade later. Yet how many politicians, activists, or intellectuals are prepared to wait that long? And if the easier path of group preferences and quotas is in place in the meantime, how much incentive will there be for the disadvantaged students to subject themselves to the painful self-discipline and hard work required to break old patterns of behavior and attitudes, in order to seize opportunities far out on the horizon? India is not the only country in which those given group preferences have shown "indifference" toward the hard task of preparing themselves to meet the standards expected of others. Similar complacency among those given group preferences has been observed in the United States, South Africa, and Malaysia. Why should anyone expect Indians to be different?

A small but encouraging sign has been an opinion survey among untouchables who are scavengers in various villages. While most see no better alternatives available for themselves, a majority have aspirations for their children to become educated for better work.[90] This longer run perspective among downtrodden people is both encouraging in itself and puts to shame the short-run expediency too often found among those further up the social scale in politics and in academia. Preferences and quotas can produce immediate increases in body counts of people from particular groups, however tenuous the position of such people may be — especially as university students who fail to finish. The make-believe equality of their physical presence can be both a mockery and an obstacle to real achievement.

How India will cope with its problems is a question with no easy answer and one obviously to be dealt with by Indians. What is clearer are the lessons that others can learn from India's experience with affirmative action. It has been said that those who refuse to heed history will be forced to repeat it. Much of the history of affirmative action in India has already begun to be repeated in other countries.

CHAPTER 3

Affirmative Action in Malaysia

Malaysia is a country of about 23 million people and one of the more prosperous countries in Southeast Asia. The population of Malaysia is 50 percent Malay, 24 percent Chinese and 7 percent Indian.[1] In earlier times, the Chinese minority was much larger — and at one time exceeded in size the Malay population. As of 1948, the population of colonial Malaya was 45 percent Chinese, 43 percent Malay and 10 percent Indian.[2] Much history lay behind those statistics, as well as the very different statistics of today. The higher fertility rate among the Malays than among the Chinese and Indian minorities[3] suggests that a Malay majority is assured for the future.

HISTORY

What is today called Malaysia is a combination of territories that were ruled by the British for about a century and a half. During most of that colonial era, which ended with independence in 1957, the central and most economically developed part of these territories was the Malay peninsula, at the tip of which is the island of Singapore, one of the leading ports in Asia. As the colony known as Malaya evolved into the independent nation of

Malaysia, it absorbed both Singapore and some territories on the island of Borneo to the east, which these territories shared with Indonesia. Most of the large island of Borneo belongs to Indonesia, whose other great island — Java — flanks Malaysia on the west.

While the two largest ethnic groups in Malaysia are the Malays and the Chinese, there is also a small Indian minority — mostly Tamils — and other indigenous peoples who, together with the Malays, make up the *bumiputeras* or "sons of the soil," for whom special provisions are made by the government. Although Malays are just half of the population of Malaysia, all the *bumiputeras* put together add up to 61 percent of the country's population.[4] In times past, the country's changing demography had much to do with its changing political structure. The first of these demographic changes began in the early nineteenth century, when immigrants began arriving from China.

British-ruled Malaya was just one of the countries in Southeast Asia to which vast numbers of immigrants from China moved during the era of European imperialism.[5] These Chinese immigrants were typically poor and illiterate, and so started at the bottom, working in hard, dirty, and menial tasks that the indigenous peoples of the region largely disdained. In British-ruled Malaya, the Chinese provided much of the labor of field hands working on rubber plantations, while people from India predominated among the miners working in the country's tin mines, as Malaya became and remained for many years the world's leading producer of these two products.

The capital and management for these enterprises were supplied by Westerners, while the labor was supplied by the Chinese and Indians, leaving little role for the Malays in the development of their own country's modern sectors. However, the Malays owned land and thus many were in a position to spurn the lowly and arduous jobs filled by the poverty-stricken Chinese and Indian immigrants. Where some Malays did work alongside the Chinese on rubber plantations, their output per worker was less than half that of the Chinese.[6] As the inflow of immigrants from China continued over the years and generations, the Chinese population of the Malay states rose from an estimated 100,000 in 1881 to more than a million just 50 years later.[7] By 1941, the Chinese out-numbered the Malays in British Malaya.[8]

Although the Chinese began at the bottom economically, their frugality enabled them to begin to move out of the ranks of laborers by setting up small businesses, usually tiny retail shops. While more than half of all the Chinese in Malaya in 1911 were laborers, either in agriculture or in the mines, just twenty years later only 11 percent were still in those occupations.[9] Even as they rose economically, however, the Chinese remained socially very separate and distinct from the indigenous Malays. The two groups spoke different languages, had different religions, and had wholly different lifestyles. The frugal Chinese lifestyle, for example, was very different from that of the Malays, who were known for free spending and for going into debt for the sake of social celebrations.[10] Population growth rates and infant mortality rates among the Chinese were both roughly half of these rates among the *bumiputeras*.[11] Given the many cultural differences among the various groups in Malaysia, it is not surprising that there have been very few inter-racial neighborhoods or inter-racial marriages in colonial Malaya or in the independent nation of Malaysia.

Over the years and generations, the Chinese built up businesses across Malaya, creating whole new industries in the process. In addition to innumerable small retail establishments, the Chinese also went into some larger ventures. For example, by 1920 Chinese-owned mines produced nearly two-thirds of the tin in Malaya, though Europeans later overtook them in tin production.[12] Retail trade, however, continued to be dominated by the Chinese, who eventually came to own 85 percent of all retail outlets in the country.[13] Although the Chinese had begun in Malaya much poorer than the Malays, their incomes rose over the years until they were earning more than double the average income of the Malays. Most of the capital invested in the country was owned by foreigners but, among the domestically owned corporate equity, most was owned by the Chinese.

Malaysia exhibits on a national scale patterns already seen in India's states of Assam, Maharashtra, Andhra Pradesh, and Karnataka — local people outperformed by outsiders, whether in education, in the labor force, or in business and industry. This situation produced the same explosive resentments found in India and in other countries, and ended with similar demands for preferential policies for those who could not meet the competition of the outsiders.

The Malays already enjoyed some preferential treatment under British colonial rule. Non-Malays faced strong restrictions against owning land in Malaya and the colonial government provided free education for Malays, while leaving others to educate their children however they could. Malays were also preferred for jobs in the colonial bureaucracy. Despite preferential treatment for Malays, however, the Chinese continued to outperform them. A higher percentage of Chinese children than Malay children received an education, even though the Chinese had to pay for their own private schooling.[14]

Inter-ethnic tensions were among the major challenges facing the British colony of Malaya when it became the independent Federation of Malaya in 1957. Later, after the addition of Singapore and other territories, the Federation of Malaya became the nation of Malaysia. The country's constitution guaranteed the political supremacy of the indigenous Malays, both directly and by weighting votes in rural areas, where the Malays predominated, more heavily than votes in the cities, where the Chinese were in the majority. The close similarity in population sizes between the Chinese and the Malays at that point made the Malays uneasy about maintaining that supremacy in the future. The Chinese were already demanding equal treatment for all citizens of Malaysia, while the Malays wanted to maintain and expand preferential treatment for themselves and other indigenous people as *bumiputeras* or "sons of the soil."

This inter-ethnic strife was resolved by one of the most remarkable political decisions: Singapore was expelled from Malaysia in 1965 — one of the few times in history when a country has voluntarily divested itself of part of its own territory. Because Singapore had a heavily Chinese population, its expulsion left Malaysia with a comfortable Malay majority, which was the whole point of the action. Now Malays held unchallengeable political control of Malaysia.

POLITICS AND PREFERENCES

Malaysia's major political parties have been ethnic parties — the United Malay Nationalist Organization (UMNO) being the largest, with the Malayan Chinese Association and the Malayan Indian Congress representing the two principal minority groups. In other countries around the world, political parties representing a single ethnic group each have been promoters of polarization. In Malaysia, however, these three ethnic parties formed a political coalition known as the Alliance Party, seeking to mollify all segments of the society. The mutual accommodations growing out of coalition politics were challenged by other ethnic parties, each demanding more for its own respective group. Yet none of these more militant ethnic parties has succeeded in displacing the ruling coalition parties, which have held power in Malaysia from the moment of its independence onward, and the country's prime ministers have all been ethnically Malay.

Government policies steered a middle course between equal rights for all — both politically and constitutionally unattainable in Malaysia — and extreme demands for an Islamic state and suppression of Chinese economic activities. The initial compromise included a continuation and expansion of preferences for the Malays in government, with various symbolic recognitions of Malay supremacy, and a raising of taxes largely from Chinese and foreign businesses, to be spent largely to benefit Malays.[15] Meanwhile, there was a more or less free hand for the Chinese, the Indians and others in the economy, and admission to university education was by performance standards that were the same for all. With admission to the University of Malaysia being determined solely on the basis of examination results, Malays gained only 20 percent of the places and most of the non-Malay students were Chinese.[16] In the Malaysian air force, more than half the officers were Chinese in 1969.[17]

Another feature of the Malaysian political landscape has been draconian emergency powers of the government, partly a holdover from colonial days, when the British had been fighting a Communist guerilla movement. Now these laws could be — and were — invoked whenever the government wished to suppress any public questioning of the country's racial policies. This severe limit on free speech was also a severe limit on the kind of racial demagoguery that has torn other multi-ethnic countries apart.

The continued and highly visible inferior position of Malays outside the political realm was galling to the pride and aspirations of the Malays, providing political fuel to those who wished to attack the compromises of the ruling UMNO-led coalition. However, when the coalition won a close victory in the elections of 1969, some jubilant Chinese began celebrating in the streets — setting off riots by angry Malays that changed the whole future direction of the country.

Malay mobs attacked Chinese and killed hundreds of them, with thousands more being made homeless.[18] In order to further mollify the Malays and spare the country more bloodshed, the government launched a sweeping set of programs called the New Economic Policy, designed to achieve what it called "racial balance." In the words of an official government publication:

If racial balance in the employment field is to be achieved such that the proportion of the various races in employment in the major sectors of the economy reflects the racial composition of the labour force, all racial groups benefit fully from full employment and existing differentials in *per capita* income between the various races are narrowed, then intersectorial movements of labour, as well as movements to higher productivity activities within sectors, of a sizeable order will be necessary.[19]

Under the New Economic Policy, the preferences which already existed in government employment were extended to employment in the private sector, including foreign firms operating in Malaysia. In addition, the New Economic Policy set as a goal the transfer of 30 percent of all corporate stock in Malaysia to Malays — either individually or to the government acting in the name of the Malay population. As of the time this goal was set, Malays owned less than 2 percent of the country's corporate equity.[20] They did not reach the goal of 30 percent ownership by the target date of 1990, but they did reach 21 percent by 1995.[21] However, the composition of those who benefitted was biased toward elites whose political support was important to the ruling coalition:

Malay businesspeople, virtually all of whom had UMNO connections, were given preference in obtaining licenses, credit, and government contracts. As part of the strategy to increase Malay participation in the modern economy, the government forced established Chinese and foreign enterprises to restructure in such a way that at least 30 percent of their shares would be owned by Malays — either government agencies acting "on behalf of" the Malay community or private Malay businesspeople. Enterprises that failed to restructure found it increasingly difficult to renew necessary licenses or obtain contracts with the expanding state sector. The normal way for large companies to restructure was through the issue of new shares that were made available to Malay purchasers at below par prices.[22]

Government loan programs were also established to offer credit preferentially to Malays. Educational preferences for Malays were also greatly expanded. The New Economic Policy provided numerous opportunities for dispensing patronage to officials and supporters of the ruling coalition parties, especially the dominant United Malays National Organization. For example, UMNO politicians have often had their own business enterprises, which receive preferential treatment from the government. A World Bank report on the issuance of housing licenses in Malaysia called it "an easy route to instant wealth" for politicians.[23]

While members of parliament and state assemblies had special opportunities to profit from the New Economic Policy, benefits were also passed down to lower level officials of government and of the ruling parties, as well as to their supporters. Preferential access to taxi or trucking licenses for Malays became, in practice, preferential access to those Malays who were members of UMNO or relatives or protégés of UMNO officials. Moreover, people who spoke out in opposition to the ruling coalition could find government benefits denied or discontinued for themselves or their localities.[24]

Loans to give Malays preferential access to credit to start businesses often became in practice gifts because of a widespread feeling that these "loans do not have to be repaid." This was especially so when "the debtors, drawn largely from the ranks of the local, ruling party stalwarts, are well-nigh untouchable."[25] Similarly with the State Economic Development Corporations. Of the 314 companies set up by the SEDCs, less than a third made a profit in 1982, while 125 operated at a loss and 86 did not even bother to file reports.[26] In short, Malaysia's preferential policies, like those in other countries, tended to benefit primarily those who were already well off and well connected. Even Chinese developers with connections to Malay politicians benefitted from government housing programs.[27]

The country's program to eradicate poverty likewise tended "to benefit the relatively better off in rural areas."[28]

Although preferential hiring of Malays for government jobs had existed since colonial times, Malay predominance in administrative and non-professional occupations did not extend to the scientific, professional, and technical branches of government, where the Chinese and the Indians continued to dominate for some time, even after independence.[29] This predominance of the Chinese in the private economy and in those government functions requiring higher levels of scientific, technical, or professional skills was too overwhelming to go unnoticed. Malaysia was not a poor country like India. The Malays' problem was not hunger or grinding poverty, but was rather the fact that they were clearly outshone by others. The New Economic Policy was designed to remedy these embarrassing ethnic imbalances in educational insitutions and in the economy.

Like so many other preferential programs, the New Economic Policy was initially designed to be temporary. It was set to expire in 20 years but, like those in India and Pakistan, has continued on long past the projected cut-off date. In a formal sense, the New Economic Policy ended in 1990 as planned, but was replaced by the National Development Policy, which continued many of the same policies under the new name. When in the year 2000 a Chinese political group suggested that preferences and quotas actually end, angry responses from the Malay public and the Malaysian government caused the suggestion to be withdrawn.

EDUCATIONAL DIFFERENCES AND CHANGES

Educationally, the Malays lagged behind the Chinese, not only quantitatively but also qualitatively. At the university level, Malay students enrolled in the least demanding courses, while there were few with the qualifications to specialize in subjects requiring mathematical or scientific knowledge.[30] As of academic year 1962–63, for example, Malay students at the University of Malaya were outnumbered by Chinese students in the faculties of agriculture, arts, engineering, and science. In the latter two faculties, Malays were outnumbered even by students from the small Indian minority.[31] In mathematical, scientific, and technological specialties, the disparities between the Chinese and the Malays were particularly extreme. In the 1960s, Chinese students received 1,488 Bachelor of Science degrees, while Malay students received just 69. In engineering, Chinese students received 408 Bachelor's degrees, while Malay students received just four.[32]

Although the government assured "other Malaysians" that the New Economic Policy to advance the indigenous *bumiputeras* would not adversely affect the minorities,[33] the changes had a particularly adverse effect in education. Among the changes in the rules was the imposition of the Malay language as the medium of instruction in schools and colleges, and the ending of admissions to the country's universities on the basis of individual performance. Both changes had devastating impacts on the Chinese and Indian younger generations.

Under the new admissions policy, the number of Chinese students attending the University of Malaysia declined absolutely between 1970 and 1980,[34] despite an increase in the total number of university students during that decade.[35] The total number of degrees received by students of Chinese ancestry in the country's institutions of higher education declined during the decade of the 1970s,[36] even though the total number of degree recipients in Malaysia more than doubled.[37]

The conversion of English-language public schools into Malay-language schools began in 1970 with the first grade of primary school. Each year another grade was converted until the process was completed in 1982. The Chinese and Indians, long used to being educated in English and seldom being fluent in Malay, found it more difficult to attend the government-provided schools and to master materials taught in a different language. While 72 percent of Malay students with six years of education passed a composition test in the Malay language in 1991, only 33 percent of the Chinese students and 19 percent of the Indian students passed. In mathematics, 87 percent of the Malay students passed, while only 57 percent of the Chinese students and 50 percent of the Indian students passed.[38] In view of the prior record of achievements in education, by the Chinese especially, clearly these new results reflected problems created by the new language policy, rather than academic deficiencies in the students.

With Chinese and Indian students having a harder time getting into Malaysia's universities, many began to look to other countries as places for higher education. By 1980, tens of thousands of students from Malaysia had left the country to study at the university level. Three-fifths of these students were Chinese.[39] A majority of all Indian students seeking higher education also left Malaysia.[40] Even at the secondary school level, more than 10,000 students left Malaysia to study in adjoining Singapore,[41] where teaching was still done in the English language. Some of those who studied abroad stayed abroad.[42]

A partial reversal in language policy occurred in 1993, when the prime minister of Malaysia announced that instruction in English at the university level would be permitted in the fields of science, technology, and medicine[43] — fields where apparently it was difficult to get enough Malays to replace the Chinese and the Indians, and where there was a shortage of highly skilled personnel.[44] In August 2001, the government announced that university admission would again be based on individual performance.[45] However, this so-called "merit" system established two different ways of gaining university admissions, the easier method being open only to Malay students. The net result was that the Malay share of university admissions rose from what it had been under the racial quota system.

ECONOMIC DIFFERENCES AND CHANGES

Expanded preferences for the *bumiputeras* or "sons of the soil" took place during a period of rapid expansion in the Malaysian economy. Over the period from 1971 to 1990, Malaysia's annual rate of economic growth averaged 6.7 percent—which then escalated to 8.7 percent over the next five years. During that whole period, real per capita income in Malaysia more than tripled.[46] The official poverty rate declined from 52 percent in 1970 to 17 percent by 1990 and fell under 10 percent by 1995.[47] In short, Malaysia's growing "sons of the soil" preferences took effect during an unusually favorable economic climate. This permitted the indigenous Malays to have both an absolute and a relative rise economically, without requiring the Chinese to suffer an absolute decline in the economy, as they did in educational institutions.

Before the New Economic Policy went into effect in 1971, Malay income was a little less than half of Chinese income. Twenty eight years later, there were apparently modest changes in relative incomes. However, official statistics have used changing definitions over the years, making comparisons inexact. The statistics are suggestive, rather than definitive, in part because the earlier data are for Malays and Chinese in "peninsular Malaysia" and later data compare "bumiputeras"—which include some indigenous non-Malays—and cover the whole of Malaysia, including communities on the island of Borneo. Mean income is compared, rather than median income, simply because data for the latter are unavailable from the later five-year plans. However, the relative ratios showed little or no differences between mean and median percentages during the years when both were available. In any event, see Table 1.

What the data suggest is that changes in the relative incomes of the Chinese and the Malays after the New Economic Policy was instituted have not been dramatic. Malay income as a percentage of Chinese income increased by 3 percentage

TABLE 1: MEAN MONTHLY INCOME OF MALAYS
AND CHINESE

YEAR	MALAY	CHINESE	PERCENTAGE
1970	172 dollars	394 dollars	44 percent
1973	209 dollars	461 dollars	45 percent
1976	237 dollars	540 dollars	44 percent
1979	309 dollars	659 dollars	47 percent

points during the decade of the 1970s and *bumiputera* income increased by 5 percentage points in the later era with a different base year. However, this is not to say that the total increase was 8 percentage points. In the one overlapping year — 1979 — there was a five-point difference between the percentages in Table 1 and those in Table 2, so the data in the two tables cannot be added because they are not comparable for the same year.

TABLE 2: MEAN MONTHLY INCOME OF BUMIPUTERAS
AND CHINESE

YEAR	BUMIPUTERA	CHINESE	PERCENTAGE
1979	296 dollars	565 dollars	52 percent
1984	384 dollars	678 dollars	57 percent
1990	940 ringgit	1,631 ringgit	58 percent
1995	1,600 ringgit	2,895 ringgit	55 percent
1997	2,038 ringgit	3,738 ringgit	55 percent
1999	1,984 ringgit	3,456 ringgit	57 percent

Sources: Fourth Malaysia Plan: 1981–1985 (Kuala Lumpur: National Printing Department, 1981), p. 56; *Fifth Malaysia Plan: 1986–1990* (Kuala Lumpur: National Printing Department, 1986), p. 99; *Buku Tahunan Peranqkaan: Yearbook of Statistics, Malaysia 2001* (Department of Statistics, 2001), p. 226.

There were a number of other factors at work, besides group preferences, during this era, which might have influenced whatever income changes took place. Between 1970 and 1995, the Malaysian economy evolved from being one where a majority of people worked in agriculture and forestry to one in which fewer than one fifth did.[48] Since the Chinese were already predominantly urban at the beginning of the period, this meant that it was the Malays whose rural-urban mix was changing dramatically. This in turn affected the relative incomes of the two groups, since urban incomes have consistently been substantially higher than rural incomes in Malaysia, as in other countries. Therefore, a mere shift of population from the countrysides to the towns would itself raise the Malay income as a percentage of Chinese income nationally, whether or not there were affirmative action policies and whether or not those policies had much impact on the average Malay.

The emigration of Chinese professionals and Chinese capital from Malaysia in the wake of the New Economic Policy is another factor, of unknown magnitude in its effects on the relative incomes of the Chinese and the Malays. Between 1976 and 1985, an estimated $12 billion worth of capital left Malaysia, more than half owned by the Chinese.[49] If the Chinese who emigrated from Malaysia were more prosperous than those who remained, as seems quite possible, then that would also affect the relative income of the two groups, as an indirect effect of group preferences.

Separating out the effect of preferences and quotas is complicated in Malaysia, as in other countries, by the fact that a dramatic increase in education among the preferred group *preceded* these policies. The number of children attending the government's secondary schools increased by 73 percent in the five years before 1970 — that is, before the New Economic Policy escalated Malay preferences. That number jumped another 86 percent during the decade of the 1970s and by another 56 percent during the 1980s.[50] The expansion of enrollments in higher education during these years further complicates any attempt to assess how much of the income changes were due to "sons of the soil" preferences, as such. Certainly policy changes did not take place in an unchanging environment.

In Malaysia, as in other countries, the principal beneficiaries of preferences and quotas were those who were already more fortunate. An early empirical study of the effects of the New Economic Policy concluded that "at most 5 percent" of the Malays benefited from such policies.[51] Within the Malay population, the income share of the top 10 percent rose significantly.[52] Dr. Mahathir bin Mohamad, a Malay political leader later destined to become prime minister, recognized the fact that it was the elite, rather than the masses, who benefitted from group preferences for the *bumiputeras* and bluntly admitted it, as well as seeking to justify it:

> These few Malays, for they are still only very few, have waxed rich not because of themselves but because of the policy of a government supported by a huge majority of poor Malays. It would seem that the efforts of the poor Malays have gone to enrich a select few of their own people. The poor Malays themselves have not gained one iota. But if these few Malays are not enriched the poor Malays will not gain either. It is the Chinese who will continue to live in huge houses and regard the Malays as only fit to drive their cars. With the existence of the few rich Malays at least the poor can say their fate is not entirely to serve rich non-Malays. From the point of view of racial ego, and this ego is still strong, the unseemly existence of Malay tycoons is essential.[53]

With the passing decades, Malays began to move into areas where they had been greatly under-represented before. Because of the country's rising prosperity, combined with its shift from an agricultural to a commercial and industrial economy, the demand for more skilled and educated people opened more opportunities for the Malays, without reducing the absolute numbers of Chinese in the same professions. For example, Malays were only 4 percent of all engineers in Malaysia in 1970, before the New Economic Policy went into effect, but this rose to 24 percent a decade later and then to 35 percent of the engineers in Malaysia by 1990. Yet, even at this latter date, the Chinese were 58 percent of the engineers. Five years later, Malays were 38 percent of the engineers and the Chinese 55 percent—and yet both groups now contained more engineers in absolute numbers, with their combined totals of engineers having risen nearly 50 percent in the years between 1990 and 1995. It was much the same story in the medical profession. Malays were just 4 percent of the doctors in Malaysia in 1970 but, by 1995, Malays rose to become 28 percent of the doctors—and again, there were both more Malay doctors and more Chinese doctors in 1995.[54] In the year 2000, the distribution of the principal ethnic groups in various professional occupations was as follows:

TABLE 3: PROFESSIONAL OCCUPATIONS, 2000

	BUMIPUTERA	CHINESE	INDIANS
ARCHITECTS	1,258	1,677	48
ACCOUNTANTS	2,673	11,944	883
ENGINEERS	15,334	18,416	1,864
DOCTORS	4,592	3,827	3,689
LAWYERS	3,118	3,861	2,588

Source: Buku Tahunan Perangkaan: Yearbook of Statistics, Malaysia 2001 (Department of Statistics, 2001), p. 215.

Although the goal of increasing the share of corporate capital owned by the Malays was not reached by 1990, as originally planned, a considerable change in the shares owned by different ethnic groups was visible. The Malay share rose from 2 percent in 1969 to 19 percent by 1990. This included about 5 percent owned by the government in the name of the *bumiputeras*. At the same time, the Chinese owned 46 percent of the corporate capital — a little more than that owned by Malays and foreigners combined. By 1995, however, the Chinese share had fallen to 41 percent while the Malay share rose to 21 percent, with the foreign share at 28 percent. Nevertheless, all of them had more capital, in absolute amounts, as the corporate capital in Malaysia grew by 11 percent per year.[55]

In short, a rapidly growing Malaysian economy, especially in its modern and industrial sectors, has allowed the Malays to advance economically, both absolutely and relative to the Chinese, without the Chinese having to suffer absolute declines in income or occupation or ownership of capital. Only in governmental institutions did the Chinese suffer absolute declines as a result of preferential policies for the Malays. This was in keeping with patterns found elsewhere around the world, where preferential policies have had their strongest effects within government and in government-controlled institutions.

A 1971 survey showed that most Malay doctors, lawyers, engineers, and other such professionals were employed by the government, while most Chinese in the same professions were employed in the private sector.[56] Moreover, within government, Malay advancement took place at the expense of the Chinese. Between 1969 and 1973, 98 percent of the new government employees were Malays. Including the armed forces makes that 99 percent.[57] While the total number of people in Malaysia's police force and the military expanded substantially between 1969–70 and 1974–80, the number of non-Malays in both organizations declined absolutely.[58] Similarly, in the government-controlled universities, as already noted, the number of Chinese students declined absolutely between 1970 and 1980,[59] even as the total number of students there was increasing.[60]

SINGAPORE

Although Singapore is an independent city-state, its experience is relevant to that of Malaysia, not only because it was once part of Malaysia back in the early 1960s, but also because the same two principal racial ethnic groups — Malays and Chinese — comprise the great majority of its population. As of 1995, 77 percent of the people in Singapore were Chinese, 14 percent Malay and 7 percent Indian.[61] Singapore is one of the principal ports in its part of the world, handling nearly one-fourth of Malaysia's exports, in addition to its own exports. Singapore is also one of the most prosperous countries in Asia, with a per capita gross domestic product more than five times that of Malaysia.

Unlike Malaysia, Singapore does not have preferential policies, and in fact tries to promote a generic Singaporean identity for members of all groups. All children in Singapore are taught English, which is the principal language of government and business there, though most Singaporeans do not speak English in their homes,[62] but instead speak Chinese, Malay, or Tamil. Here, as in Malaysia, the Malays have been outperformed by the Chinese in both the schools and the economy. Nor has this been demonstrably changed by the Singapore government's policy of scattering Malay families among Chinese families in housing developments. However, some Malays express a preference for Chinese neighbors "because they consider that the Chinese will not intrude or interfere in their personal or family lives." Some Malay parents and children "choose schools where there are more Chinese and few Malays, in the hope that the student will learn good study habits from the Chinese while also avoiding Malay company."[63] Chinese as well as Malay parents recognize such differences. As one study found:

> Some parents note with pride that their children have mostly Chinese friends, because they mix with fellow Chinese students at

school and avoid Malay company in the neighborhood. In the process of attempting to gain social mobility through education, it is not only non-studious children who must be avoided but *Malay* children in general, since non-studiousness is a trait taken by Malays (as well as non-Malays) to characterize Malays as an ethnic group.[64]

While it is fashionable in some quarters to dismiss such views of groups as "stereotypes," the people who hold these views are in daily contact with the groups in question, while those who dismiss their beliefs are often far removed from the scene. Moreover, the same view is shared by both ethnic groups in this case.

Although Singapore and Malaysia follow entirely different policies as regards ethnic groups, both have for many years avoided intergroup outbreaks of violence of the sort plaguing India and other countries. The common factor behind relative peace between the Chinese and the Malays in the two places cannot be affirmative action because Singapore does not have affirmative action. What both governments do have are very severe repressions of free speech, preventing individuals from following careers as racial agitators or fomenters of intergroup strife. Both countries have also had long periods of economic prosperity.

A minor flap erupted in 2001 when Singapore's prime minister pointed out that Malays in Singapore are economically better off than Malays in Malaysia. More Singaporean Malays have an upper secondary or higher education than do Malays in Malaysia. Accordingly, a higher percentage of the Malays in Singapore have administrative or professional jobs.[65] Clearly, Malays have done better as a minority without affirmative action in Singapore than as a majority with preferences and quotas in Malaysia.

SUMMARY AND IMPLICATIONS

Affirmative action in Malaysia has produced results similar to those in India and other countries with preferential policies, in some respects, but very different results in other respects. Just as the actual beneficiaries of preferences and quotas for untouchables in India have been estimated to be no more than 6 percent of the designated beneficiary group, so in Malaysia no more than 5 percent of the Malays have been estimated to have actually benefitted from such programs. In both countries, those people who were initially more fortunate were the most benefitted. In both countries — and in others — the supposedly temporary preferences have been extended past the point projected for their termination. Similarly, the "indifference" noted among untouchable students admitted preferentially to higher education in India has been also been observed in Malaysia: "Malay students, who sense that their future is assured, feel less pressure to perform."[66] Even Malaysia's own long-time Prime Minister, Mahatir bin Mohamad, one of the advocates and architects of the country's affirmative action policies, said in August 2002:

> Getting scholarships and places in the universities at home and abroad is considered a matter of right and is not valued any more. Indeed, those who get these educational opportunities, for some unknown reason, seem to dislike the very people who created these opportunities.
>
> Worse still, they don't seem to appreciate the opportunities that they get. They become more interested in other things, politics in particular, to the detriment of their studies.
>
> In business, the vast majority regarded the opportunities given them as something to be exploited for the quickest return.
>
> Very early on, they sold off their opportunities in order to become sleeping partners in an arrangement known cynically as 'Ali Baba,' in which Ali merely obtains the licenses, permits,

shares or contracts, and immediately sells these to non-Malays, mainly Chinese.

They learn nothing about business and become even less capable of doing business and earning an income from their activities.[67]

Dr. Mahathir declared: "I feel disappointed because I achieved too little of my principal task of making my race a successful race, a race that is respected."[68]

In other respects, Malaysia has had one of the most successful programs of affirmative action in the world, where success is defined solely in terms of the relative advancement of the designated beneficiary group and avoidance of the kind of widespread violence found in India and elsewhere. But Malaysia has paid the price in other ways.

Draconian sedition laws stifle public criticisms of the preferential policies and of racial policies in general. Educational standards declined in the country's universities after student admissions and faculty hiring were no longer based on individual performances, but on group membership. Shortages of highly trained people in highly technical fields have developed, as members of those groups who previously excelled in these fields have been systematically kept out of the universities and have often left the country for their education and not returned. However, like some other countries promoting group preferences and quotas, Malaysia did so in the name of "national unity,"[69] however little unity it actually produced or however such disaffection it created.

While the degree of success of affirmative action in Malaysia compares favorably with that of similar programs in other countries today, it is not historically unique. Similar success, in terms of benefitting one group at all costs, was achieved by apartheid in South Africa and by the racial laws in Germany under the Nazis. What has yet to be achieved is similar "success" in democratic nations with freedom of speech. Moreover, even in Malaysia, the benefits of preferential policies have gone disproportionately to those who were already more fortunate. Nor is it clear, after more than 30 years of such policies, that even the fortunate Malay beneficiaries have reached the point where they are able to compete on equal terms with members of the Chinese or Indian minorities.

Prime Minister Mahathir, who had declared in 1966 that Malays must become prepared to compete with other groups on equal terms,[70] declared in August 2000: "There are some who think that they can progress on their own. They are mistaken. Without the government's help, those who think they are strong will fall flat." Moreover, he was keenly aware of the explosive dangers of allowing racial agitators to stir up the country's various groups against one another, creating a "conflagration" that would "engulf us all."[71] The history of many multi-ethnic societies around the world makes this no idle paranoia — especially where one group's achievements have greatly outstripped another's, as in Fiji, Sri Lanka, India, Rwanda and much of pre–World War II Central and Eastern Europe, where envy and resentment of Jews was stirred up to a fever pitch that culminated in widespread cooperation with the Holocaust, run by the Nazis but with a chilling amount of cooperation from others in Eastern Europe.

If there is any lesson from the history of affirmative action in Malaysia, it is that extraordinary economic prosperity and growth, combined with extraordinary repression of free speech, can make preferential programs politically viable and repress mass intergroup violence. But to say that the country as a whole is better off with affirmative action would be to ignore many counterproductive consequences. The fact that the adjoining city-state of Singapore, which has no affirmative action program, has likewise had extraordinary prosperity and extraordinary repression of free speech — as well as being ruled by one political party, in power since its independence, decades ago — suggests some of the other factors responsible for racial peace between the Malays and the Chinese. Neither country's experience can serve as a guide to racial peace in countries where free speech and other democratic rights prevail.

Malaysia's experience is very relevant, however, to a widespread belief in some countries that ethnic imbalances can only be a result of discrimination against the under-represented group—and that any suggestion that this is due to a failure of the group itself to achieve the same qualifications as others is "blaming the victim," if not racism. No one in Malaysia has been in any position to discriminate against the Malays or to victimize them otherwise. When admission to the University of Malaysia was based on individual performance, this university was run by Malays and was responsible to a government that was also run by Malays. Yet Chinese students predominated in many areas of the university and even the small Indian minority supplied more students than the Malay majority in some fields. There were simply not enough qualified Malays.

Even after the imposition of "some of the soil" preferences for their benefit, there were still not enough qualified Malays in scientific, medical, and technical fields to satisfy the Malaysian government, dominated by Malays, leading to a reversal in language policy in 1993. A reversion to an admissions policy based on individual achievement in 2001 further strengthens the conclusion that even a government dominated by Malays found the qualifications of Malay students inadequate. The fact that some groups are less qualified than others cannot be arbitrarily dismissed as a mere "stereotype" or "perception" by outsiders. Nor are performance differences limited to academic performances. According to *The Straits Times,* published in Singapore, in January 2002 Malaysia's Prime Minister Mahathir "lamented the fact that bumiputeras are not serious in completing government projects because they tend to sell them to second, third, and fourth parties. According to the prime minister, nearly 85 percent of the projects have not been completed."[72]

CHAPTER 4

Affirmative Action in Sri Lanka

The island nation of Sri Lanka, located about 20 miles off the southeast coast of India, stretches 270 miles from north to south and 140 miles from east to west. It has a population of 19 million. Roughly three-quarters of its people are Sinhalese and the principal minority, the Tamils, are less than one-sixth of the population. Since the middle of the twentieth century, Sri Lanka has undergone one of the most remarkable — and catastrophic — changes in the relationship between its majority and minority populations.

Formerly the British colony of Ceylon, Sri Lanka achieved independence in 1948 with a promising future being anticipated by its own people and by outside observers alike. There was a basis for such optimism. Although the Sinhalese and the Tamils differed in ethnicity, language and religion — and seldom intermarried — there was much evidence of goodwill across the social lines that divided them. The elites of both groups were Westernized, English-speaking, and cosmopolitan, and were used to working together in the British civil service and in private British businesses. Both elites tended to live in Westernized enclaves together, and apart from the more traditional masses of their respective groups. Moreover, the country's political leaders were committed to a secular, democratic state, recognizing the rights of all its citizens, regardless of their ethnicity or religion. This live-and-let-live pattern was not confined to the elites or to politics. Whatever the historic clashes of Sinhalese and Tamils in centuries past, there had never been a race riot between them during the first half of the twentieth century.[1]

Other groups in the population of the country included Moslems and Christians. Relations among the various ethnic and religious groups in Sri Lanka were described by an American scholar as "cordial, unmarred by the sort of friction that exists between Hindus and Moslems in India." It was not unusual for Buddhists to appear at Hindu festivals or Christmas celebrations, for example. As a Sri Lankan scholar described the situation:

> In striking contrast to other parts of South Asia (including Burma), Sri Lanka in 1948 was an oasis of stability, peace and order. The transfer of power was smooth and peaceful, a reflection of the moderate tone of the dominant strand in the country's nationalist movement. More important, one saw very little of the divisions and bitterness which were tearing at the recent independence of the South Asian countries. In general, the situation seemed to provide an impressive basis for a solid start in nation-building and national regeneration.[2]

Yet this all changed radically within a decade after independence, as a result of politicizing intergroup differences and instituting preferential policies. The basis for such policies was the familiar fact that different groups were not proportionally represented in the universities or the professions or in businesses. More specifically, the Tamil minority was more favorably situated in all these respects than the Sinhalese majority. As with other such differences in other countries, the reasons go back into history.

HISTORICAL BACKGROUND

A succession of European conquerors arrived in Ceylon over the centuries — first the Portuguese (1597–1658), then the Dutch (1658–1796), and finally the British (1796–1948). The first two invaders conquered the coastal regions of the island, but the British eventually conquered all of it, though not all at one time. One lasting consequence of this history was that different regions of the country experienced Westernization of different kinds for differing periods of time and therefore differed among themselves culturally. Such differences existed within the Sinhalese and Tamil populations, as well as between them.

The Tamils were concentrated in the geographically less promising and less prosperous northern part of the island, with a dry climate and a lack of natural resources, while the Sinhalese lived where there was more fertile soil and more ample rainfall. When the various conquerors established Christian missionary schools, the Tamils more readily seized upon education as a way out of their geographically disadvantaged circumstances. During the era of British rule, Americans also established a missionary school that eventually became Jaffna College, located in the northern region, where Tamils were concentrated. American educators put more emphasis on mathematics and science than did the British schools, where a more literary education was offered. This meant that the Tamils were particularly well trained in subjects that would permit them to enter the sciences, engineering, and the medical field in the years ahead.

Historic head starts had enduring consequences in Ceylon, as in other parts of the world. Nor were Tamils the only group to benefit from Western education. The much earlier Dutch colonial rule had left as part of its legacy a racially mixed Ceylonese group known as "Burghers" (many being part-Dutch), whose earlier assimilation to Western culture enabled them to prosper in later colonial regimes, including that of the British, where they served in the colonial civil service. As of 1870, these Eurasian Burghers constituted the great majority of physicians and surgeons employed by the colonial government, even though Burghers were less than one percent of Ceylon's population.[3] Although descended from the Dutch and the Ceylonese, most Burghers spoke English after the imposition of British rule, since English facilitated employment by the British authorities. As late as 1911, less than ten percent of the Sinhalese or Tamils spoke English, compared to more than three-quarters of the Burghers.

Geography has complicated the cultural differences within both the Sinhalese and the Tamil groups. As has often happened in other parts of the world, the highlands resisted the invaders longer than the lowlands. It was not until 1815 that the British conquered the Kandyan highlands in the south of Ceylon. What this meant culturally was that the lowland Sinhalese began to be Westernized before the Kandyan Sinhalese. After the British conquest of the Kandyan highlands, they began to import Tamils from India to work on British-owned plantations there. This meant that there were now two culturally different groups of Tamils in Ceylon as well, often referred to as the "Ceylon Tamils" and the "Indian Tamils." Separated geographically as well as culturally, these two Tamil groups had little interaction with or impact on one another. The "Indian Tamils" — still called that a hundred years after their settlement in Ceylon — were the poorest, most isolated and uneducated portion of the country's population and were generally of lower caste than the Ceylon Tamils.

Against this historical background, it is hardly surprising that there remained in the twentieth century great differences in the relative representation of the various groups and subgroups at the university level or in business and the professions. With the passing years and the spread of education among the

Ceylon Tamils and the Sinhalese, the tiny minority of Burghers was overtaken in government employment by these much
larger groups. Moreover, among all these various groups, the
timing and degree of their Westernization, education, and ability to speak English in colonial times was reflected in their
educational and employment patterns for generations, extending well into the post-colonial era of Sri Lanka.

As of 1921, half the lawyers in Ceylon were Sinhalese, the
lowlanders being 46 percent and the highlanders 4 percent,
even though the highlanders were about half as numerous as
the lowland Sinhalese. Ceylon Tamils, who were only about half
as numerous as the highland Sinhalese, nevertheless provided
28 percent of the lawyers, despite being only 12 percent of the
total population at that time.[4] But there were no Indian Tamil
lawyers at all, even though Indian Tamils at that point outnumbered Ceylon Tamils.[5]

It was much the same story in the medical profession. The
Ceylon Tamil minority actually produced more doctors than
any other group — 44 percent of all doctors or other medical
practitioners, compared to 34 percent who were Sinhalese
(only a tenth of whom were highland Sinhalese). Burghers
provided another 12 percent — and, again, none at all were
Indian Tamils.[6] Similar patterns continued over the years. In
Ceylon University College in 1942, 30 percent of all the students were Ceylon Tamils, nearly three times their representation in the population.[7]

Although the top echelons of the colonial civil service were
dominated by Englishmen, and the Sinhalese were a majority
of the native Ceylonese civil servants, the Ceylon Tamils were
still much over-represented relative to their percentage of the
population.[8] Over the years, the Sinhalese began catching up
with the Tamils in English education and by 1946 there were
205 Sinhalese doctors, compared to 115 Tamils.[9] However, the
Ceylon Tamils continued to be over-represented relative to

their share of the population. That same year, two years before independence, Ceylon Tamils occupied 30 percent of the positions in the Ceylon government and 40 percent of the judicial posts.[10] In keeping with their educational backgrounds, Ceylon Tamils were especially successful in scientific and technical fields.[11] As of 1948, the year of national independence, 40 percent of the engineers in the government's irrigation department were Tamils.[12]

Although the vast majority of Indian Tamils remained plantation laborers, on into the second half of the twentieth century, there were other immigrants from India who came to Ceylon in other capacities. While many of these other Indians worked in lowly occupations such as laborers, servants, and rickshaw pullers, some of these later Indian immigrants became traders, businessmen, and money-lenders. These latter were typically from groups with an entrepreneurial history in India, such as the Gujaratis and the Chettiars. In business as elsewhere, the Sinhalese were eclipsed by minorities, as well as by Europeans. At one point, 40 percent of all the credit extended by pawn-brokers in Ceylon was extended by Chettiars. Nearly 90 percent of all the imported rice was imported by Indians — and the rest by Europeans. As of 1945, there were an estimated 750 Chettiar firms in Ceylon, with an aggregate capital of £7.5 million.[13] The retailing, wholesaling, and textile trades were also largely in the hands of Indians.[14]

None of this went unnoticed, least of all by politicians looking for issues with which to mobilize voters. Even during British colonial rule, laws passed in 1938 began restrictions against Indian businessmen and these restriction were tightened in later years.[15] Despite such restrictions, however, a Sinhalese politician could still complain in 1955, "in the towns and villages, in business and in boutiques most of the work is in the hands of the Tamil-speaking people."[16] The stage was set for affirmative action.

AFFIRMATIVE ACTION AND ITS AFTERMATH

When Ceylon achieved its independence in 1948 and later changed its name to Sri Lanka, its positions of power, wealth and prestige were largely in the hands of an educated, English-speaking, often Christian, elite, both Sinhalese and Tamil. Yet the great majority of the country's population was Buddhist and Sinhala-speaking, while most members of its principal minority were Hindu and spoke Tamil. However historically understandable this situation might be, its political viability was another story. In Sri Lanka, as in some other countries, there was a growing number of newly educated people seeking employment in positions dominated by other groups — especially as government employees — and this newly educated group created political pressures for group preferences and quotas.[17]

At first, the rising numbers of educated but non-English-speaking Sinhalese spearheaded a reaction against Western culture, language and religion.[18] Buddhists resented the large role of government-subsidized Christian missionary schools in the education of Sri Lankans. There was also an understandable demand that the affairs of the government no longer be conducted in English but in the people's "own language." Like so many political catchwords, the demand for their "own language" instead of English concealed more than it revealed. There was no "own language" of the Ceylonese people as a whole, but two different languages representing the two largest population groups. While this demand was made as far back as the early 1940s, before independence, when it meant a transition to the two languages of the principal groups in the country, the transition from English was still not yet implemented as the 1950s began, largely due to the caution of Prime Minister D. S. Senanayake, who sensed the explosive potential of issues like language and religion in a newly independent and ethnically divided country.

Amid rising agitation over the language issue, an ambitious

member of the government, Solomon Bandaranaike, went into opposition in 1951, establishing his own party dedicated to a quick implementation of the "own language" policy. At this point, that still meant the two languages of the two principal groups in the country but, in response to growing demands from the Sinhalese majority, there was a swift transition in just a few years to demands for "Sinhala only" as the language of Sri Lanka. As in other countries, such as India, behind the language issue was the issue of access to jobs, especially jobs in the government. For this purpose, a change from English to *both* indigenous languages as the official language of government and free competition for civil service jobs could have meant a displacement of an English-speaking elite by a largely, or disproportionately, Tamil elite.

The key figure in the transformation of a general resentment against the old elite and what they stood for into a specific program of preferential treatment of the Sinhala language — which entailed preferential access of the Sinhalese population to jobs and education — was Bandaranaike. Like so many militant group leaders in other countries, Bandaranaike himself was not at all representative of those in whose name he spoke stridently. He was an Oxford-educated, Christian, Sinhalese aristocrat (his godfather was the British colonial governor), who grew up speaking English and unable to speak Sinhala. But, like some other Sinhalese politicians of his time, Bandaranike became Buddhist, Sinhala-speaking and an extremist on language, religion, and Sinhalese culture.[19] His own goals were neither religious nor ideological. He wanted to become prime minister — and he succeeded.

In 1956, Bandaranaike was elected in a landslide victory that swept away the old elite so thoroughly that only he and one cabinet member in the new government had ever held high office before. Bandaranaike's new government produced legislation requiring "Sinhala only" as the official language of Sri Lanka — the language not only of government itself, but also the language in which businesses and other institutions had to communicate with government. As in India and Malaysia, language policy in Sri Lanka became a focus of intergroup strife, because of its potentiality for having profound effects on educational and economic opportunities. However, once having achieved the prime minister's office by whipping up intergroup resentments, Bandaranaike then attempted to moderate the anti-Tamil policies, but this only set off howls of protest from other Sinhalese demagogues with political ambitions of their own, including a future president, J. R. Jayawardene.[20]

The Tamils' disproportionate representation in institutions of higher learning continued for some time, despite preferential treatment in favor of Sinhalese students. This overrepresentation of Tamil students was especially striking in engineering and medical science, where students from the Tamil minority were 48 and 49 percent, respectively, of all the students. The Sinhalese students were heavily concentrated in the liberal arts, while the Tamils were concentrated in the sciences.[21] However, a series of policies providing preferences and quotas for the Sinhalese progressively reduced the Tamils' prospects in education and employment.

Christian missionary schools also were a special target. In 1960, the government took over more than 2,000 private schools "to ensure equality of educational opportunity to all children regardless of race, religion, economic condition or social status" and to provide a kind of education "which is national in its scope, aims and objects and in conformity with the cultural, religious and economic aspirations of the people."[22]

At the university level, Sinhalese applicants could gain admission by meeting lower standards than those required for Tamils to gain admission.[23] In the civil service, in 1963 the government began sending Sinhalese employees to staff their offices in the northern region, where the Tamils were concentrated. A year later, the government began the compulsory retirement of Tamil civil servants who could not speak Sinhala.[24] Sri Lanka's constitution was modified to eliminate a section that guaranteed minority rights.[25]

Declining prospects for education and employment now facing many Tamils — especially the young, looking forward to university education and professional careers — led to protests. Although these were peaceful protests in the tradition established by Gandhi in India, in the frenzied atmosphere whipped up by Sinhalese politicians and Buddhist monks, these protests led to Sinhalese mob attacks on Tamils. Despite the absence of race riots between these two groups in the first half of the twentieth century, a number of such riots erupted from 1956 to 1958,[26] but these were only the first in what would become a long series of bloody and lethal riots in the years ahead. Trains and cars were stopped by angry mobs, their passengers assaulted and some burned alive. Such horrifying scenes would be repeated many times in outbreaks of riots over the years.

The Tamils' political responses at first included relatively moderate demands for the use of their own language in official communications and then for some autonomy in the regions where they were concentrated. Such demands were in response to the central government's unabashed favoritism toward the Sinhalese and to such weakening of the Tamils politically as the disfranchisement of the Indian Tamils and the pressuring of them to "return" to an India that many of them had never seen.

Bandaranaike created an accord with the Tamils, compromising on some issues, but political outcries from the Sinhalese prevented this accord from being carried out. In 1959, a Sinahalese Buddhist extremist assassinated Bandaranaike for having betrayed the cause. As in other countries, the illusion of being able to control the course of events was shattered. Sinhalese political parties across the ideological spectrum all jumped on the bandwagon of group rights and tried to outbid one another for the Sinhalese vote. The disfranchisement of the Indian Tamils meant that the Tamil vote was now so small that it could be disregarded, leaving the only question how best to compete for the votes of the Sinhalese majority.

Despite preferential admissions policies at the university level, and despite attempts to reduce the Tamils' educational edge in the schools, Tamil students continued to be over-represented in the science-based fields. The next attempt to change this was called "standardization." Instead of basing admissions decisions on the actual scores made by individual students, each student was given a "standardized" score based on his score *relative to other students from his own ethnic group.* Such preferences were later supplemented by quotas. In 1972, a "district quota system" was introduced, to allocate university admissions on the basis of the population in each district. Since Sinhalese and Tamils were concentrated in different districts, district quotas were, in effect, ethnic quotas. Under this system, the proportion of Tamil university students in the sciences fell from 35 percent in 1970 to 19 percent by 1974.

Because the Tamil plantation laborers in the Kandyan region were counted as part of the population, but were unlikely to use any of the university places set aside in the district quotas, this made it especially easy for Sinhalese students from that region to get into universities. Many of these students preferentially admitted were "from the affluent classes," according to a study of these policies and their effects.[27] Protests against quotas and preference by academics were futile, as university admissions policies were determined by political authorities at the Cabinet level.[28]

A drying up of educational opportunities was especially serious for Tamils, because of their concentration in a part of Sri Lanka with poor geographic conditions for making economic progress without relying heavily on education. As attempts to salvage opportunities at the national level proved unavailing, Tamils began to seek more autonomy in their own regions of the country, notably on the northern Jaffna peninsula. After appeals, protests, and civil disobedience campaigns all failed to produce the autonomy that Tamils were seeking, armed guerilla warfare began — and the Tamils' demands now escalated to include a separate, independent nation of their own. Moderate leadership among the Tamils gave way to more militant and extreme leadership, eventually led by a guerilla group called the Tamil Tigers, formed in 1975. Sri Lanka was now on the road to civil war.

It was a war filled with atrocities on both sides. Moreover, a substantial number of Tamils living in regions of the country where the majority population was Sinhalese found themselves singled out as targets for mob violence. A hundred and fifty people were killed and 20,000 made homeless in riots in 1977.[29] This was only a prelude to new riots in 1981 and worse riots in 1983 — the riots in both these years bearing the marks of deliberately organized activity by Sinhalese gangs, with indifference or complicity on the part of the police and the military.[30] Nor were such explosions of violence due solely to hooligans. After the 1981 riots, President Junius Jayawardene said: "I regret that some members of my party have spoken in Parliament and outside words that encourage violence and the murders, rapes and arson that have been committed."[31]

In July 1983, there were "five days of pillage and slaughter aimed at Tamils living throughout the south and their businesses and property." It was a large-scale outbreak, beginning in the country's capital city of Colombo:

> As many as 3,000 Tamils are said to have been killed, nearly 60 percent of the Tamils in Colombo were turned into refugees, and most of the Colombo Tamil business community, which had accounted for over half the city's commercial infrastructure, was ruined. Many Sinhalese burned down their own workplaces, targeting, in particular, Tamil-owned garment factories. Much of the wholesale food district of Colombo was destroyed. The stately Victorian railroad station in the center of the city had to be converted into a morgue to accommodate the corpses.[32]

Not only the numbers, but also the nature of the atrocities, suggested the levels of hatred that had developed in a once peaceful and harmonious country. For example, a bus was accosted by a mob and the bus driver ordered to turn over a Tamil. He pointed to a woman passenger who was then taken out into the street, where her belly was ripped open with a broken bottle and she was set on fire. People in the mob "clapped and danced" as she died in agony.[33]

Meanwhile, in the Tamil areas, similar savagery was inflicted on Sinhalese who lived there. Moreover, the Sinhalese army units sent into the Tamil areas were equally cavalier about the lives of the civilians they encountered. After being ambushed by guerrillas, the army sometimes lashed out with indiscriminate attacks on Tamil civilians. *The New York Times* of August 7, 1983, reported:

> Sri Lankan Army troops pulled 20 civilians off a bus and executed them two weeks ago in retaliation for a Tamil guerrilla attack that killed 13 soldiers a government spokesman confirmed today.[34]

Nor was this an isolated episode. A year later *The Economist* of London reported, "random acts of revenge by soldiers or riot policemen continue."[35]

Tamils began to flee, not only from the areas with a Sinhalese majority, but also from Sri Lanka as a whole. By 1985, nearby India had received 40,000 Tamil refugees.[36] Other Tamils emigrated to European or European offshoot societies, including Australia, Britain, and the Scandinavian countries.[37] Meanwhile, the Tamil Tigers took over de facto control of the northern areas between 1977 and 1987, fighting the Sinhalese army and slaughtering other Tamils who opposed them, killing in the process more Tamils than the Sinhalese army killed.[38]

As violent incidents escalated into full-scale civil war in Sri Lanka, nearby India was drawn into the conflict. The Indian state of Tamil Nadu, across the water from Sri Lanka, became a base for the training of Sri Lankan guerrillas, who returned to their native land to fight for independence. In August 1987, the Indian army intervened directly by landing 50,000 troops as peace-keepers in the northern Tamil regions of Sri Lanka — a move which outraged the Sinhalese population and was initially welcomed by the Tamils. The Indian troops' mission was to take over the maintenance of order from the Sri Lankan army and police forces and to disarm the Tamil guerrillas. But the Tamil guerrillas resisted being disarmed and the process cost the Indian army more than 400 lives in the first year. Now engaged in hostilities, the Indian army's own brutalities and atrocities alienated many Tamils, while their very presence — ostensibly at the invitation of President Jayawardene, who actually had no choice, given the relative sizes of the two countries — spurred the formation of Sinhalese terrorists, as opposed to any peace effort as their Tamil counterparts in the north.

Sinhalese terrorists killed more than 200 supporters of the international accord that had ratified the intervention of Indian troops, and narrowly missed an assassination attempt on President Jayawardene himself.[39] An assassination attempt which did not miss was one in which a Tamil suicide bomber from Sri Lanka killed herself and Indian Prime Minister Rajiv Gandhi in India in 1991.

Sri Lanka had now reached a stage where the initial issues that ignited the conflict were buried under a large overlay of mutual hatreds, distrust, vengeance and counter-vengeance. Perhaps most ominous of all was the formation of murderous extremist organizations among both the Sinhalese and the Tamils — organizations with a vested interest in the continuation of conflict and prepared to kill those who sought reconciliation. A provision in a new constitution in 1978 recognized language rights of the Tamils, but this could not restore the status quo ante. It was, in a World War II phrase, "too little and too late." The civil war continued on for decades more.

With all the lives that it has claimed, what did affirmative action accomplish in Sri Lanka? By 1973, the Sinhalese had overtaken the Sri Lankan Tamils in education and incomes,[40] and of course they were already better off than the Indian Tamils in both respects, even before group preferences and quotas were instituted. Contrary to widespread assumptions, it was not when economic disparities were greater that intergroup strife was greater. On the contrary, the Sinhalese and Tamils co-existed peacefully in the 1920s, when the Tamil minority produced more doctors than the Sinhalese majority. It was a decade after the Sinhalese had overtaken the Tamils in numbers of doctors in 1946 that the first mob violence against the Tamils erupted, and it was a decade after the Sinhalese had overtaken the Tamils in income and education — with the help of preferences and quotas — that the majority unleashed its biggest and most savage riots against the minority. In short, it was not the disparities which led to intergroup violence but the politicizing of those disparities and the promotion of group identity politics.

SUMMARY AND IMPLICATIONS

The history of Sri Lanka in the second half of the twentieth century represents the most blatant, painful, and tragic mockery of the underlying assumption of being able to control the course of events — an assumption implicit in affirmative action policies in countries around the world. The actual course that events took in Sri Lanka was foreseen by no one and made all groups worse off, on net balance, as the country as a whole suffered repeated race riots, civil war, atrocities, widespread terror and the assassinations of the country's national leaders, not to mention the assassination of the prime minister of India by a Tamil extremist, as a result of the Indian army's intervention. Such a record of carnage and atrocities would be shocking in any country, but was especially shocking in a country with a record of intergroup toleration that was once among the best in the world.

If nothing else, Sri Lanka demonstrated that complacency is never in order when racial or ethnic relationships are concerned, for even generations of peaceful co-existence can quickly turn ugly when the right circumstances and the right demagogue come together. Nor are such developments as readily stopped as they are started. Even concessions that would have brought peace in the past can fail to bring peace after many bitter experiences have hardened both sides and produced extremists with a vested interest in the continuation of the struggle itself, which enhances their power, rather than concern for any social results likely to be produced by the struggle. In September 2000, *The New York Times* reported this scene of casual deaths in Jaffna:

> A young woman riding a bicycle near her home was struck by shrapnel that severed her femoral artery. A cow, lazily chewing its cud, was taken out by a stray shell. A 5-year old boy, whose grandmother had sent him to the store to buy fruit juice, was struck in the spine by shrapnel from a shell that had crashed into a drumstick tree. Two people died when incoming fire hit a home for elderly residents.[41]

The same account also reported this:

> A plaintive, unsigned poster, pasted to walls all over town, asks, "Can't we stop this madness?"

Stopping such madness was not nearly so easy as starting it, as was done nearly half a century earlier, by a man who was not even a racial fanatic but simply someone who wanted to become prime minister and decided that stirring up intergroup conflict was the easiest way to achieve that political goal. The net result has been a decades-long civil war in which a small island nation has suffered more deaths than the United States suffered during the long years of the Vietnam war. The 2001 election in Sri Lanka brought to power a party pledged to trying to negotiate a peace with the Tamil political leaders.[42] In the worldwide revulsion against terrorism after the September 11, 2001, attacks against the United States, many foreign governments pledged to stop Tamil Tiger fund-raising in their respective countries, which had been financing a civil war in which roughly 64,000 Sri Lankans died.[43]

Early in 2002, the Tamil Tigers announced a cease fire and the end of suicide bombing. Their leader emerged from the jungle, for the first time in more than a decade, to pledge to work for peace. By the end of the year, an accord between the government and the Tamil Tigers set in motion a process for the final settlement of their differences. It was the first hopeful sign in nearly half a century. Near the end of the year, the *New York Times* reported:

> The unexpected concessions during the second round of talks raised hopes of a permanent solution to the 19-year war that has killed 64,500 people. But a final settlement could be years away, as both sides and the Norwegian mediators brokering the talks conceded.[44]

CHAPTER 5

Affirmative Action in Nigeria

L ike many a country which emerged from colonial rule, Nigeria was never a country before colonial rule. Its very name was given to it by its British rulers. More important, it was an amalgamation of many very diverse West African communities—a fact that was to have fateful implications for its future as a multi-ethnic state. The regions brought together under British hegemony were not only different ethnically, they were different economically, culturally, and geographically.

Islamic conquests from the north were in progress when British conquest intervened. The Moslem Fulani tribe had conquered the Hausa tribe in the north, but not the Yoruba or Ibo tribes in the South, when British rule was extended over them all. Although these were and are the largest ethnic groups in Nigeria, there are numerous other tribes, some exclusive to a given territory and others scattered among larger tribal groups. While these various groups are called "tribes" in Nigeria, they are by no means all small bands of people. Some tribes number in the millions and are scattered over areas larger than some nations in Europe. Nigeria has the largest population of any nation in Africa and one out of every eight Africans is a Nigerian.

Internally, Nigeria is fragmented by language, religion, and ethnicity. There is no majority group in any of these respects. The largest of the ethnic groups are the Hausa-Fulani tribes of the northern region, constituting about 28 percent of the country's population. The next largest group—about 18 percent of the population—are the Ibos, with the Yorubas from the southwestern region being very similar in size at 17 percent.[1] Altogether, there are hundreds of smaller tribes.

More than demographic or even cultural differences are involved. These tribal divisions are accompanied by deeply felt alienation and hostility among many of these groups. A 1970 study of Nigerian students studying abroad in Edinburgh found that, among the Yoruba, more than 40 percent of the males and more than 60 percent of the females excluded the possibility of friendship with a Hausa. Marriage with a Hausa was excluded by more than 80 percent of the males and more than 90 percent of the females. Among the Ibos, similar proportions would exclude marriage with Hausas—or with Yorubas.[2] Such alienation has social, political, and economic implications. An econometric study in 1997 estimated that Nigeria's economic growth rate would have been almost double its actual rate if its ethnic diversity were only average for African nations, instead of being nearly double the average.[3]

HISTORY

Geographically more fortunate than many other parts of sub-Saharan Africa, the region of West Africa now called Nigeria contains the Niger River and its tributaries, facilitating the development of towns and villages, which have long been more common in this region than in most of tropical Africa. About half the population of Nigeria lived in these urban communities before the beginning of the twentieth century. Nigeria has also had larger and more complex indigenous political systems than those in other parts of sub-Saharan Africa and has been more advanced in other ways. For example, iron was smelted in what is now Nigeria, five centuries before Christ.[4]

Islam came to the northern regions of the country five centuries ago, while the southeastern region inhabited by the Ibos became predominantly Christian in the wake of British missionary activity and, later, British political hegemony. The southwestern region, inhabited by the Yoruba, has become roughly half Islamic and half Christian, while indigenous African religions also continue to be practiced. In centuries past, the coastal peoples of the region were more powerful and more advanced than the peoples of the interior, as in much of the rest of the world. As elsewhere in sub-Saharan Africa, these coastal peoples raided and enslaved their less fortunate brethren in the interior—in this case, the Ibos. The Ibos have been described, by a scholar largely sympathetic to Africans, as having barely advanced beyond the state of savagery in the early twentieth century. This was said not in denigration of the Ibos, but rather to accentuate their rapid rise later in that century.[5]

The British became involved in West Africa in the nineteenth century, seeking to advance and protect various British interests, including British missionaries and traders, by establishing a sphere of influence. Britain's historic decision to ban the international slave trade in 1808 led not only to the banishment of slave trading from the British Empire, but also to the suppression of the slave trade in other places, including its principal sources in sub-Saharan Africa.

Whether or not the colonial officials realized it at the outset, this entailed a long-run political and military involvement in the region, while the British navy patrolled the Atlantic off the west coast of Africa to deter and intercept slave shipments to the Western Hemisphere. Reluctant to incur the expense of establishing and administering a colony, the British were nevertheless drawn into local political and military conflicts among the various contending Africans. Eventually, the British sphere of influence evolved into British rule in the twentieth century—though "indirect rule" through local indigenous authorities.

What the British attempted was what might be called low-budget imperialism, with local societies, political structures, and cultures left as much as they had been as possible. Despite this conservative agenda, however, the British presence was itself a transforming and even revolutionary influence. Unwilling to bear the high costs of staffing their colonial administration from top to bottom with people from Britain, the British hired local Nigerians as clerks and in other subordinate occupations. This in turn meant creating a whole new class of Africans with English-language education, familiar with Western concepts and experienced in Western ways of doing things. This class tended to become critical of indigenous African institutions and authorities—and eventually also critical of British authorities and their colonial rule.

Group Differences

British rule also had major effects on the relationships among the various peoples of Nigeria. Some of these peoples were more receptive than others to the Western education now being offered by missionaries, leading to great disparities in the numbers of educated indigenous people in the different regions. The Moslem authorities in the north, for example, did not want Christian missionaries establishing schools in their region. Since virtually all schools in Nigeria were missionary schools during the colonial era, this left the north lagging far behind the south in modern education and the skills and economic experience growing out of it. Moreover, after the British established their hegemony over the various African tribes, it was now safe for people from one region of Nigeria to travel and even settle in what had once been enemy territory before the colonial era. This led to a large influx of southern Nigerians into the north, not only to staff colonial institutions but also to establish themselves in business and in various modern occupations in the private sector.

One of the groups particularly prone to seize upon the opportunities presented by Western education were the Ibos of southeastern Nigeria, a group once lowly and backwards,[6] who now rose up the occupational ladder, often above their erstwhile superiors. These erstwhile superiors, particularly in the north, did not take this social reversal with good grace. As Nigeria approached its independence in 1960, intergroup jealousies and friction delayed the creation of a constitution and a government—which in turn delayed independence itself. The British were prepared to grant independence before the various ethnic groups within Nigeria were prepared to agree to accept it, since they had first to iron out their disagreements on a constitution.

Although the upstart group whose rise was particularly resented were the Ibos, the Yorubas had the highest per capita income of any of these groups. The southeastern region where the Ibos originated had less fertile land and had long lagged behind other regions in economic level and urbanization, a fact which led many ambitious and Western-educated Ibos to migrate elsewhere to pursue their careers. This in turn led to their being widely interspersed among other peoples hostile to them. Northern authorities, for example, insisted that Ibos live in separate communities and send their children to segregated schools.[7] Around the middle of the twentieth century, as independence approached, per capita income in the western (Yoruba) region was twice that in the northern (Hausa-Fulani) region, with the eastern (Ibo) region income being in between.

These economic differences reflected in part the fact that educational differences among the tribes and regions remained extreme throughout the colonial era. As of 1912, for example, there were fewer than a thousand students in elementary school in northern Nigeria, where more than half the population of the country lived, while there were 35,000 students attending primary schools in the southern regions. While Western education grew over time in all regions of Nigeria, the huge disparities continued.

By 1957, when there were approximately 185,000 children enrolled in elementary school education in the northern regions, there were 2.3 million in the other regions whose combined populations were not as large. Similar disparities existed and persisted in secondary and higher education. As of 1951, only one person out of the 16 million people in the northern region had a university degree. Virtually all the Nigerian students in institutions of higher learning, whether overseas or at home, were from southern Nigeria. In academic year 1959–60, on the eve of independence, northern Nigerians were just 9 percent of the students at the country's University of Ibadan. Among the much larger number of Nigerian students receiving a higher education abroad, only 2 percent were Hausa-Fulani as late as 1966, six years after independence.

Such disparities in higher education were reflected in occupational disparities, especially in the higher professions. Of the 160 physicians in Nigeria in the early 1950s, 76 were Yorubas, 49 were Ibos, and only one was from the Hausa-Fulani group, the largest group in the population.[8] In the army, three-quarters of the riflemen were Hausa-Fulani, while four-fifths of the officers were southerners. As late as 1965, one-half of the officer corps were specifically Ibos.[9] Even within the northern region, southern Nigerians outnumbered northern Nigerians in many coveted occupations. These included not only occupations requiring medical or technical skills,[10] but also clerical and other semi-skilled jobs in the postal service, banks and the railroad, and southerners were also prominent as traders, artisans, merchants and factory workers in northern Nigeria.[11]

Among senior public officials in northern Nigeria, more than four-fifths were expatriates — mostly Europeans but a few from other African countries — and about one-third of the Nigerians in such positions in the north were southerners. This dependency on outsiders was very different from the situation in the eastern and southern regions of Nigeria. In each of these other regions, Nigerians were roughly three-quarters of the senior public officials.[12] Among the spoils of independence were government jobs currently held by Europeans, and while a policy of "Nigerianization" of such jobs was proclaimed, in the northern region the policy was more specifically "northernization." There the emphasis was on expelling southern Nigerians from these jobs, even if that required replacing them for the time being with European expatriates, because of a lack of qualified northern Nigerians.[13]

National Independence

Demands for independence came first from the southern and eastern regions of Nigeria, while northern Nigerian officials resisted until they could get some constitutional guarantees that the country's administrative apparatus would not be dominated by officials from the other regions. Northern Nigeria, where a majority of the country's population lived, was the politically dominant region of the country, but the central government apparatus required to carry out policy—the bureaucracy—would clearly not be, if hiring for government positions were to be on the basis of individual qualifications alone. Those positions were important not only as a means of controlling the application of whatever policies the political leaders might choose, but also as a source of patronage assuring the continuation in power of incumbent northern politicians.

Both the northern resistance to early independence and its insistence on group representation in federal government positions put them in conflict with the leaders and peoples of the other regions. All clearly understood the high stakes involved in these conflicts and both sides reacted with hostility and bitterness. As one northern leader later confessed, "We had to teach the people to hate the southerners; to look at them as people depriving them of their rights," so as to gain the political support of the northern population.[14] Another northern spokesman said:

> The South with its many schools and colleges, is producing hundreds of academically and technically qualified people for the public services. The common cry now is Nigerianisation of the public services. It is most important that the federal service shall be fully representative of all units which make up the federation. Now, what do we find in Nigeria today? There are 45,000 men and women in the Federal Public Services. I have not been able to obtain the figures of the number of northerners in the service but I very much doubt if they even amount to one percent . . . [15]

In short, the northern position was that group representation was more important than individual skills. One advocate of group representation rejected what he called "the tyranny of skills."[16] This was not simply an issue to be settled in the political arena after independence. Northern fears of southern domination of the administrative apparatus of government led to opposition to early independence without some prior guarantees of northern representation in the bureaucracy. In turn, this provoked southern hostility to northern leaders. In 1953, after a motion in the House of Representatives, located in Lagos in the south, asking the British to grant independence in 1956, was opposed by northern members, those members were later surrounded by groups of Ibos and Yoruba who called them "thieves," "slaves of the white man" and "stupid Hausas."[17]

Afterwards, when advocates of early independence took their case to the people in the north, they were met with riots, fomented by northern political leaders, in which dozens of people were killed and more than a hundred wounded.[18] In an effort to defuse the situation, the British held a conference in London at which it was decided to allow more regional autonomy. As a result of this, between January 1954 and August 1958 more than 2,000 southerners were fired by the Northern Public Service and urged to go south. Nor could they be immediately replaced by qualified northern Nigerians; hence the large number of expatriates employed. Before 1954, there was not a single northern Nigerian in the administrative cadre of the Northern Public Service. Immediately after the "northernisation" policy, five were appointed and by 1958 there were a little over 300. But they had still not replaced all the southerners fired earlier.

Although such group preferences were initially limited to government employment, they began to spread into the private sector as a result of northern government actions. European firms in northern Nigeria, which tended to hire southern Nigerians for responsible positions, found themselves under political pressure to hire northerners instead. In addition, the local government itself provided loans to northern Nigerian businessmen trying to compete with southern Nigerians, who were more successful. Ironically, one of the political advocates of the northernization policies himself hired Ibos rather than other northerners in his private businesses.[19] Apparently the belief that southern Nigerians were more efficient was not just a "perception" or "stereotype."

Given such intergroup hostility, it was perhaps not surprising that the first decade of Nigeria's independence was marked by riots, plots, and coups. The country's first census had to be nullified, amid charges of fraud. Early in 1966, the prime minister was assassinated in the course of a military coup. Because he was from the Moslem northern region and most of the coup leaders were Ibo military officers from the Christian south, this set up a fateful backlash, in which the new military government was rebelled against and then overthrown in a counter-coup in July of the same year by Moslem military officers. By September, the backlash against the Ibos took the form of new and bloodier riots in the north:

Northern soldiers chased Ibo troops from their barracks and murdered scores with bayonets. Screaming Moslem mobs descended
on the Ibo quarters of every northern city, killing their victims
with clubs, poison arrows and shotguns. Tens of thousands of Ibos
were murdered in the systematic massacres that followed.[20]

After these traumatic events, more than a million Ibos fled
the northern region to join their fellow Ibos in the southeastern part of the country. This region then decided to secede
from Nigeria, where they no longer felt safe, and form their
own independent country, which they named Biafra. This is
turn set off a civil war that lasted two years. The Nigerian government blockaded this landlocked region, to prevent food or
military supplies from reaching it. Ibos then starved to death at
a rate of a thousand a day.[21] Altogether, more than a million
people died in Biafra from a combination of starvation, military actions, and disease. Biafra collapsed and was re-absorbed
into Nigeria.

After this catastrophic episode, and after all the years of intergroup hostility that preceded it, Nigeria changed to a policy
of reconciliation. The devastated economy in the southeastern
region was rebuilt and Ibo political and military personnel were
rehabilitated, including some officials of the former Biafran
government. Years later, in 1982, even the exiled leader of
Biafra was pardoned. Ibos in general resumed their role as a
prosperous element in Nigerian society.

The Federal Military Government which took power in the
July 1966 coup remained in power until 1979, when a new
constitution was written for a return to civilian rule. The new
constitution was designed to mitigate ethnic politics by reorga-
nizing political regions, in an attempt to break up ethnic blocs.
Nevertheless, in the 1979 elections held under the new constitution, each of five presidential candidates received an absolute majority of the votes in at least one state and less than five
percent of the vote in another state or states.[22] Since Nigeria's

major ethnic groups live in different states, this voting pattern represented a continuation of extreme ethnic polarization.

What also continued was a large role for government in the economy and rampant corruption in the carrying out of that role. In a very poor country, the central government's control of much of the country's wealth makes the struggle to control the central government desperate and the use of that control shameless. Although not unique in these respects, Nigeria is usually ranked among the most corrupt countries in the world and in some years an international survey has ranked it as *the* most corrupt country in the world.[23] Widespread and large-scale financial corruption — $30 million stolen by one state governor, for example — has been accompanied by equally gross electoral fraud, in which a "defeated" candidate later turned out upon investigation, years later, to have won by more than a million votes.[24] Meanwhile, civil servants' pay fell in arrears, inflation soared, and total national output declined.

As public confidence in their elected officials also declined, this set the stage for another military coup in 1983, part of a history of short-lived civilian governments and long-lived military regimes in Nigeria. Even in its more or less legitimate activities, the government of Nigeria has served as an instrument for milking one ethnic group for the benefit of another. In 1961, for example, the northern region paid only 9 percent of the country's personal income taxes and received 45 percent of the money dispensed to the various regions by the federal government. Meanwhile, the western region paid 64 percent of the country's personal income taxes and received less than one-quarter of the regional funds.[25] In essence, the Yoruba were being drained financially for the benefit of the Hausa-Fulani.

PREFERENCES AND QUOTAS

In addition to various informal ways in which Nigerian governments at state and national levels have practiced favoritism toward one ethnic group over another, more formal systems of ethnic preferences and quotas have been imposed under the requirement that numerous activities must "reflect the federal character of the country." This expresses ethnic preferences in regional terms. According to a provision of the 1979 constitution, "the composition of the Government of the Federation and any of its agencies, shall be carried out in such a manner as to reflect the federal character of Nigeria, and the need to promote national loyalty, thereby ensuring that there shall be no predominance of persons from a few states or from a few ethnic or other sectional groups in that government or any of its agencies."[26] Even before this constitutional provision was written, special efforts were made to recruit northerners into the national government's civilian branches and into its military services.

Seeking to redress regional—and therefore ethnic—imbalances in education, the federal government established both universities and pre-university remedial educational institutions in the more educationally backward regions. Then it established a Joint Admissions and Matriculation Board to control admissions to the country's universities, using ethnic quotas. Moreover, similar principles of regional and ethnic balance were applied to a wide range of government activities and projects:

> With the enunciation of the principle of federal character, politicians and ethnic champions as well as ethnic entrepreneurs now watch assiduously every aspect of life to make sure that they are not denied any possible benefits arising from the implementation of the concept. Hence demands have arisen over the siting of industries by the government, the building of roads, hospitals and schools in various parts of the federation in conformity with the principle of federal character. Emphasis is placed on balancing the location of socio-economic projects in the North with those in the South. In fact, the iron and steel project of the country was delayed over the demands for balancing in the location of signifi-

cant national projects. Similarly, the construction of the oil refinery in Kaduna, an area where no crude oil is produced, is motivated in part by the principle of ethno-regional balancing. The location of federally-sponsored specialist hospitals has followed the same principle of balancing that inspired the geographic location of the federal government colleges.[27]

As in other countries, the things made available through ethnic balancing have been primarily those things of interest and concern to the more fortunate members of the various ethnic groups, such as university admissions, rather than free and universal compulsory education for the poor. In Nigeria, group preferences concentrate on those things which serve the interests of those people who have already moved out of traditional ways of life and into the modern sectors of the economy and society, with little concern for those still left behind.[28] The "federal character" principle has been extended to promotions, school admission, and even membership on the national soccer team.[29] Intergroup hostilities have been especially sharp in those modern sectors, such as in the cities, where locally indigenous and non-indigenous groups have confronted one another:

> Native urban dwellers resent migrants and often seek preferential treatment with respect to urban administration and planning. Non-indigenous dwellers, on the other hand, feel alienated and reluctant to participate in the development of the city. This is especially evident in northern Nigerian cities and in Lagos where 'sons of the soil' regularly harass 'strangers.'[30]

Because the "federal character" principle is administered by the federal government, these affirmative action programs have strengthened the role of the central government vis-à-vis state and local governments, which have lost much of their taxing authority and have therefore been forced to rely for the bulk of their income on money received from the national treasury. Moreover, competing ethnic and regional claims on the federal treasury have made something as ordinarily mundane as a census a matter of heated controversy and bitter charges and counter-charges of corruption and fraud. Yet, far from settling or defusing intergroup tensions, the administration and application of the federal character principle became itself a matter of unending contention.

Regional autonomy allowed the dominant tribal or ethnic group in each region to show favoritism to its own members in the allocation of government jobs, subsidies and other benefits. Because these represented essentially preferences and quotas for the majority population of each region, the ability of other groups to challenge such policies politically was limited. However, with the concentration of power in the federal government, more evenly matched regional majorities could more effectively vie with one another for the favors of those holding the power of the central government. Whether or not this resulted in more fairness, it resulted in more conflict.

SUMMARY AND IMPLICATIONS

Territorially separated and politically polarized ethnic groups have been a formula for disaster in many countries around the world. Some of these countries have degenerated into civil war, like Sri Lanka and Yugoslavia, or have broken apart, either with or without military action — like Czechoslovakia, the Soviet Union, and first Pakistan from India and then Bangladesh from Pakistan. Nigeria's civil war was part of this general pattern, and its re-uniting after breaking apart was one of the more favorable outcomes, tenuous as its national unity has continued to be.

Against this background, the effects of group preferences and quotas are harder to assess. Given the huge differences in education and cultures among the different tribes in Nigeria, would a policy of equal opportunity for all—with its inevitable predominance of southern Nigerians in coveted positions, even in northern Nigeria—have been politically viable? It is hard to imagine how such a situation would not have led to political demands for group preferences and quotas—and to mutual recriminations, demonization and polarization among the different groups. Perhaps a country with a long history of national concerns predominating over regional or tribal differences, or a tradition of equal treatment for all, could have avoided the tragedies which have racked Nigeria. But Nigeria was not such a country. The very idea of making such disparate regions of the British empire in West Africa into one country was a belated and perhaps ill-advised decision. As far back as 1899, early colonizers recommended breaking the territory of Nigeria into two separate provinces. In the years immediately following independence in 1960, more than one region threatened secession before the Ibos actually seceded to form the ill-fated nation of Biafra.[31]

If the goal of group preferences and quotas was to create a sense of national unity, as often proclaimed, there is no evidence that it has in fact advanced that goal or even moved the country in that direction. As a study in 2001 concluded: "Nigerians seldom categorize others by their wealth or occupation but by ethnicity."[32] This is more than a social custom. It has political implications. As an earlier study put it:

> To the average Nigerian, a political leader is good only if he is able to patronise members of his family at the expense of other families, to promote the cause of his tribe at the expense of the nation, and, if need be, to defend the wrong of a brother at the expense of justice.[33]

In October 2001, the president of Nigeria acknowledged continuing ethnic clashes and found it necessary to re-assert the right of any Nigerian citizen "to live and enjoy full citizenship anywhere within this country." He urged all Nigerians "not to see any fellow Nigerian as a settler—in our country where he or she is a citizen by birth—so that we can feel justified to demand that he or she departs our neighborhood, when it suits our whims."[34] Nor had such ethnic clashes subsided months later, when a correspondent in Lagos reported:

> Gangs of youths armed with machetes, swords and bows and arrows took to the streets of Lagos yesterday in a third day of ethnic conflict in which at least 55 people have been killed.
>
> Grabbing what possessions they could, thousands left their homes as plumes of black smoke rose from the city's slum. . . . Soldiers were deployed yesterday to help contain the violence, which began on Saturday between Yoruba and Hausa tribal fights in the impoverished northern areas of Idi Araba and Mushin.[35]

Estimates of the number of deaths in intergroup clashes between 1999 and early 2002 ranged from 6,000 to 10,000.[36]

If it is difficult to isolate the effects of preferences and quotas, as such, on Nigeria's troubled history, it is much clearer that the group polarization which preceded and produced the preferences and quotas has been deadly in its effects, both in peace and in war, and under both civilian and military governments. So much rancor and bitterness had been built up in Nigeria before policies "reflecting the federal character of the country" were instituted, that both the policies and the disasters which followed may be seen as consequences of the same underlying polarization. This situation is somewhat different from that in a country where a majority chooses to grant preferences and quotas to a minority, whether out of a sense of guilt, fear, or magnanimity. In such countries, good will may prevail, at least initially, and subsequent polarization may later be attributed to the effects of the policies themselves. In Nigeria, however, both the policies and the poisonous politics which produced them have been inextricably bound up together from the beginning, in a situation which unfolded with virtually the inevitability of a Greek tragedy.

Only in the wake of repeated disasters have there been steps taken to dampen the ethnic polarization through political restructuring, aimed at requiring candidates to demonstrate political support in different regions of the country—which is to say, among different ethnic groups. That such efforts have largely failed thus far may be less important in the long run than the fact that the problem has been identified and its importance recognized, which is a necessary prelude to any future actions that might succeed.

While preferences cannot be said to have created ethnic polarization in Nigeria, as they did in Sri Lanka, nevertheless the question may be asked whether these preferences have eased or accentuated the pre-existing frictions and hostilities among the country's many minorities—in a country with no majority. The prestigious Economist Intelligence Unit in London made this assessment:

> Various explanations have been given for the sharp rise in sectarian and communal violence in Nigeria since 1999. The unrest is said to stem from the release of pent-up anger and frustration following years of authoritarian military rule. Unease in the country has also increased as historically fragile relations between predominantly Muslim northerners and mainly Christian southerners have been critically strained by the introduction of sharia (Islamic law), including harsh punishments for offenders in many parts of the north. But the most widely accepted reason for Nigeria's enduring civil unrest is the mistrust between its more than 250 ethnic groups that make up Nigeria, many of which consider themselves separate nationalities. The persistence of racial mistrust reflects the failure of nation-building in Nigeria, where most people's loyalty is to their ethnic group rather than the nation.[37]

From the standpoint of others seeking to glean some lessons from the experience of Nigeria, clearly the spectacle of ethnic groups organized into different political parties—each party exclusively dependent on the votes of one group, and all fighting over the dispensation of government largess—is not one to encourage emulation elsewhere. It is not the simple fact that one group gives the vast majority of its votes to one party that is crucial. That happens in many countries, including the United States, without producing ethnic parties in the sense in which such parties have existed in Nigeria or Sri Lanka, where these parties have freely insulted, demonized, and alienated other groups—and led both countries into civil wars. What must also exist to produce such tragedies is such exclusive preoccupation with intergroup struggles that attacks on other groups provoke no backlash from voters offended by such polarization. That situation existed in the American South during the era when "white supremacy" was loudly proclaimed during election campaigns. But, in the absence of such extreme conditions, parties based on a variety of issues and constituencies have tended to play down or paper over inter-ethnic conflicts that could cost them votes among the general public.

What has saved the United States from the fate of Nigeria is that polarizing political tactics have for more than a century been confined to one region of the country and that the disapproval of many other Americans limited how far such tactics could go. Where there was no such disapproval of unbridled polarization, Americans also had a civil war, even though between two groups that were not racially or ethnically different, but territorially separate. In Nigeria, there was no such concern over polarization or even violence directed against other ethnic groups. For example, during the bloody outbreaks of violence in northern Nigeria that killed tens of thousands of Ibos in 1966, the Yoruba expressed little concern, either from a humanitarian point of view or from the standpoint of the damage to the nation as a whole.[38]

India has not had an outright civil war between territorially separated groups, though it has had escalating violence around the country, in the wake of polarization among many groups, including in recent years polarization by Hindu politicians targeting Moslems. Malaysia and Singapore have avoided the fates

of Nigeria and Sri Lanka partly by not having territorially separate ethnic groups, and has avoided the fate of India by essentially banning free speech on ethnic issues. But where none of
these restraints or countervailing forces is at work, Nigeria has
been a painful example of what can happen. What has been
clear from its experience is that the often repeated idea that
attempts at equalizing outcomes through group preferences
and quotas would enhance "national unity" has been proven
to be as false in Nigeria as in other countries. The goal of
national unity behind policies "reflecting the federal character
of the country" has given the various groups something to fight
over, rather than something to bring them closer together.

The underlying assumption that the degree of economic or
other inequality is not only correlated with the degree of intergroup antagonism, but is the main cause of it, may seem plausible to some and may be accepted without question by others,
but it does not fit the facts in Nigeria, nor in other countries.
While the region where the Yoruba are indigenous has long
had a higher economic level than the region inhabited by the
Ibos, the hostility of the Hausa-Fulani toward the upstart Ibos,
who were historically closer to their own economic level, has
long been far more fierce than that toward the more prosperous Yoruba. Moreover, it was precisely when the Ibos began
to close the economic gap between themselves and the Yoruba
during the late 1940s that hostilities between Ibos and Yoruba
then erupted and escalated.[39] In the 1990s, when the Katafs,
formerly lagging behind the Hausa economically, had closed
the gap, the relations between these two groups likewise became more polarized than ever, so that "the slightest disagree-
ment tends to explode into violence." The same phenomenon
has been found among other Nigerian tribal or ethnic groups.[40]
Similar patterns have existed in other African countries, as well
as in Asia, Europe, and the Western Hemisphere. In Sri Lanka,
for example, the disproportionate success of the Tamils in educational institutions and professional occupations was even

greater in the peaceful first half of the twentieth century than in the tragically bloody second half. There, as in Nigeria and elsewhere, it was not the economic or other differences, as such, which provoked polarization and violence, but the politicizing of those differences.

Intergroup strife within various regions of Nigeria has led to the creation of more states — first a dozen in 1967 and then 36 in 1996.[41] Having suffered the deadly consequences of conflicts growing out of ethnic heterogeneity, Nigeria has sought to create more homogeneity within separate enclaves, in order to defuse the polarization that has threatened to tear the country apart.

CHAPTER 6

Affirmative Action in the United States

Affirmative action policies by the government of the United States confront a problem not found in many other countries. Both the American Constitution and statutes such as the Civil Rights Act of 1964 mandate equal treatment of individuals. Advocates of official group preferences and quotas in the United States have therefore often sought to deny that these were in fact group preferences and quotas. Instead, such policies have been depicted as a correction or forestalling of discrimination, or as promoting "diversity," whose social benefits are sweepingly asserted or assumed, without actually being tested or demonstrated.[1]

The historical evolution of affirmative action in the United States would be difficult to understand without first realizing the legal obstacles which such policies must overcome in order to be acceptable in American courts of law, as well as in the political arena. Group preferences and quotas in the United States evolved out of laws initially seeking to ban discrimination against individuals — including laws explicitly repudiating the principle of group preferences and quotas.

The central statute in this evolution was the Civil Rights Act of 1964 and the central group whose plight provided the impetus and rationale for this law were blacks. As in other countries, however, these policies spread far beyond the initial beneficiaries. Blacks are just 12 percent of the American population, but affirmative action programs have expanded over the years to include not only other racial or ethnic groups, but also women, so that such policies now apply to a substantial majority of the American population. Put differently, failure to have statistical representativeness among employees can be equated with job discrimination for a wide range of groups, with the burden of proof to the contrary falling on the employer.

Official group preferential policies go far back in American history. Religious discrimination existed in much of colonial America. Different laws applied to whites and free blacks in the antebellum South, and continuing legal distinctions between blacks and whites persisted during the long Jim Crow era that began after the Civil War and extended past the middle of the twentieth century. Nor were blacks the only racial group discriminated against in law and policy, for the sake of the white majority. The indigenous population of American Indians were also subject to different — and worse — laws than the white majority, as were Chinese and Japanese immigrants. Ironically, however, the first official preferential policy for a racial minority in the United States appeared in the 1830s, long before racial discrimination laws were repealed. American Indians were given preferential employment status in the Bureau of Indian Affairs.[2]

Rather than attempt to follow in detail the changing laws and policies affecting the many religious, racial, ethnic and other groups at various times in American history, we can see in broad outline what has happened to American blacks, because this is the group most often used as justification for affirmative action policies, however more widely such policies have been applied to others. While this history is rather straightforward, what is a challenge is disentangling the myths which have become intertwined with that history.

MYTHS VERSUS HISTORY

In a history geared toward justifying current political policies and movements, blacks have been seen as a group whose economic and social disparities today are a direct consequence of their enslavement and maltreatment in the past, as well as continuing racism and discrimination in the present. Whether it is the lower incomes of blacks, compared to other Americans, or their higher infant mortality rates, lower levels of marriage and labor force participation, or other social pathology, the general cause has been believed to be the behavior of whites. Accordingly, the socioeconomic rise of blacks in the second half of the twentieth century has been seen as a consequence of laws and policies countering the discrimination inflicted on blacks by whites and attempting to redress past inequities. Virtually all these widespread explanations of social pathology among black Americans are demonstrably false.

Blacks have indeed been maltreated — first enslaved for more than two centuries and then subjected to gross official discrimination for another century in the South, where most blacks have always lived. Nor was the rest of the country free of either racism or discrimination. But neither the initial poverty of blacks, nor the later rise of most blacks out of poverty follows the path sketched by those who promote preferential policies. The facts of history contradict much of today's prevailing vision.

While such things as the much lower labor force participation rates of blacks and the much lower marriage rates among blacks today are often attributed to "a legacy of slavery," in reality blacks had higher rates of labor force participation than whites, and slightly higher marriage rates than whites, in the late nineteenth century, when they were just one generation out of slavery.[3] Indeed, this continued to be true well into the twentieth century. The drastically different patterns seen today began after the 1960s.

Undoubtedly, racial discrimination has contributed historically to blacks having lower incomes than whites. But that is very different from saying how much or in what ways. It cannot simply be assumed that blacks would have had the same incomes as whites in the absence of racial discrimination, given that various groups of American whites have had very different incomes from one another at various periods of history. In addition, a number of non-white groups in the United States — Chinese, Japanese, Asian Indians, and black Barbadians — have had higher incomes than white Americans. Moreover, one of the most serious forms of discrimination against blacks has historically been discrimination by government in its provision of education. Black-white differences in per pupil expenditure, especially in the South during the Jim Crow era, have been extensively documented. Inferior education would assure income differences, even in the absence of employer discrimination. The point here is not to deny employer discrimination, either in the public sector or the private sector, but simply to point out some of the difficulties in determining its nature and magnitude — difficulties that are too often overlooked when equating statistical disparities in income or employment with employer discrimination.

Although simple quantitative differences in education are not the only criteria of educational discrimination against blacks, historically the differences in this respect have been sufficiently dramatic to make it unnecessary to go into qualitative differences as well. Suffice it to say that blacks lagged substantially behind whites in education for most of American history. As late as 1940, non-white males had completed just 5.4 years of school, compared to 8.7 years for white males. For young adult males, aged 25 to 29 years of age, the black-white difference was four years. Twenty years later, the black-white difference in schooling among young adult males in these age brackets had shrunk to less than two years. By 1970, the years of schooling for young black men in these age brackets was less than one year — 12.1 years of schooling for young black men, compared to 12.7 years for their white counterparts.[4]

In short, black education rose substantially, both absolutely and relative to white education, in the decades *preceding* the civil rights legislation of the 1960s and the affirmative action policies that began in the 1970s. What economic changes accompanied this rise in black education? As of 1940, 87 percent of black families had incomes below the official poverty line. By 1960, this was down to 47 percent of black families.[5] This dramatic 40-percentage-point decline came at a time when there was no major federal civil rights legislation. But this was a time not only of rising black education, but also a time of a massive exodus of blacks out of the South — more than 3 million people[6] — escaping both the Jim Crow laws and the substandard Southern black schools. In short, this was a time when vast members of blacks lifted themselves out of poverty — "by their own bootstraps," as the phrase goes.

Beginning in the 1960s, there were also major federal civil rights laws. While the percentage of black families with incomes below the poverty level continued to decline, to 30 percent during this decade, it is not so clear which factors contributed most to this. But it cannot be assumed arbitrarily that it was all due to civil rights laws, as too often it is in various political discussions. While it is an often repeated fact that the number of blacks in professional and other higher level occupations increased in the five years following passage of the landmark Civil Rights Act of 1964, it is an almost completely ignored fact that the number of blacks rising into such occupations was even greater in the five years *preceding* passage of the Civil Rights Act of 1964.[7]

While the role of the 1960s "equal opportunity" legislation and policies epitomized by the Civil Right Act can be debated, the effect of the federal affirmative action policies that began in the 1970s are clearly less impressive. During the decade of the 1970s, the poverty rate among black families fell from

30 percent to 29 percent.[8] Even if all of this one-percentage-point decline were arbitrarily attributed to affirmative action, it would still not be a significant part of the history of the economic rise of blacks out of poverty, however crucial affirmative action has been made to seem politically. Nor should this be surprising, given that preferences and quotas in India and Malaysia have benefitted primarily the already more fortunate, rather than those in poverty.

In the United States as well, affirmative action has been a boon to those already more fortunate. A study of a random sample of minority beneficiaries of government contracts set aside by the Small Business Administration showed that more than two-thirds of these beneficiaries had net worths of more than a million dollars each. These include a black businessman in a position to offer to arrange a buy-out of the multibillion-dollar Viacom media conglomerate. This entrepreneur had previously been a government official at the Federal Communications Commission and thus knew from the inside how minority set-aside programs worked in the media. These programs also benefitted wealthy black athletes like Lou Brock, Julius Erving and O. J. Simpson. Yet when some members of Congress publicly opposed such programs, Congressman Charles Rangel from Harlem compared them to Hitler and depicted any attempt to roll back affirmative action as an attack on all blacks.[9]

In reality, during the period from 1967 to 1992 — most of this being in the affirmative action era — the top 20 percent of black income-earners had their income share rising at about the same rate as that of their white counterparts, while the bottom 20 percent of black income-earners had their income share *fall* at more than double the rate of the bottom 20 percent of white income earners.[10] In short, the affirmative action era in the United States saw the more fortunate blacks benefit while the least fortunate lost ground in terms of their share of incomes. Neither the gains nor the losses can be arbitrarily attributed to affirmative action, but neither can affirmative action claim to have advanced low-income blacks when in fact those blacks fell behind.

Because minority immigrants are eligible for affirmative action, even though they have obviously suffered no past discrimination in the United States, members of the Fanjul family from Cuba — with a fortune exceeding $500 million — have received government contracts set aside for minority businesses.[11] An absolute majority of the money paid to "minority"-owned construction firms in Washington, D.C., during the period from 1986 to 1990 went to European businessmen from Portugal. Asian entrepreneurs have likewise immigrated to the United States and then acquired preferential access to government contracts.[12] Such results once again demonstrate how far the reality of affirmative action departs from its rationale of remedying past discrimination.

Although affirmative action began as a program primarily intended to benefit blacks, most of the "minority and women-owned businesses" favored by government preferences are owned by groups other than blacks. More than four times as many businesses are owned by Hispanics and Asian Americans and thirteen times as many businesses are owned by women as by blacks. Moreover, even within this omnibus category of minority and women-owned businesses, some evidence suggests that the vast majority of firms receive nothing from these preferences, while a relatively few receive the bulk of the benefits. In Cincinnati, for example, the city vendor list identified 682 such firms, but 13 percent of these firms received 62 percent of all the preferential contracts and 83 percent of the money. Nationally, only about one-fourth of one percent of minority-owned enterprises were even certified as entitled to preferences under the Small Business Administration. Then, even among this tiny fraction of minority firms, 2 percent received 40 percent of the money.[13]

A special benefit has been created for American Indians who run gambling casinos on reservations. But here, again, there has been the same skewed distribution of benefits seen in many other contexts. Five states, with almost half the total American Indian population of the country, receive less than 3 percent of all casino proceeds, amounting to about $400 per Indian. Meanwhile, three states with only 3 percent of the Indian population receive 44 percent of all casino revenue — and average of $100,000 per Indian. One casino in California brings in more than $100 million a year, or about $900,000 per Indian. These are revenues, rather than profits, and many non-Indian investors reap profits from Indian casinos.[14]

THE EVOLUTION OF AFFIRMATIVE ACTION

The Civil Rights Act of 1964 was not only a law mandating equal rights for individuals, both the Congressional debates leading up to its passage and particular provisions of the Act itself explicitly repudiated the concept of group preferences or quotas. The term "discrimination" which sometimes has very different meanings to different people, was specifically defined in the Civil Rights Act of 1964 to mean *intentional* actions by an employer against individuals, as distinguished from disparate consequences of particular tests or other criteria on different groups. The principal advocate for the Act, Senator Hubert Humphrey, put it this way:

> The express requirement of intent is designed to make it wholly clear that inadvertent or accidental discriminations will not violate the title or result in entry of court orders. It means simply that the respondent must have intended to discriminate.[15]

While guiding the Civil Rights Act of 1964 through the Senate, Senator Humphrey assured his colleagues that it "does not require an employer to achieve any kind of racial balance in his work force by giving preferential treatment to any individual or group."[16] He pointed out that subsection 703(j) under Title VII of the Civil Rights Act "is added to state this point expressly."[17] That subsection declared that nothing in Title VII required an employer "to grant preferential treatment to any individual or group on account of any imbalance which may exist" with respect to the numbers of employees in such groups "in comparison with the total number or percentage of persons of such race, color, religion, sex, or national origin in any community, State, section or other area."

While the Civil Rights Act clearly did not create affirmative action in the United States, it is much less clear just what specifically did. In part this is because group preferences and quotas arose and evolved incrementally and even surreptitiously. The very phrase "affirmative action" meant different things at different times.

In the American context, there has been what might be called generic affirmative action, as well as highly specific affirmative action. Generic affirmative action is distinguished from a policy of passively adhering to a non-discrimination principle, while waiting to respond to particular problems as they arise. Thus the National Labor Relations Act of 1935 required employers to take "affirmative action" to ensure that their employees had a free choice as to whether or not to vote to be represented by a labor union. Such actions might include posting relevant federal laws on the subject in the workplace and/or announcing the end of any anti-union activities or policies previously engaged in by the management. In other words, it was not considered sufficient simply to "cease and desist" from anti-union activity and passively comply with the new federal laws giving workers the right to choose collective bargaining, it was necessary to affirmatively proclaim that right and repudiate any pre-existing policies whose lingering effects might intimidate workers in exercising their rights.

Similarly, in the much later application of this principle to racial and other groups, it was not considered sufficient for the employer simply to cease and desist from discriminating. It was necessary for the employers to take "affirmative action" to ensure that previously excluded groups were made aware of new opportunities now open to them, so as to be able to take practical steps to prepare for and apply for such opportunities. Affirmative action might also include voluntary efforts, both inside and outside the workplace, by both employers and others, to advise and train people for new opportunities in employment, college admissions and other benefits.

Such generic affirmative action has long had far wider support from the general public, and from both conservatives and liberals in the political arena, than more specific affirmative action in the form of group preferences and quotas.[18] In short, there has been widespread support in the American population at large for efforts to bring less fortunate groups up to the existing standards, even among people completely opposed to bringing the standards down to these groups.

The first official use of the term "affirmative action" in a racial or ethnic context was in President John F. Kennedy's Executive Order No. 10,925 in 1961, where he said that federal contractors should "take affirmative action to ensure that the applicants are employed, and that employees are treated during employment, without regard to their race, creed, color or national origin." This first in a series of Executive Orders, extending over several administrations, was clearly *not* calling for group preferences or quotas. On the contrary, it was calling upon employers to hire and promote *without regard* to group membership — and to make that fact clear to all. It was generic affirmative action.

The next major development in the evolution of affirmative action was the creation of the Office of Federal Contract Compliance in the U.S. Department of Labor by President Lyndon Johnson's Executive Order No. 11,246 in 1965. In May 1968, this office issued guidelines containing the fateful expression "goals and timetables" and "representation." But as yet these were still not quotas, for 1968 guidelines spoke of "goals and timetables for the prompt achievement of full and equal employment opportunity." By 1970, however, during the Nixon administration new guidelines referred to "results-oriented procedures," which hinted more strongly at what was to come. In December 1971 the decisive guidelines were issued, which made it clear that "goals and timetables" were meant to "increase materially the utilization of minorities and women," with "under-utilization" being spelled out as "having fewer minorities or women in a particular job classification than would reasonably be expected by their availability . . ."[19] Employers were required to confess to "deficiencies in the utilization" of minorities and women whenever this statistical parity could not be found in all job classifications, as a first step toward correcting this situation. The burden of proof — and remedy — was on the employer. "Affirmative action" was now decisively transformed into a numerical concept, whether called "goals" or "quotas." Affirmative action in this specific sense was thus a product of the decade of the 1970s.

Many have seen the emergence of affirmative action, in the sense of group preferences and quotas, as a later perversion of the initial equal-opportunity intent of the law. However, even before the Civil Rights Act of 1964 was passed, there were already developments which foreshadowed the shift to preferences and quotas. Moreover, this shift was in keeping with the underlying social vision of the problems of black Americans. If economic differences between groups were presumed to be strange and/or sinister, then the obvious remedy was to eliminate such differences. The fact that such differences can be found in countries around the world and over centuries of history — often on a larger scale than differences between black and white Americans — may be known to some scholars and their students and readers, but these are still a minuscule fraction of the population, and certainly too small to have any political or even intellectual effect on widespread beliefs.

When the Civil Rights Act of 1964 was being debated in Congress, there was already a prominent state case in Illinois, in which the Motorola Company was judged to have violated state laws against discrimination by refusing to hire a black applicant who had failed a test they had given him. An examiner for a state agency considered the test to be "unfair to culturally deprived and disadvantaged groups."[20] Here the charge was not that this *individual* was given a test not required of other individuals, but that the *group* to which he belonged was less likely to pass such tests. The question of whether the law should focus on individuals or groups was joined early on at the state level, while the federal Civil Rights Act was still under consideration in Congress.

Supporters of the Civil Rights Act dismissed the Illinois case as an oddity unlikely to survive the normal legal processes, as a case where one examiner "went too far" and as a "red herring" as regards Congressional debates over federal anti-discrimination law.[21] But when one of the critics of the Act, Senator John Tower of Texas, introduced an amendment to declare that an employer "may give any professionally developed ability test to any individual seeking employment" and use such tests in making hiring or promotions decisions, Senator Humphrey said: "These tests are legal. They do not need to be legalized a second time." He also said: "The Motorola case has been discussed, discussed, and cussed."[22]

Despite this clear legislative history, the U.S. Supreme Court later ruled in *Griggs vs. Duke Power Company* (1971) that tests and other procedures which "act as 'built-in headwinds' for minority groups" could not be allowed to stand, even if they were "neutral on their face, and even if neutral in terms of intent," when they are "unrelated to measuring job capability."[23] This last proviso meant that employers had to "validate" any tests they used which had a disparate impact on minority groups. This apparently innocent requirement concealed costly and complicated statistical validation processes, open to endless legal challenges, that became for many employers simply prohibitions against using tests.[24]

The *Griggs* decision was not the only example of courts

reading the Civil Rights Act of 1964 to mean precisely what the Act and its legislative history had clearly said that it did *not* mean. A case that was decided by the U.S. Supreme Court in 1979 was brought by a white employee of Kaiser Aluminum named Brian Weber, who had been rejected for a job training program for insufficient seniority, even though black employees with less seniority were accepted. This was because of the company's affirmative action plan — a plan "voluntarily" established by the company to retain its status as a government contractor. Weber sued on grounds that the Civil Rights Act of 1964 had been violated by discrimination based on race. Section 703(a) of the Act declared it unlawful for an employer "to discriminate against any individual with respect to his compensation, terms, conditions, or privileges of employment, because of such individual's race, color, religion, sex, or national origin" and Section 703(d) more specifically declared it unlawful to "discriminate against any individual" in "apprenticeship or other training."

Notwithstanding this plain language, the Supreme Court voted against Weber's claim of discrimination. Writing for the majority, Justice William J. Brennan rejected "a literal interpretation of these words." He claimed that the "spirit" of the Act had as its "primary concern" the economic problems of blacks, so that it did not bar "temporary, voluntary, affirmative action undertaken to eliminate manifest racial imbalance in traditionally segregated job categories." Quite aside from the fact that these racial quotas were neither temporary nor voluntary, this interpretation ignored both the language and the legislative history of the Civil Rights Act of 1964, which had rejected discrimination against anyone of any clor, as well as rejecting ideas of correcting racial "imbalances." Brennan's complete evasion of the plain words of the statute was described in a dissenting opinion as reminiscent of the great escapes of Houdini.[25]

The Weber case became both a legal landmark and a

political model for evasions of the law by citing such rationales as remedial action or "diversity" — and for taking the issue out of the realm of government-sponsored discrimination, which would be a violation of the Fourteenth Amendment, by maintaining that affirmative action quotas and preferences created by employers in order to maintain their eligibility for government contracts were "voluntary" and "private." Although the Weber case was the high-water mark for advocates of group preferences and quotas, the Supreme Court continued to go back and forth on the legality or illegality of particular affirmative action programs. Judicial vacillation was signalled not only by differing decisions on very similar cases — the same nine justices had invalidated a University of California medical school quota in the Bakke case just one year before affirming the job training quota in the Weber case — but also by 5 to 4 decisions and by decisions in which there was no overall majority for the decision as a whole, but only shifting majorities, made up of different justices, for the particular sections that added up to the whole decision. Reconciling equal treatment of individuals with group preferences was not easy.

Despite a zig-zag pattern of judicial decisions over the years, the general trend has been toward ever more expansive definitions of "discrimination," leading to more and more "remedial" group preferences and quotas. In the controversies swirling around both judicial and political policies involving affirmative action, there has been much confusion between generic affirmative action, such as "outreach" efforts, and more specific affirmative action in the sense of group preferences and quotas. Indeed, much of that confusion has been cultivated by defenders of affirmative action who decry the notion that nothing should be done to help the less fortunate — which is of course not the issue at all.

The real issue is what specifically shall and shall not be done, for whom, for what reason, and for how long. Such issues remain unresolved. As late as 2003, the Supreme Court of the

United States declared in *Grutter v. Bollinger* that "all government use of race must have a logical end point." Yet the Court neither imposed such a time limit nor provided any criterion by which anyone could know when that limit had been reached.

EXTENSIONS OF AFFIRMATIVE ACTION

As in other countries, affirmative action in the United States has not merely evolved but spread. It has spread to a succession of groups, to a wider range of activities and industries, and the meanings of words have also spread, so that "discrimination," for example, now encompasses things that no one would have considered to be discrimination when the Civil Rights Act of 1964 was passed.

Extensions of "Discrimination"

Because discrimination so often serves as a predicate for preferences and quotas under American laws and policies, the definition of discrimination has tended to expand over time, along with the groups and activities to which affirmative action has been successively extended. The "intentional" act which constituted discrimination, as described by Senator Hubert Humphrey when he successfully led the effort to get the Civil Rights Act of 1964 passed, has long since been superseded by more expansive concepts and more vague and shifting standards of proof.

The most decisive shift in the burden of proof has been to make the accused disprove a prima facie case of discrimination, based on statistical disparities in group results. These may be disparities in test results or disparities in group "representation" among employees of businesses or students admitted to college, for example. The *Griggs* decision by the U.S. Supreme Court shifted the burden of proof to employers whenever tests were passed at very different rates by different segments of the population. This became known as the principle of "disparate impact," which was applied not only to tests but also to other criteria such as academic credentials or a non-criminal history, when these criteria led to different proportions of different groups being accepted.

The policies of federal administrative agencies codified and extended the principle that lesser performances by A were to be regarded as presumptively the fault of B, the latter being left to try to prove a negative, so as to avoid a charge of discrimination. Guidelines issued by the Equal Employment Opportunity Commission declared that "a selection rate for any race, sex, or ethnic group which is less that four-fifths . . . of the rate for the group with the highest rate will generally be regarded by the Federal enforcement agencies as evidence of adverse impact" of the selection process.[26]

The redefinition of "discrimination" was often accompanied by denials that this represented a lowering of standards. The argument has been made that no one was being forced to hire people who were not "qualified." But this word sidestepped the real question, which was whether people of lesser qualifications were to be hired in preference to people of greater qualifications, simply because of the respective groups to which they belonged. The word "qualified" essentially homogenized applicants who met whatever minimum standard might be arbitrarily set by third parties. If that standard were to be set as correctly answering half the questions on a test, then someone who answered 51 percent correctly was just as much a part of the "qualified" pool as someone who answered 99 percent. More important, an employer who hired proportionately fewer black "qualified" applicants than white "qualified" applicants could be considered to be engaging in racial discrimination, even if the average test scores of the black applicants were substantially lower. Moreover, this was not officially considered to be a policy of racial preferences, but only an application of anti-discrimination law.

The boldest application of this principle was "race-norming" of tests. The U.S. Employment Service, for example, reported the percentile rankings of job applicants to employers, without informing those employers that these were *separate* percentile rankings according to the racial group to which the applicant belonged. Thus a black job applicant who ranked at the 90th percentile among fellow blacks might have a lower absolute score than a white applicant who ranked at the 80th percentile among whites. In Sri Lanka, the same practice was called by the innocuous name "standardization," which offset the higher average academic performances of Tamil students as compared to Sinhalese students. In both countries, it was simply a disguised form of group preferences.

When the clandestine practice of race-norming became known and a matter of public controversy in the United States, it was banned in the Civil Rights Act of 1991. However, the kind of thinking it involved was not banned and has continued in other guises. Moreover, that such a practice could have been imposed secretly in the first place — and persist undetected for a decade[27] — suggests some of the difficulties of attempting to ban affirmative action — and especially of trying to have a "nuanced" reduction of it, to "mend it, not end it," as some have said. Anything short of unequivocally banning it outright simply invites such subterfuges. Indeed, even outright bans on group preferences in admissions to state colleges and universities in Texas and in California have set off searches for non-objective criteria, such as have already been used in India to circumvent court limitations on group preferences there.

In addition, laws have been passed to admit students who finish in the top 10 percent of their high school classes, in disregard of the highly disparate qualities of different high schools — and, more particularly, the very low quality of the high schools from which many minority students graduate. Thus students with composite SAT scores below 900 have been admitted to the University of Texas because they were in the top

10 percent of their high schools, while other students with SAT scores hundreds of points higher—some over 1500—have been rejected.[28] In California, the search for non-academic criteria for granting admissions to the University of California has in practice meant the use of such criteria to admit more Hispanics, but not Asian Americans who meet those same non-academic criteria, in addition to having higher academic credentials.[29] It is race-norming by another name.

The ease with which discrimination charges can be made with statistics alone, and the difficulty or impossibility of proving a negative when the burden of proof shifts to the employer, provide incentives for businesses to locate away from concentrations of blacks, for example. Whether the jobs lost by blacks as a result of such locational decisions are greater or less than the jobs gained by blacks as a result of racial preferences is another empirical question seldom asked, much less answered. Here, as in other countries, affirmative action tends to be discussed and debated primarily in terms of its rationales and goals, rather than its actual consequences.

Extensions to New Groups

The rationale of remedying or forestalling the effects of discrimination extends well beyond the various racial or ethnic groups originally used as a reason for creating affirmative action policies. The largest of these new groups—indeed, larger than all the other groups put together—are women. And, of course, in the United States most of those women are white. Although the rationale has wandered far from the "legacy of slavery" argument, the practices growing out of affirmative action have not wandered far from the practices used in situations involving blacks. Women have become entitled to employment quotas and business set-asides like other groups. The need for specific evidence of prior specific harm has likewise been evaded, in this case by the phrase "glass ceiling"—that is, discrimination that cannot be seen but which is simply assumed as a basis for preferential treatment.

Women have even had a fictitious history created for them, much as there has been a fictitious history of the rise of blacks from poverty. In reality, the socioeconomic history of women in the United States is very different from the socioeconomic history of blacks—and even more radically different from the history depicted by those seeking affirmative action for women. Unlike the more or less continuous rise of blacks from lower to higher levels of education and from lower to higher occupational levels during the twentieth century, women's educational and occupational trajectories varied considerably during that century. Although the conventional explanation of women's lag behind men in the economy is discrimination, and their rise in more recent times has been credited to feminist or "women's liberation" movements that began in the 1960s and the government laws and policies created in response to such political efforts, the cold fact is that women were in many ways better represented in higher occupational levels in the 1930s or earlier than in the 1960s. This can scarcely be credited to movements that had not yet begun in these earlier times, much less to affirmative action policies that began in the 1970s.

Unlike what happened in the history of blacks, women's percentage share of the jobs in professional and technical occupations *declined* in the middle decades of the twentieth century—and then rose later. A similar pattern of fall followed by rise can be seen in women's percentage shares of the college and university degrees required for such occupations.

Women's representation in professional and technical occupations declined by 9 percent from 1940 to 1950 and then by another 9 percent from 1950 to 1968.[30] As far back as 1902, women's share of the people listed in *Who's Who* was more than double their share in 1958.[31] Women received 34 percent of the Bachelor's degrees in 1920 but only 24 percent in 1950. They received just over 15 percent of the doctoral degrees in

1920 but just under 10 percent in 1950.[32] In mathematics, women's share of doctorates declined from 15 percent to 5 percent over a period of decades, and in economics from 10 percent to 2 percent.[33] There were similar declines in women's shares of doctoral degrees in the humanities, law and chemistry. For no year during the 1950s or 1960s did women receive as high a percentage share of all master's degrees, or of all doctoral degrees, as they had back in 1930.[34]

If statistical disparities between women and men are attributable to discrimination by men, then this remarkable history would suggest that men inexplicably became more discriminatory toward women during the first half of the twentieth century and then relented later in the second half, causing the trend to reverse. However, this whole puzzling — and politically inconvenient — question does not even arise in discussions where the educational and occupational history of women in the early twentieth century is ignored and trends are plotted only for the period since 1960. Such ignoring of an inconvenient earlier history has been the rule, rather than the exception, in discussions of discrimination against women and of the presumed need for affirmative action to overcome that discrimination.

In reality, the fall and later rise of women in their education and occupations, relative to men, is far more strongly correlated with demographic trends than with political, legal, or ideological trends. As women began having fewer children — a trend that began in the nineteenth century and continued on into the 1930s — they became better represented in higher levels of education and professional occupations. Then, when birth rates began to rise again, from the 1930s to the 1950s,[35] women began to be less well represented in these higher educational and occupational levels. The role of men in all this was primarily that of fathers of the children born to women. If this period of relative occupational retrogression were due to men's actions as employers, then it would be hard to see why the very same trends occurred in the hiring of faculty at women's colleges, run by women administrators.[36] Alumni of women's colleges, returning for class reunions in the later period, were often surprised to find male professors far more common in women's colleges than in the days when these alumni were students.

After the birth rate began to decline again in the 1960s,[37] women's representation in higher levels of education and occupations began to rise again. The crucial role of marriage and child-bearing on women's economic level can also be seen by breaking down the female population as a whole into those who do and those who do not become wives and mothers, those whose careers are continuous and those who interrupt their careers to assume domestic responsibilities. As far back as 1971, women who remained unmarried into their thirties and who had worked continuously since high school earned slightly *more* than men of the same description.[38] Academic women who never married averaged slightly higher incomes in 1968–69—before affirmative action—than academic men who never married.[39]

Substantial male-female differences in income reflect the fact that most women do get married, do have children, and do interrupt their careers for domestic responsibilities more often than men do. Different occupations have different rates of obsolescence of their respective skills, so that interruptions of careers in some fields are more damaging to one's career than in other fields. For example, a physicist loses about half the value of his or her knowledge from a six-year layoff, but it would take a historian more than a quarter of a century to suffer a similar loss.[40] Women tend to specialize in occupations where career interruptions are easier to accommodate—teaching rather than computer engineering, for example.

Another factor in male-female differences in earnings is that men tend to specialize more in hazardous occupations that pay higher compensation. Although men are 54 percent of the workforce, they account for 92 percent of job-related deaths.[41] Innumerable other economically relevant differences between the sexes exist, even with men and women who seem to be "the same" superficially,[42] and whose different incomes cannot therefore be automatically attributed to employer discrimination.

As for the effect of "women's liberation" movements and government legislation in increasing women's income relative to that of men, there is no evidence of any such trend for those women who worked full-time and year around over the period from 1960 to 1980.[43] What was happening over this span was that more women were working full time and year around, both absolutely and relative to men.[44] This says nothing about how employers were treating given women or how successful "women's liberation" was. A significant increase in the ratio of female to male earnings began in the 1980s[45] — during the Reagan administration — which is not when most feminists would claim that their influence began to be felt.

While women are the largest group to whom affirmative action has been extended, there are others who have benefitted from similar extensions of this principle — and who are similarly remote from the "legacy of slavery" rationale or rationales based on lingering effects of past discrimination. These include not only various immigrants from Latin America, Europe and Asia, but also Eskimos who have been granted preferential status in Virginia, where it is doubtful that many of their ancestors ever lived, much less suffered discrimination. Even for women, the "lingering effects" of past discrimination argument is far less weighty than it is for blacks or American Indians, for example. Since women are descended from men as well as women, there is no evidence that whatever disadvantages their mothers, grandmothers, etc., suffered had more impact on their current socioeconomic condition than the corresponding advantages enjoyed by their fathers, grandfathers and other male ancestors.

Successive extensions of the principle of affirmative action to more and more groups adversely affect both blacks and whites. As of 1970, blacks were two-thirds of all people in racial or ethnic groups legally entitled to affirmative action but, a quarter of a century later, blacks were just 49 percent of such groups.[46] Moreover, this does not count the effect of the extension of affirmative action to women, mostly white women. With the addition of women, what affirmative action amounts to is legalized discrimination against the residual non-preferred population, mostly white males. None of this takes into account the illegal or semi-legal uses of affirmative action which have occurred in the United States, as in other countries.

Minority businesses preferentially awarded government contracts, for example, can then turn over the actual work of fulfilling those contracts to others, in essence collecting a royalty for letting non-minority firms rent their minority status to acquire business from the government. The "Ali-Baba" enterprises found in Malaysia and Indonesia have their counterpart in American firms ostensibly owned by blacks but in fact serving as "fronts" for whites. A Baltimore grand jury was kept busy for months exposing such fronts, and an investigation of "disadvantaged business enterprises" in Indianapolis ended up decertifying more than one-third of all businesses with that designation. At the individual level, jobs, promotions and government contracts may go to people with only minute traces of some minority ancestry—an entrepreneur who was 1/64th Cherokee Indian won a set-aside contract in California—or with the effrontery to claim minority status fraudulently.[47]

The successive extension of preferred status to more groups, both legally and illegally, not only dilutes the benefits for those for whom the original rationale is strongest, it changes the terms of competition in ways that can work to the further disadvantage of genuinely less fortunate groups. For example, where group preferences must masquerade as anti-discrimination policies, employers have incentives to use employment and promotion criteria which can pass muster in court, so as to avoid discrimination charges—whether or not these are the best criteria for assessing the ability to do the jobs in question. Objective criteria, such as diplomas and degrees, thus acquire greater weight than they might otherwise have. As in other countries, the genuinely less fortunate—black males from the ghetto, for example—are less likely to have these credentials as compared to white women, who are also legally entitled to affirmative action. Whether the advantages that black males acquire over white males, as a result of affirmative action, outweigh the disadvantages they have relative to white women is an empirical question. But it is a question unlikely to be asked.

PRIVATE BUSINESSES

In the United States, as in other countries, businesses closely controlled by government have tended to have different hiring standards for different groups to a greater extent than businesses operating more freely in a competitive marketplace. In the United States, blacks were more likely to be discriminated against in government-regulated businesses before the civil rights era and more likely to received preferential hiring in such businesses after that era. The telephone industry, before the break-up of the American Telephone & Telegraph Company, was a classic example of a heavily regulated enterprise with a monopoly in its markets nationwide.

As of 1930, there were approximately 235,000 telephone operators in the United States, of whom just 331 were black. In all categories of telephone company employees, black males were 1.2 percent and black females 0.2 percent. Male employees included many manual laborers doing such work as digging holes for telephone poles, while the women were predominantly operators.[48] As late as 1950, black women held only one percent of all jobs in the telephone industry nationwide. In the South, few blacks were employed as telephone operators during the entire decade of the 1950s and they failed to reach even one percent as late as 1960. Between 1950 and 1960, the number of telephone operators employed in the Southern states increased by 6,611, while the number of black telephone operators increased by just 20.[49]

Meanwhile, outside the South, the number of black telephone operators rose rapidly during the decade of the 1950s, both absolutely and relative to white telephone operators. In fact, the increase in the number of black telephone operators nationwide exceeded the total increase in the number of telephone operators nationwide. In short, there were dramatic changes in the employment of black telephone operators during the decade of the 1950s, virtually all of it outside the South, with more than two-thirds of this increased employment of black women employed in the telecommunications industry occurring in just five states — New York, Pennsylvania, Illinois, Michigan, and Ohio.[50] How can this pattern be explained — and what does it imply?

Although A.T.&T.'s nationwide operations, such as long-distance service, were regulated by the Federal Communications Commission, the individual phone companies were regulated by their respective state governments. The immediate postwar years saw changes in racial attitudes and in *state* anti-discrimination legislation[51] — outside the South. The number of black women working as telephone operators in New York City, for example, tripled during the 1950s, even though the total number of telephone operators in the city remained virtually unchanged during that decade. In San Francisco, the number of black women hired as telephone operators tripled during the same decade, while again the total number of telephone operators remained virtually unchanged. In Detroit, the number of black women who were telephone operators increased five-fold, despite a slight decline in the total number of telephone operators in the city. No such dramatic changes occurred in such Southern cities as Atlanta, Birmingham, Dallas, or New Orleans, nor in such border state cities as St. Louis or Washington, D.C.[52]

The point here is not to claim that these racial employment policies were a direct consequence of orders from state regulatory commissions. Prior to 1970, public utility commissions generally did not seek to influence the racial hiring policies of the companies they regulated.[53] Instead, the point here is that the very fact of being a regulated public utility made preferences for or against any given group less expensive than they would have been in a free, competitive market. For a regulated monopoly, any additional costs associated with discrimination against qualified applicants could simply be passed on to customers. Thus it was virtually costless to discriminate against blacks in an earlier era and it was virtually costless to show them preferential treatment in a later era. In other words, public utilities could reflect prevailing social views at little or no costs to themselves, whether those views favored or opposed the hiring of blacks.

To some extent, the same reasoning applies to non-profit organizations, such as academic institutions, hospitals, and foundations. Accordingly, it is not surprising that most American colleges and universities had no black tenured professors until 1940 and few black or Jewish professors at Ivy League institutions until well after World War II. As of 1936, only three black Ph.D. holders were employed by all the white colleges and universities in the United States. By contrast, more than three hundred black chemists alone were employed in private industry at the same time.[54] To private industry, these black chemists represented profits that could be made by hiring them. But, to a college or university chemistry department, there was no such incentive and they could easily afford to pass over these chemists.[55]

In later decades, the evolution of affirmative action, along with the still surviving anti-discrimination laws, created a dilemma for many businesses. If they failed to have "enough" black employees, they were liable to be sued for discrimination by individual blacks, by civil rights groups, or by government agencies acting on their behalf. However, if they engaged in preferential hiring of blacks, they could be sued for discrimination by whites. Court decisions legitimizing affirmative action under prescribed conditions then provided businesses with a set of guidelines that could minimize their legal jeopardy. Therefore, when efforts were made to end group preferences and quotas during the 1980s by some within the Reagan administration, big business support for the continuation of affirmative action helped doom the efforts to rescind it.[56] In addition, large corporations tend to have their own internal affirmative action officials and departments, with their own vested interests in the continuation of such policies. In the year 2000, several large corporations filed briefs supporting the continuation of affirmative action at the University of Michigan.[57]

THE ACADEMIC WORLD

Nowhere is affirmative action more deeply entrenched than in the academic world. Moreover, that world has a special importance as the gateway to upward mobility. Various arguments have been made for the admission of black, Hispanic, and American Indian students to colleges and universities under lower standards than those applied to white or Asian American students. Chief among these is the claim that conventional criteria such as test scores and academic records do not reveal these students' "real" ability or likelihood of success. Over the years, this has been one of the most repeatedly studied — and repeatedly refuted — claims. Black students with low test scores do not perform better academically than white students with the same low test scores. On the contrary, black students tend to perform slightly *less* well than white students with the same test scores — and this applies across the board, not just with low-scoring students.[58]

Other claims made as rationales for preferential admissions of black or other minority students have tended to be either not testable empricially or not to have been subjected to any empirical test. One of these claims is that "diversity" enhances the educational experience for all students. Typical of this genre of claims was an article in *The Chronicle of Higher Education* titled "Why Affirmative Action Works at Michigan" — but the article in fact provided no empirical evidence of either *why* or *whether* it "works" by any definable standard, but only assertions and anecdotes.[59]

Often a related claim is made that black students must be admitted in numbers sufficient to provide a certain "critical mass" on campus that will enable individual black students to feel socially comfortable and secure enough to be able to do their best work. Again, empirical evidence in support of this proposition is neither asked nor given. Conceivably, one might get data from colleges and universities with relatively few black students and comparable institutions with more substantial numbers of black students, and then compare these students' academic performances. Nothing of the sort has been done by proponents of the "critical mass" theory.

Alternatively, one might compare the academic performances of black students in past eras in predominantly white academic institutions, where there were only a relative handful of black students at the time, with the academic performances of later generations of black students in the same institutions which now have a better approximation of the "critical mass." But this too remains undone. Nor is there any incentive for proponents of affirmative action to do such studies when their unsubstantiated assertions are so widely accepted and repeated.

Some data that might be relevant to the "critical mass" theory come from the history of all-black Dunbar High School in Washington, D.C. Between 1892 and 1954, Amherst College admitted 34 graduates of this school. Of these, 25 graduated from Amherst — 74 percent of the admittees — and 21 percent of these black graduates were Phi Beta Kappas.[60] There were never enough black students at Amherst during this period to constitute a "critical mass." The contrast between the academic achievements of these early black pioneers at Amherst and the widespread academic failures of black students of a later era is much more consistent with the opposite theory of John H. McWhorter, a black professor at the University of California at Berkeley, that an anti-intellectual black subculture reduces black students' performances well below what they are capable of.[61] If so, then a "critical mass" is likely to be counterproductive academically.

Further evidence of the negative potential of a "critical mass" comes from numerous reports by observers of black students in schools across the country that these students have developed a habit of referring to fellow black students who are academically oriented and academically achieving as "acting white" — a charge that can bring anything from social ostracism to outright violence. A recent empirical study published by the National Bureau of Economic Research found that "a higher percentage of Black schoolmates has a strong adverse effect on achievements of Blacks and, moreover, that the effects are highly concentrated in the upper half of the ability distribution."[62] In other words, black students with higher ability perform less well when there are more black students present.

Another bit of empirical evidence comes from a study of the academic consequences of ability-grouping in schools, which concluded: "Schooling in a homogeneous group of students appears to have a positive effect on the achievements of high-ability students' achievements, and even stronger effects on the achievements of high-ability minority youth."[63] In other words, black youngsters with high ability improve particularly well when put among other high ability youngsters, rather than being educated in the presence of other students of lesser ability. An *intellectual* critical mass produces opposite results from a racial critical mass.

Still another bit of evidence comes from a study of graduation rates in state colleges and universities in Colorado. This study found that, in general, whites graduated at higher rates than blacks at most of the institutions studied. However, "for the two instances in which blacks graduate at higher rates than whites, we are dealing with extremely small sample sizes for the blacks."[64] In short, it was precisely where they *lacked* a racial "critical mass" that the black students did markedly better.

All this is more consistent with the McWhorter thesis than with the "critical mass" theory. However, it is not necessary to claim that this evidence is conclusive or even to choose between competing theories of the effects of a "critical mass" on black students in a given institution. The more fundamental point here is that the assumption that a "critical mass" is not only academically beneficial, but academically essential, has become prevailing dogma without empirical evidence being asked or given.

A companion dogma is that black "role models" are essential to the education of black students—another widely trumpeted belief for which evidence has seldom been asked nor given. In 2003, long after "role models" had become a mantra, a survey of empirical studies concluded, "there is no systematic evidence that same-gender or same-race/ethnicity role models have significant influence on a range of dependent variables that they are assumed to influence, including occupational choice, learning, and career success."[65]

Certainly most Dunbar High School students who succeeded at Amherst College between 1892 and 1954 were unlikely to have seen a black professor. The spectacular rise of the Nisei generation of Japanese Americans after World War II came at a time when they were at least equally unlikely to have been taught by a Japanese American teacher or professor, or to have seen or known a Japanese American scientist or engineer, since the majority of their parents were farmers.

Although racial preferences and quotas in admissions to American colleges and universities began in the 1960s, usually without much real discussion of pro's and con's—and with instant dismissal of any critics, some of those critics nevertheless made the case against such preferences at length and with considerable logical and empirical support. One of the most cogent of these critics was Professor Clyde W. Summers of the Yale Law School. Like many other critics of affirmative action, Professor Summers had in previous years written in opposition to discrimination against blacks, even before that was a popular position to take.[66] Nor was he entirely comfortable when finding himself now arguing against affirmative action:

> Anyone who is at all aware of our historic brutal discrimination against minority groups, and is sensitive to our continued pattern of deprivation, wants to believe in measures which promise to open doors of opportunity and provide some recompense for past injustices. To raise questions about this program in which so many so deeply believe almost inevitably leads to misunderstanding, no matter how one tries to make himself understood. More troublesome, what one writes may be seized upon and used by those who seek excuses for doing nothing and thus preserving the present pattern of deprivation.[67]

Summers called preferential admissions policies "an unreal solution to a real problem." His first objection was that preferential admissions, beginning at the top elite institutions, would create a nationwide mismatching of minority students and the institutions they attended, all up and down the academic pecking order. Since his own field was law, he illustrated the pattern with the admissions policies of law schools:

> If Harvard or Yale, for example, admit minority students with test score 100 to 150 points below that normally required for a non-minority student to get admitted, the total number of minority

students able to get a legal education is not increased thereby. The minority students given such preference would meet the normal admissions standards at Illinois, Rutgers or Texas. Similarly, minority students given preference at Pennsylvania would meet normal standards at Pittsburgh; those given preference at Duke would meet normal standards at North Carolina, and those given preference at Vanderbilt would meet normal standards at Kentucky, Mississippi and West Virginia. Thus, each law school, by its preferential admission, simply takes minority students away from other schools whose admissions standards are further down the scale.... In sum, the policy of preferential admission has a pervasive shifting effect, causing large numbers of minority students to attend law schools whose normal admission standards they do not meet, instead of attending other law schools whose normal standard they do meet.[68]

Because of this "pervasive shifting effect," minority students would find themselves in serious academic difficulties all up and down the scale of law schools and other institutions, because they would be systematically mismatched with institutions at all levels. Put bluntly, many minority students with all the prerequisites for success would be artificially turned into failures because of this pervasive mismatching. This argument would for decades remain at the heart of objections to affirmative action. Attempts to get data on which to confirm or refute this argument were met by blanket refusals of academic authorities to release such information. Instead, there were assurances issued that no "unqualified" students were being admitted—a virtually meaningless statement when coming from those who arbitrarily define what "qualified" meant, without revealing what that definition is.

Despite academic policies secreting the data needed to resolve this key issue, some such data did become public, in one way or another. Almost invariably, such data completely undermined the academic defenders of affirmative action.

At the University of California at Berkeley, for example, a

1988 study showed that the average composite Scholastic Aptitude Test scores of black undergraduates was 952, which was above the national average of 900, but well below the university's average of 1232 for white students and 1254 for Asian American students. Black students with above-average SAT scores cannot be called "unqualified" but they were certainly mismatched — and 70 percent of black students failed to graduate from Berkeley. Despite rising numbers of black students at Berkeley during the 1980s, the number of black *graduates* declined.[69] At M.I.T., the average black student's math SAT score was in the top 10 percent nationwide — and in the bottom 10 percent at M.I.T. Nearly one-fourth of these extraordinarily high-ranking black students failed to graduate from M.I.T.[70]

At the University of Texas, where the average SAT score of black undergraduates was more than 100 points below that of white undergraduates, the grade point average for black freshmen was 1.97, compared to 2.45 for white freshmen.[71] At the Georgetown University Law School, the median test score of black students on the Law School Aptitude Test was at the 75th percentile — again, hardly "unqualified," but that score was lower than the score of *any* white student admitted to this elite law school.[72] Incidentally, the student who released this Georgetown data was denounced as "racist" in the national media, as well as on campus, despite a lack of any evidence of racism, unless the release of the data is arbitrarily defined that way, making the whole argument circular.

As Professor Summers had predicted, the failures were not confined to the elite institutions. Thus San Jose State University had 70 percent of its black students fail to graduate, just like Berkeley,[73] though it is doubtful that the minority students at Berkeley would have failed at San Jose State. That is the domino effect of mismatching. Moreover, these costs of affirmative action would not stop with unnecessary academic failures among minority students.

Professor Summers and others predicted, back in the 1960s,

that black students who were completely overmatched at many colleges and universities, would not only find their position intolerable, but would then proceed to find academic standards and much else about academic life intolerable, leading to a shift of their focus from academics to ideological crusades on campus and beyond. Demands for "relevant" courses, black studies departments, and quota hiring of black faculty without regard to "irrelevant" academic credentials proliferated across the country, often backed up by campus disruptions and violence. As in other countries, the illusion of being able to control the course of events from the top down under affirmative action was painfully dispelled.

Easier courses in black studies and in some other departments were accompanied by what Harvard professor David Riesman called "affirmative grading." Many professors inflated grades all around, reducing failure rates and making most students A students. The credible threats represented by organized black students also tended to lead to preferential treatment of behavioral offenses.[74]

White students were not unaware of all this. As Summers and others had predicted in the 1960s, whites who saw their black classmates consistently at the bottom academically and allowed to get away with things that would not be tolerated in others, began to manifest increasingly negative attitudes, despite draconian punishments for saying or doing anything that could be construed as "racism." White students on a number of campuses have had outbursts of violence against black students of a sort unknown on those campuses in the era before preferential admissions programs and double standards on campus.[75] Even in the absence of overt hostility, black students at M.I.T. complained that other students there did not regard them as being desirable partners on group projects or as people to study with for tough exams.[76] Similar reports came from other academic institutions — and from black professors as well as black students. Blacks regarded as "quota" professors have complained of being less often invited to collaborate on research, which is crucial to their advancement.[77] Even liberal academic supporters of affirmative action began commenting on the increasing hostility toward black students on campus and coined the term "the new racism."[78]

At the heart of the problem, for both black students and black professors, is the unyielding fact that the numbers who have the credentials required for being at selective institutions are nowhere near the numbers required for fulfilling arbitrary quotas based on their "representation" in the population at large. As far back as 1969, those black professors with Ph.D.s from top universities and numerous publications were earning *more* than white professors of the same description.[79] It was just that there were not very many black professors like this. The problem was not discrimination, but inadequate numbers with the requisite qualifications.

Similarly with black students. When elite law schools began admitting black students preferentially in the 1960s, the total number of black students who met their usual standards who met their usual standards on Law School Aptitude test scores and grade-point average was 39—in the entire country.[80] Two decades later, there were just sixteen.[81] At the college level, the number of black students who scored 650 or higher on the verbal SAT was less than 700 nationwide in 1995.[82] Most Ivy League institutions average at least 650 in verbal SAT scores. But there are not enough black students in the whole country with a 650 verbal SAT score to be admitted to the eight Ivy League institutions in proportion to their "representation" in the general population, much less to other elite institutions from coast to coast.

Although test scores and grade-point averages were pooh-poohed as predictive factors by advocates of affirmative action, early factual studies showed the standing of black law school students averaging at the 8th percentile.[83] That is, 92 percent of their classmates had better academic performance in law

schools. Moreover, disproportionately higher numbers of black
law school graduates failed the bar exam and disproportionately higher numbers of black medical school graduates failed
medical licensing board exams.[84] In the face of such mounting
evidence, in medicine, law and other fields, defenders of affirmative action have argued that black doctors, lawyers and other
professionals are so much needed in black communities that it
was still a good thing for them to be preferentially admitted to
colleges, graduate schools and professional schools. [85] Nor has
this argument been forced to confront the fact that many doctors who are not black serve in inner city hospitals, with no
evidence that black patients are any the worse for that.

One example who was repeatedly singled out over the years
as a justification for affirmative action was a young black man
named Patrick Chavis, who had been admitted under affirmative action to the medical school at the University of California
at Davis, where Allan Bakke had been initially rejected. Chavis
had gone back to practice medicine in the black community, in
contrast to Bakke, who went on to become an anesthesiologist
in Minneapolis after graduating from the same medical school,
to which he was admitted in the wake of the landmark Supreme
Court case that bears his name. Senator Edward Kennedy of
Massachusetts was among the many people who extolled Chavis as an example of what affirmative action was meant to accomplish. The Lawyers Committee for Civil Rights made the
usual comprison between Chavis and Bakke — to Chavis' advantage — in 1997, just two weeks before the Medical Board of
California suspended Chavis' license to practice medicine in
the wake of a suspicious death of one of his patients.[86] The
Board cited Chavis' "inability to perform some of the most
basic duties required of a physician," according to an administrative law judge when he ordered the emergency suspension
of Chavis' license.[87] A year later, after a fuller investigation of
his treatment of several patients, Chavis' license was revoked.[88]

Those who had been using Chavis as an example before

now switched to the position that one isolated example does not prove anything. Unfortunately, Chavis was not an isolated example. Plans to use double standards to maneuver black students through medical school were reported to me back in 1969 and published in a 1972 book of mine.[89] Four years later, Professor Bernard Davis of the Harvard Medical School reported in the *New England Journal of Medicine* that black students there and at other medical schools were being granted diplomas "on a charitable basis." He said, "It is cruel to admit students who have a very low probability of measuring up to reasonable standards" and that it was "even crueler to abandon those standards and allow the trusting patients to pay for our irresponsibility."[90] The only response to his revelations was a predictable denunciation of him as a "racist."

Discussions of college admissions policies often proceed as if the issue is the distribution of benefits to various applicants, when in fact the issue is selecting those applicants who can best master the kind and level of academic work at the particular institution. Those who see the issue as distributing benefits to applicants object to admissions "criteria that benefit primarily white middle-class students."[91] Arbitrarily focussing on different groups of applicants ignores those who have the largest stake of all — in this case, people needing medical attention. In other fields as well, it is the ignored third parties who have the biggest stake in what institutions of higher learning do and how well they do it. Applicants for engineering schools do not have nearly as large a stake as those millions of other people whose lives depend on the quality of the engineering that goes into the bridges they drive across or the planes they fly in or the equipment they work with.

Colleges and universities were not created to distribute benefits to applicants but to develop minds and create skills that serve society at large. The criteria that matter are the criteria which best enable these institutions to carry out that responsibility. Such a responsibility cannot be subordinated to the impossible task of equalizing probabilities of academic success for people born and raised in circumstances which have handicapped their development, even if for reasons that are not their fault and are beyond their control. Perhaps if we were capable of fully understanding everything that had happened to Patrick Chavis from the moment he was born, we might judge him less harshly. But the role of academic institutions is not to play God in judging individual souls. It is, among other things, to see that people like Patrick Chavis do not end up with scalpels in their hands and "M.D." after their names to lure unsuspecting patients to their deaths.

Empirical Studies

While many of the crucial assumptions behind preferences and quotas are widely accepted without evidence being asked or given, there have been some empirical studies which bear on these assumptions. However, the same uncritical acceptance which has allowed conclusions favorable to affirmative action to prevail without evidence has also allowed studies done in questionable ways to be accepted as proof when those studies reached conclusions favorable to the continuance of group preferences and quotas.

One of the most widely praised of these exercises in defense of affirmative action in the academic world was the 1998 book *The Shape of the River* by former university presidents William Bowen and Derek Bok, of Princeton and Harvard, respectively.[92] This book's premise was that admitting black applicants to colleges and universities with lower qualifications than those required of other applicants has not produced the bad results claimed by critics of affirmative action. The authors mobilized and displayed voluminous statistics, in an attempt to show that such students succeeded academically and succeeded later in life. Unfortunately, however, these many statistics, tables, graphs and equations were not about black students who were admitted with lower qualifications than other students. They were about black students in general in the institutions covered, *including black students admitted under the same standards as white students.* This much-touted study is *Hamlet* without the prince of Denmark.

The controversies about preferences and quotas in college admissions are not about whether any black students should be admitted to colleges, but is precisely about the admission of those particular black students who do not meet the normal standards applied to other students at the particular institutions they attend. The failure of Bowen and Bok to single out such students raises the first of many serious questions about their study — especially since other studies have separated out such students and found the opposite of what Bowen and Bok claim to have found. Submerging black students who were admitted with lower qualifications in broad statistics about black students in general is particularly suspicious when the raw data behind the published numbers are not available to others, who might break down the statistics differently and get at the key information that these authors excluded. Scholars whose request for the same data was flatly denied noted that Bowen and Bok had "access to student records that schools have never made available to investigators before."[93] While the institutional decision to release this data only to two long-time defenders of affirmative action raises doubts, the way the statistics were then used casts a further cloud over the Bowen-Bok study.

The sample used in the Bowen-Bok study consists of 24 private and just 4 public institutions of higher education, when in fact only 9 percent of black students attend private institutions, which constitute the bulk of the Bowen-Bok sample.[94] Moreover, other minorities such as Hispanics and Asians are omitted from the study. As for the black students in this sample, 64 percent had at least one parent who had graduated from college — more than five times the proportion among all black, college-age youths.[95] In short, Bowen and Bok used a highly atypical sample of minority students attending highly atypical colleges and universities — and from this they draw conclusions about affirmative action admissions policies in general, despite a pro forma caveat against this early in the preface.[96]

More specifically, Bowen and Bok deny the claims of critics of affirmative action that minority students admitted under lower standards (1) do not perform as well as other students, (2) do not survive to graduate as often, and (3) do not do as well in their post-college careers. The key problem seen by these critics is that minority students admitted to elite institutions under lower standards are *mismatched,* rather than *unqualified,* and could have been more successful at other institutions geared to students of their own academic ability levels, many of which colleges and universities are good institutions. In short, the argument is that there is no point failing at a big-name institution when you can succeed at a good quality institution without such a big name.

How do Bowen and Bok answer such critics of preferential admissions policies? First of all, *The Shape of the River* redefines preferences and quotas as "race-sensitive admissions," and Bowen and Bok say that they are against "quotas" — which apparently means that they are against the word "quotas," since they make the usual arguments for numerical representation and assert (without evidence) the educational benefits of "diversity."

Their most triumphant finding is that black students "graduated at *higher* rates, the more selective the school that they attended" (emphasis in the original).[97] The implication is that mismatching does not hurt black students' prospects of graduating, after all. But closer scrutiny reveals a very different story.

As Bowen and Bok themselves say elsewhere: "There has been a much more pronounced narrowing of the black-white gap in SAT scores among applicants to the most selective colleges."[98] This is substantiated more clearly by data from others' research, which show that the gap between black and white composite SAT scores has been 95 points at Harvard but 184 points at Duke and 271 points at Rice.[99] The crucial question is not how selective the college is, but how wide is the gap between the qualifications of its black students and the normal standards of the institution, as indicated by the qualifications of the other students.

A study of racial differences among students in state colleges and universities in Colorado found that, although in general a higher percentage of whites than blacks graduated within a six-year period, 50 percent of blacks and 48 percent of whites graduated within that span at the University of Colorado at Denver, where the difference in SAT scores was only 30 points. Where there were negligible differences in test scores, there were negligible differences in graduation rates. In Colorado, it so happened that there were smaller differences in test scores at the lower ranked institution. At the flagship University of Colorado campus at Boulder, where the test score difference between blacks and whites was more than 200 points, only 39 percent of the black students graduated, compared to 72 percent of the whites.[100]

Clearly racial preferences were greater at the University of Colorado at Boulder, where 75 percent of both black and white applicants were accepted, despite a 205-point difference in SAT scores. Meanwhile, at the University of Colorado at Denver, only 68 percent of black applicants were accepted, compared to 82 percent of white applicants, leading to a student body with only negligible differences in test scores between black and white students — and negligible differences in graduation rates.

A study of five state-run medical schools around the country found similar patterns. Among these five medical schools, black-white differences in scores on the Medical College Admission Test were greatest at the medical school at the State University of New York in Brooklyn and least at the medical school at the University of Washington. The racial difference in the percentage of students later passing the U.S. Medical Licensing Examination was likewise greatest at SUNY Brooklyn (20 percentage points' difference) and least at the University of Washington (9 points' difference). Even this understates the difference between these institutions, since 25 percent of the black medical students at SUNY Brooklyn did not even take the U.S. Medical Licensing Examination, compared to 10 percent at the University of Washington.[101]

Although blacks in general have had a higher rate of dismissal from medical residency programs than other groups, those particular blacks with academic credentials comparable to whites have had dismissal rates comparable to whites. Although black physicians in general obtained board certification only half as often as white physicians, those black physicians who had college grades and Medical College Admissions Test scores comparable to those of white physicians actually obtained board certification more often than whites.[102] In short, the crucial factor in the success or failure of black students has not been whether an institution was highly ranked or lower ranked, but whether the gap between the qualifications of black and other students was large or small. Bowen and Bok, however, consider their sample results "much more conclusive"[103] than other studies — though apparently not so conclusive that the raw data can be allowed to be seen by other researchers. Yet their results not only differ from what others have found in studies of particular institutions, they differ from national patterns:

> Blacks with SAT scores between 851 and 1,000 have a 77 percent graduation rate from colleges whose overall SAT average is 900. By contrast, blacks who score between 700 and 850 on the SAT graduate from those same schools only 56 percent of the time, and blacks whose SAT scores are below 700 have just a 38 percent chance of graduating.[104]

The institutions compared by Bowen and Bok differ in more than just test scores. The most selective group of institutions — Yale, Stanford, Princeton and the like — averaged an undergraduate student body of fewer than 3,000 students, while the least selective group of institutions in this particular sample — Michigan, Penn State, University of North Carolina at Chapel Hill, etc. — averaged more than 13,000 undergraduates. Indeed, the largest number of undergraduates on any campus in the first group was smaller than the median number of undergraduates on campuses in the second group. Moreover, even the least selective set of institutions in the Bowen-Bok sample are by no means mediocre. They appear regularly in various lists of leading American universities and no one considers them "average."

Given this context, what the Bowen and Bok data show is that, within a very narrow range of institutions, black students who attend the most elite institutions, whose average size is less than one-fourth of that in another set of elite institutions, graduate at a higher rate. This may say more about large versus small undergraduate institutions, especially for students who may need more individual help from their professors, than about anything else. A well-known study of college students found that their satisfaction with faculty was inversely related to the size of the college or university.[105]

Data from other sources reinforce the importance of college size in the survival rates of black students. For example, 13 percent of black students at Stanford failed to graduate in six years, compared to 42 percent who failed to graduate in the same time at the University of California at Berkeley. There were nearly three times as many undergraduates at Berkeley as at Stanford and the student:faculty ratio at Berkeley was more than double the Stanford ratio. Similarly, 12 percent of black students attending Yale failed to graduate in six years, compared to 41 percent at the University of Michigan at Ann Arbor. Here again, Michigan's student:faculty ratio was more than double that at Yale and there were four times as many undergraduates at Ann Arbor.[106]

The conclusions of the Bowen-Bok study are further under-mined by the nature of their sample of institutions, as well as by their atypical sample of students. Because their comparison is between different sets of elite institutions with differing average SAT scores, but with all having scores above the national aver-age, this creates what statisticians call the "restricted range" problem. You cannot tell the general importance of some fac-tor by seeing what difference it makes in a sample where there is only a very limited range of variation in that factor. For exam-ple, you may find very little correlation between height and performance among professional basketball players, but pro-fessional basketball players as a group are much taller than most other people, so the fact that a player who is 6 foot 11 inches tall is just as good as another player who is 7 foot 2 inches tall does not disprove the role of height in basketball. No one would hire a midget to play professional basketball because of a low correlation between height and performance among exist-ing basketball players.

Bowen and Bok point out that even the lowest scoring black students graduate at a higher rate in their sample of the most elite institutions than in the other elite institutions in their sample.[107] This might be more weighty evidence if was not (1) based on such an atypical sample of students and institutions, and (2) contradicted by so much evidence based on others' statistics that were not such tightly held secrets.

What makes affirmative action urgently needed, according to Bowen and Bok, is that (1) without it, few black students would be admitted to the most elite colleges and universities and that (2) these particular institutions are the gateways to high-level professions in which blacks are currently under-represented, so that otherwise these young blacks' prospects are bleak. A critic has parodied this argument as suggesting that "It's Yale or jail." So long as the big-name colleges and univer-sities are able to acquire a disproportionate share of the best-qualified black students, it should not be surprising that such students do well after graduation. The only meaningful question is whether such students would have done well at other colleges whose normal admissions standards they met. Many lesser known colleges have outperformed big-name colleges when it comes to getting their graduates into top postgraduate, earning Ph.D.s, or ending up in *Who's Who in America*.[108]

In the case of black students, there is a whole history of their going to predominantly black colleges — none of which is ranked in the top tier — for generations on end. Today, black colleges enrol only about one-fourth of all black students in higher education, but their graduates receive 40 percent of all science and engineering degrees received by black students nationwide. Of the ten undergraduate institutions whose black students go on to receive the most Ph.D.s in science, six are black institutions.[109] Apparently it is not Yale or jail, after all. In fact, none of the institutions in the large Bowen-Bok sample was among the top ten as the undergraduate home of black Ph.D.s — and only one — the University of Michigan — was among the top eighteen.[110] Again, what is salient is not simply that the Bowen-Bok thesis is inconsistent with the empirical facts but that it was so widely accepted with the relevant facts being neither asked for nor given.

Post–Affirmative Action Results

In 1995, racial preferences and quotas in university admissions were banned by the Regents of the University of California, and in 1996 a statewide referendum confirmed that ban. In Texas, the Fifth Circuit Court of Appeals banned preferential admissions at the University of Texas Law School in 1996. In both states, there were predictions of dire consequences. President Bill Clinton said that the California ban on group preferences would "resegregate" the universities.[111] Jesse Jackson likewise spoke of a "radical resegregation of our schools and reduction in opportunity"[112] and called the ban on affirmative action "ethnic cleansing."[113] Much the same message was echoed by many others.

What actually happened?

Black freshmen enrolment in the flagship of the University of California system—the Berkeley campus—dropped substantially. So did black freshmen enrolment at the other leading campus of the system, UCLA. However, these did not represent similar reductions in the total number of black freshmen going to college in the University of California system as a whole. Moreover, the UC system is not the only state-supported university system in California. There is also the California State University system, which in fact enrolls more students.[114]

Within the University of California system as a whole, the enrolment of black freshmen dropped from 917 in 1997 to 739 the following year but rose again to 832 in the year 2000 — a decline of 9 percent over this period—and then rose to 936 in 2002. While there was only a temporary and relatively modest decline in the number of black freshman throughout the University of California system as a whole, on the flagship Berkeley campus the decline was much sharper, from 222 in 1996 to 122 by 1999 and the recovery was only to 142 by the year 2002. At UCLA, the decline from 230 black freshmen in 1996 was likewise never fully recovered and by 2002 there were just 161 black freshmen on that campus. However, on some other campuses within the University of California system— Santa Barbara, Riverside, Irvine, Santa Cruz—there were *increases* in the number of black freshmen.[115] What this meant was that black students redistributed themselves within the University of California system, with no net decline at all between 1996 and 2002. It was much the same story in the California State University system, where there were more black freshmen enrolled in 2002 than there had been back in 1996, before the end of affirmative action[116]—a fact receiving remarkably little attention or comment in the media, which had widely publicized earlier hysterical claims about an impending "resegregation" of higher education.

In the University of Texas system, there was likewise a decline in black undergraduate enrolment at the flagship campus in Austin, but a rise on almost every other campus. In 1996, there were 1,479 black undergraduates enroled on the Austin campus and that fell to 1,298 by 2000—a decline of 12 percent. But, for the University of Texas system as a whole, the total number of black undergraduates *rose* from 5,250 to 5,657.[117] Although the total number of undergraduates in the system also rose over these same years, black undergraduates nevertheless increased from 4.6 percent of all undergraduates to 4.8 percent.

In short, despite many hysterical media reports and dire predictions of minorities losing "access" to higher education in the wake of bans on affirmative action, there were very modest changes in the numbers and proportions of black students in the state university systems of both California and Texas—and, in the end, a rise. The more substantial change was in black students' redistribution among the campuses within these systems. The crucial question, however, is not how many black or other minority students are *on campus* at any given moment, but how many *graduate*. There may well be more minority graduates, now that minority students are no longer so mismatched with the institutions they are attending. Existing data on variations in test score differences and graduation rate differences already point in that direction. But data on survival to graduation have not yet been forthcoming—and may never be forthcoming, if such data substantiate what critics of affirmative action have been saying for decades.

While there are more data available for making comparisons between blacks and whites than among other racial or ethnic groups, there is also a vast amount of data on Asian Americans. However, proponents of affirmative action tend to avoid discussing Asian Americans, even though Asian American experiences might be very relevant to testing many of the theories behind affirmative action. Indeed, the experiences of Asian Americans often flatly contradict much that is said by those making a case for affirmative action.

For example, black-white differences in test scores are often attributed to cultural biases in the test favoring white, middle-class students. Yet a higher percentage of Asian Americans students score above 700 on the mathematics SAT than among whites. Despite an emphasis on the lower incomes of the families of black students, as a factor in these students' lower test scores, Asian American students from families with low incomes average higher scores on the mathematics portion of the SAT than black students from high-income families.[118] Claims of culturally biased tests are also used to back up the claim that these tests under-estimate the future performances of black students. Although such claims have been refuted repeatedly for black students, it is a claim that has in fact turned out to be true for Asian American students, who outperform whites with the same IQs in academic institutions and in their later careers.[119] But those who use the unsubstantiated allegation that blacks will perform better than their scores indicate, and so should be admitted to colleges and universities with lesser scores than whites, never use the empirically verified fact that Asian Americans perform better than whites with the same scores to argue for larger quotas for Asian Americans.

Finally, the argument is often made that objections to affirmative action are due to "angry white males" who resent blacks taking places in college that would normally go to them. In reality, Asian Americans take more places than blacks in many leading colleges and universities—and especially in engineering schools. They have outnumbered blacks at seven of the eight Ivy League colleges and on all nine campuses of the University of California, as well as at Stanford, the University of Chicago, and Cal Tech, among other places. Yet there is no such backlash against Asian Americans, who are admitted without any group preferences and quotas. This suggests that it is not the places but the processes that are resented. Again, however, it is not a question of one set of evidence against another, but of one set of beliefs becoming prevailing dogma without evidence being either asked or given.

SUMMARY AND IMPLICATIONS

In the United States, as in other countries, the rationale for affirmative action has had little to do with its actual operation or consequences. Supposedly a means to redress the harm created by discrimination in the past, preferences and quotas established under affirmative action policies require neither the individual beneficiary nor even the group from which that individual comes to demonstrate any specific harm from prior discrimination. Thus recent immigrants from Asia or Latin American are eligible for affirmative action benefits in the United States, though obviously there was no past discrimination against these individuals or their forebears in this country, simply because they were not living in this country. Moreover, even among blacks, benefits to black millionaires under affirmative action are far more demonstrable than benefits to blacks in poverty. Rationales produce political support but the policy produces results far removed from those rationales.

The costs of affirmative action are as seldom scrutinized as to the benefits or alleged benefits. Among the costs are lowered standards of performance in order to get numerical results. Moreover, these standards are sometimes lowered for all, in order to avoid the political embarrassment or legal liability of obvious double standards for favored groups. Grading systems may be changed to pass-fail or grade inflation may occur all around. Physical strength requirements may be reduced, so that more women can be hired, but if that requirement is reduced for all, then that can lead to more men, as well as women, with inadequate strength in such life-and-death occupations as firefighters, soldiers, or policemen. Indeed, there may be more low-performing men than low-performing women in some fields after the physical standards are lowered to allow more women to become eligible.

In addition to the hostilities between groups created or exacerbated by preferences and quotas in other countries, affirmative action in the United States has made blacks, who have largely lifted themselves out of poverty, look like people who owe their rise to affirmative action and other government programs. Moreover, this perception is not confined to whites. It has been carefully cultivated by black politicians and civil rights leaders, who seek to claim credit for the progress, so as to solidify a constituency conditioned to be dependent on them, as well as on government.

In this context, there has been a virtual moratorium on recognition of achievements by blacks, except in so far as they are collective, political milestones or otherwise serve current ideological or political interests. Thus, despite much hand-wringing and finger-pointing over the abysmal education performances of black students in ghetto schools, there has been at best utter indifference among black organizations and movements to documented examples of black schools that have been academically successful.[120] Nor has there been much interest in the fact that some very ordinary black schools in Harlem performed as well on city-wide tests in the 1940s as the predominantly white working class schools on the lower east side of Manhattan — much less that a black high school in Washington outperformed most white high schools in D.C. as far back as 1899.[121] While the rise of many prominent individuals from the lower east side of Manhattan has been justly celebrated, there has been little or no interest in blacks who have done the same thing, for that would be a distraction from the politics of grievance and demands.

The transparent dishonesty with which quotas and preferences have been instituted and maintained — a dishonesty reaching into the highest court in the land, as the Weber case, among others, demonstrates — has produced cynicism and bitterness. As another insult added to injury, airs of moral superiority on the part of those perpetrating deception add to a galling sense of grievance among many people who are part of the non-preferred population. That all of this has done relatively little for the genuinely poor in ghettos and barrios across the United States is part of the painful irony of the situation.

Many defenders of affirmative action ignore or dismiss unwelcome facts in favor of more palatable assumptions. Thus, higher failure rates for blacks on bar exams or medical board exams are taken as evidence that there is something wrong with those exams. Fewer blacks made partners in big law firms mean that there is something wrong with those law firms[122] — and so on down the line. The very possibility that preferential policies may have put some people in settings where their chances of success are reduced is arbitrarily banished from the realm of possibility. Affirmative action continues to be judged by its rationales, rather than its results.

———•◆•———

CHAPTER 7

The Past and the Future

If studying history is one way to avoid repeating it, there is much in the history of affirmative action policies around the world that should never be repeated. In too many countries, such policies have turned out to be ways of producing relatively minor benefits for a few and major problems for society as a whole. Both advocates and critics of such policies have tended to over-estimate the benefits that have been transferred. Moreover, the distribution of benefits from group preferences and quotas often shows the same disparities as the broader social inequalities which they are supposed to be remedying.

Allowing black millionaires in the United States to have preferential access to the purchase of radio station licenses does not reduce inequality among Americans, nor does it benefit people living in ghettos. Affirmative action does little for the poor in America, as elsewhere. The poverty rate among blacks was cut in half before there was affirmative action and has changed very little since then.

Whatever the peculiarities of particular countries, the general patterns which have emerged in one country after another strongly suggest that similar incentives and constraints tend to produce similar consequences among human beings in widely disparate circumstances. The fact that so many of these consequences were not anticipated by those who promoted group preferences creates a painful contrast with the confident and sweeping assertions with which such policies were often begun. Those who thought that they were directing the course of events often discovered that they had simply opened the floodgates and that events were taking a course far different from what had been envisioned.

The spread of preferences from group to group and from activity to activity is just one symptom of the floodgates' being open. The whole mindset behind preferences and quotas has spread as well. France has passed a law requiring political parties to have equal numbers of male and female candidates.[1] In Pakistan, places have been reserved in educational institutions for the children of "sportsmen," military officers, government employees, attorneys, doctors, and university employees.[2] The American Society of Newspaper Editors keeps statistics on the percentage of minority journalists — out to two decimal places — lamenting a decline in "journalists of color" from 11.86 percent to 11.64 percent in one year and expressing satisfaction when this rose again to 12.07 percent a year later.[3]

Too often, sweeping assumptions about the past and sweeping assertions about the future have served as substitutes for the difficult task of analyzing hard facts. These facts include a bitter history of escalating intergroup violence where affirmative action has existed longest, in India, and outright civil war in Sri Lanka. There has also been a moral dimension to these illusions — namely, the assumption that we can compensate individuals today for what was done to groups in the past, that we can make right among the living the wrongs done to people long dead. Galling as it may be to acknowledge, every evil of past generations and past centuries will remain indelibly and irrevocably evil, despite anything that we can do now. Acts of symbolic expiation among the living simply create new evils.

The illusion of compensation for disadvantages too often ignores the reality that those individuals most likely to be compensated are often those with the least disadvantages, even when the groups they come from may suffer misfortunes. In Pakistan, for example, quotas favoring people from the less developed districts of the country turned out to favor "the relatively well-off candidate from both backward and developed regions."[4] Conversely, those individuals who end up being sacrificed for the sake of symbolic expiation are likely to be the least advantaged of the non-preferred population, even if that population as a whole may be more fortunate than the group that has been given preferences.

Those whites displaced from admission to elite American colleges when blacks are admitted with lower qualifications are unlikely to be named Rockefeller or Vanderbilt and are more likely to be named Bakke or Grutter. The same pattern can be found in other countries. When affirmative action was instituted in Bombay to increase the number of Maharashtrians among business executives there, the biggest losses of these executive positions were not among the dominant Gujaratis but among the less represented South Indians.[5] In Malaysia, the requirement that businesses take in Malay partners was more easily circumvented by the larger Chinese and foreign firms:

> Both Chinese and foreign companies began to actively solicit business ties with politically-influential Malays willing to lend their names for a price without taking on executive roles after becoming owners and directors of the companies. . . . Small, predominantly manufacturing, enterprises, which were not privy to such avenues to bypass the state were those most affected by the government's new constraints.[6]

THE VOCABULARY OF AFFIRMATIVE ACTION

Failure to come to grips with the actual consequences of affirmative action policies has been due not only to an unfamiliarity with the history of such policies, or to a dearth of statistics in a particular country, but is also due to words and conceptions which obscure and confuse. The desirability of one policy versus another cannot even be discussed seriously when words have chameleon-like changes in meaning during the course of a discussion. Such expressions as "a level playing field" can have diametrically opposite meanings when no distinction is made between performance differences and favoritism. Whether one advocates or opposes affirmative action, its consequences have been too serious to be ignored or hidden behind a fog of words with vague and shifting meanings.

Blurring Distinctions

In the context of affirmative action, blurring the distinction between performance differences and favoritism serves the political purpose of providing a rationale for government intervention with preferences and quotas for particular groups, as ways of offsetting the supposed favoritism or "advantages" enjoyed by other groups. However, if we are serious about wanting to confront realities, then our vocabulary cannot confuse performance differences with favors or advantages.

The expression "a level playing field" cannot mean *both* (1) having the same performance receive the same evaluation or reward, regardless of the group from which the individual comes, and (2) equal outcomes or equal statistical probabilities of success for different groups. It is a matter of semantic preferences which of these definitions one chooses, but it is a matter of simple clarity and honesty not to choose both, nor to drift back and forth between these very different concepts in the course of a discussion. Where it is clear that those whom one is addressing mean the first and the expression is used to mean the second, then that is sheer deceit. Among advocates of affirmative action, the phrase "a level playing field" has often been used to describe — not even-handed rules applied to all — but a deliberate tilting of the rules to produce a preconceived equalizing of results.

These shifting definitions serve to evade facts which challenge the central dogma behind many discussions of discrimination and affirmative action—namely, that statistical differences between groups are due to how others treat these groups, not due to differences in the performances of the groups themselves. Yet all around the world, there are performance differences among groups.

People from higher socioeconomic classes tend to score higher on mental tests, whether in China, the Philippines, or the United States.[7] People from some geographic settings tend to score higher than people from other geographic settings: Indonesians from the island of Java have scored higher than Indonesians from the outer islands, Filipinos from Manila have scored higher than Filipinos from other parts of the country, Pakistanis from the Punjab score higher than people from other parts of Pakistan, and Tamils from the Jaffna peninsula consistently outscored the Sinhalese who predominate in the rest of the country.[8] In the United States, regional differences in mental test scores among soldiers tested during the First World War sometimes outweighed even racial differences, as whites in some Southern states scored lower than blacks from some Northern states.[9] Indeed, test score differences between different generations of the same people have, in various countries, been greater than those between black and white Americans.[10]

In countries where there are minority students who have dramatically outperformed students from the majority population which controls the educational institutions, as in Sri Lanka and Malaysia, then clearly this is not a matter of discrimination or bias. Nor can the above-average incomes of Japanese Americans be attributed to any ability on their part to discriminate or otherwise get an advantage over white Americans. Superior economic performances by minorities have been common around the world—not just in the countries studied here. Germans in Russia, Armenians in Turkey, Lebanese in West Africa,

Italians in Brazil, Indians in Fiji, and Jews throughout Eastern Europe have been just some of the minorities who have excelled economically, without any ability to discriminate against the majority populations of these countries. In short, the automatic dismissal of evidence that one group performs better or worse than another by blaming "test bias," "covert racism" or other such convenient explanations may sound plausible within the confines of one country, but not against the background of large and numerous performance differences in countries around the world.

Groups are often said to be "excluded" from various institutions or activities because they do not meet the qualifications for those institutions or activities as often as members of some other groups do, or do not perform as well in these institutions or activities. But when the Malays are referred to as a "deprived" group in Malaysia[11] and non-Malays as having "privilege,"[12] it would seem that surely no one really means that there are either legal rights of a lesser nature for Malays or economic activities which anyone can prevent Malays from engaging in within Malaysia. Yet it is hard to know whether such statements represent only current verbal fashions or a serious belief about the real world, especially when a writer for the British newspaper *The Guardian* described the situation before the New Economic Policy in Malaysia this way:

> Malays were on the sidelines in their own society, with hardly any place in economic life, little role in the media, and not much more in intellectual and academic life.
>
> So action which would normally be inadmissible, interventions in the economic, cultural and education sphere to give Malays a chance to catch up, ought to be permitted. Foreign firms and governments which blocked Malay progress could be similarly treated.[13]

When others are said to have "blocked" the progress of Malays in Malaysia, the clear implication seems to be that the outcome was due to what others did, rather than to what the Malays did not do. In other words, this implies that it was not any lack of skills, experience, or other capabilities on the part of the Malays which was responsible for their not ending up with the same achievements as others in Malaysia. But if this was meant as a serious statement about the real world, there was no attempt to specify just what this blocking consisted of.

No doubt there are reasons why one group excels over others in particular fields. Nor are these reasons necessarily innate or due to personal merit. The Tamils in Sri Lanka, for example, were in colonial times educated in American missionary schools that emphasized mathematics and science more so than the British missionary schools in which the Sinhalese were educated. The Chinese who immigrated to Malaysia came from circumstances in southern China that had long made hard work and frugality necessary for survival, while the Malay culture developed in easier circumstances, permitting an easier-going way of life. Much the same distinction could be made between the Indians who settled in Fiji and the indigenous Fijians. Many other influences may have been behind other differences between other groups in other countries. But that does not make those differences any less real or automatically make them simply results of discrimination by others.

Words can confuse the vagaries of fate with the sins of man. Philosophically, we might regard it as unjust, in some cosmic sense, that one group was better prepared for a particular kind of competition than other groups, even if its advantage consisted only of prior adversity. However such a conception might be debated in the abstract around a seminar table, the empirical question in public policy issues is whether one group outperforms another or is simply rewarded more for the same (or lesser) performances. At the very least, these are *different* questions, even if these differences are blurred or confused by words and phrases about one group's greater "access," "advantages," "opportunity" and the like.

A common complaint in countries around the world is that some groups have less "access" to credit, making it harder for them to start businesses or to buy homes, for example. Yet both government programs and private lending organizations have suffered devastating losses when lending to groups who are said to have been denied "access" to credit in a market economy. In Malaysia, for example, "of the 55,000 loans that had been given to Malay businesses, only 6,000 had been paid back."[14] In the United States, when the Bank of America set up a special subsidiary to lend to people in the "subprime market" — that is, people with lower credit ratings — it lost hundreds of millions of dollars and announced that its offices "will stop making subprime loans immediately."[15]

When people with a track record of not repaying loans as often as others are not granted loans as often as others, or not at as low an interest rate as others, is that a denial of equal "opportunity" or a reflection of unequal prospects of repayment? When those students or workers who do not perform as well as others do not advance as well as others, does this mean a lack of "access" beforehand or a lack of achievement afterward? These are not semantic questions but questions about the real world. Beclouding the realities of these situations with tendentious words does not facilitate determining either causes or cures.

The widely accepted doctrine that prior favoritism predetermines the future likewise cannot withstand scrutiny. The clear favoritism of the British colonial government in providing free education to Malays did not prevent the Chinese from excelling the Malays in education, either during colonial times or in the first decades after independence. Only affirmative action preferences and quotas enabled Malays to increase their share of places in the universities. Moreover, even this quantitative increase did not lead to a sufficient qualitative performance to satisfy the Malay government, which began to take steps to allow other groups to enter university programs needed to supply scientific and technical skills that the Malays still failed to supply.

Hiding Asian Success

Not only particular facts, but whole groups of people, have been hidden behind a fog of words. For example, in the Bowen-Bok study of affirmatve action in higher education in the United States, black students admitted to American colleges under lower standards have been hidden within a larger group of black students, which included those who met the same standards of admission as white students. Although the Bowen-Bok study has been widely accepted as proving that affirmative action "works," those for whom it supposedly works are never allowed to appear alone anywhere in the voluminous statistics presented in that study. The performances of those blacks admitted under the same standards as whites prove nothing about affirmative action.

Many other statistical comparisons of blacks and whites by those supporting affirmative action policies often omit other ethnic groups, whose data are readily available and whose experience might serve as a check on theories about the causes of the black-white differences. If the central premise of affirmative action is that groups cannot on their own rise to parity in American society when they have a history of poverty and low occupational status, and are indelibly different in skin color, then the history of Chinese Americans or Japanese Americans might be relevant to testing this belief empirically, since both groups have in fact done what has been said to be impossible.

At the beginning of the twentieth century, Japanese immigrants were agricultural laborers and domestic servants to an even greater extent than the blacks.[16] It was only after the Second World War that the younger generation of Japanese Americans went into very different occupations and rose up the socioeconomic ladder. By 1979, Japanese American males had higher incomes than white American males.[17]

Current socioeconomic differences between blacks and whites, which are routinely ascribed to racial discrimination or cultural bias, might look very different if data were examined showing that Asian Americans often have the same "advantages" over whites that whites have over blacks. For example, whites' applications for home mortgages are approved at a higher rate than those of blacks, but applications from Asian Americans are approved at a higher rate than those of whites.[18] Blacks tend to lose their jobs during an economic downtown more often than whites, but whites are more likely to lose their jobs than are Asian Americans.[19] The fact that whites score higher than blacks on the mathematics SAT has been taken as proof of the cultural bias of this test, but the fact that Asian Americans score higher than whites[20] has been passed over in silence. Higher infant mortality rates among black women than white women has been blamed on the failure of society to provide equal access to prenatal care, but the fact that Chinese American women have lower infant mortality rates than white women — despite not having prenatal care as often[21] — has likewise been passed over in silence.

Clearly Asian Americans are an embarrassment to those making the usual arguments for affirmative action. Therefore Asian Americans are either ignored or are submerged statistically in larger aggregates. These larger aggregates include "non-whites" where they are swamped by the much larger number of black Americans. More recently Chinese Americans and Japanese Americans have been lumped together with Samoans, Hawaiians, Vietnamese and others under the omnibus category "Asian and Pacific Islanders," whose heterogeneity is suggested by the fact that Japanese Americans have nearly double the income of Samoans — as well as incomes higher than that of white Americans.[22]

This burying of inconvenient facts in heterogeneous statistical aggregates is not peculiar to the United States. In Canada, the popular omnibus category is "visible minorities," submerging the highly successful Japanese minority there in a category with less successful minorities. In Britain, people of Chinese ancestry are submerged in the omnibus category "black," as are Indians, Pakistanis and others. These are just some of the ways words are used to obscure evidence that could be dangerous to clarify, from the standpoint of those defending the social vision behind affirmative action. A study in New Zealand says: "Bitter resentment of Asian immigrant success is expressed" in a government document from the Maori Development Ministry.[23] In all these countries, the facts about Asian success are a deadly threat to the social vision used to explain away the failures of others and to claim preferential treatment as compensation for the presumed failures of society.

An official report titled *Ethno-Racial Inequality in the City of Toronto* declares: "Combining all the non-European groups, the family poverty rate is 34.3 percent, more than twice the figure for Europeans and Canadians."[24] In other words, this is presented as a racial difference by lumping together "all the non-European groups." But a detailed breakdown of the family poverty rates of the many European and non-European groups shows that Canadians of Japanese ancestry in Toronto have poverty rates lower than those of Canadians of British, French, German, Polish, or Hungarian ancestry in that city.[25] In classic rhetoric that evades achievement, the report says, "The Japanese are among the most privileged groups in the city."[26] Anyone familiar with the history of severe racial discrimination against the Japanese in Canada — including internment during World War II longer than Japanese Americans[27] — must surely regard the word "privileged" as Orwellian Newspeak.

It is much the same story when it comes to median family income in Toronto. The median family income of people of British ancestry living in Toronto is above the median family income for the city as a whole, but that of Japanese Canadians in Toronto is above that of the British.[28] Among the many other differences among various groups in Toronto are differences in the percentage of their families which include couples rather than single parents — 41 percent among blacks and 91 percent among Japanese[29] — and in how recently they arrived in Canada, as well as in their median ages, their knowledge of English, and other factors. Clearly those who lump together "visible minorities" in Canada are able to bury social differences that are highly relevant and empirical evidence that is highly inconvenient for those attempting to explain differences in group success by racial discrimination.

Nothing has been more common, in countries around the world and over centuries of recorded history, than large disparities in the success or failure of different groups — whether these groups have been of the same or a different color. The attempt to ascribe the same phenomenon in particular countries today to barriers against non-whites must not only ignore all this history but also bury the facts about Asian minorities statistically.

INTERGROUP RELATIONS

Among the most remarkable rationales for group preferences and quotas is the claim that such things promote a more cohesive society — "national unity" being a popular phrase in India, Malaysia, and Nigeria, for example[30] — despite a history of increasing intergroup resentments, polarization, violence, and even civil war in the wake such policies in a number of countries. Nor are India, Malaysia, and Nigeria the only countries where affirmative action is promoted as a means of better intergroup relations. The actual track record of group-identity politics is in sharp contrast with the mystical benefits of "diversity," endlessly asserted but seldom tested empirically, and never proved.

In India, for example, the number of people killed in intergroup violence during the decade of the 1980s was four times
as high as in the 1970s.[31] In Nigeria, the phrase "national
unity" has appeared repeatedly in official pronouncements justifying group preferences, even as members of different tribes
slaughtered each other before, during, and after that country's
civil war. Despite incessant repetition of the word "diversity"
and sweeping dogmas about its social benefits, countries that
have suffered the intergroup strife which has so often accompanied the politicization of intergroup differences have then
gone to great trouble to try to create enclaves of homogeneity
as a means of reducing internal strife. Both India and Nigeria
have split existing states or provinces into smaller political
units, in which some former minority group can become a
majority. In short, those who have suffered the most severe
consequences of group identity politics have then turned to
local *reduction* of diversity as a way to defuse polarization and
violence.

A related, and equally unsubstantiated, assumption is that
disparities in income and wealth promote intergroup strife. As
a corollary, reductions in such disparities are assumed to reduce resentments and the hostility and violence growing out of
such resentments. Seldom, if ever, is this widespread belief
subjected to empirical scrutiny. Among the countries studied
here, all the evidence points in the opposite direction. In Malaysia, Nigeria, and Sri Lanka, there was far less intergroup
violence in the first half of the twentieth century, when intergroup disparities were greater, and far more violence after
these disparities had been politicized and group identity politics promoted.

In the United States as well, the worst ghetto riots occurred
during administrations which most sympathetically publicized
and dramatized the grievances of blacks — especially the administration of President Lyndon Johnson. Moreover, such riots
declined abruptly with the election of Richard Nixon as presi-

dent, and major ghetto riots became virtually unknown during the eight years of the Reagan administration, when group identity politics were ignored or frowned upon. Here again was the same pattern found in other countries, where it was not disparities, but the politicization of those disparities and the promotion of group identity politics, which was the harbinger of intergroup hostility and violence.

Other countries not covered here show similar patterns. The Volga Germans in Russia co-existed peacefully for more than a century with their Russian neighbors, despite the greater productivity and prosperity of these Germans. But this prosperous minority became targeted as "exploiters" after the Bolshevik revolution and suffered spoilation and violence. Indians, Pakistanis, and Lebanese likewise lived peacefully for years among Africans whose economic level did not approach their own — until political demagogues made Asians targets of envy, resentment, discrimination, and violence. It was much the same story with Indians in Fiji, Jews in Germany, Armenians in Turkey, and other groups in other places.

A study of group preferences and quotas in Pakistan concluded: "Paradoxically, Pakistan's redistribution policies have been effective in increasing ethnoregional proportionality, but they have done little to restrict, or in some cases have served to enhance, the level of ethnoregional conflict in the state."[32] Such conflict escalated to the point of civil war when East Pakistan seceded to become the new nation of Bangladesh.

Those who imagine themselves to be promoting intergroup harmony by attempting to reduce economic disparities between groups seldom consider whether their politicizing of those differences may have the opposite effect. What has actually happened seems to carry far less weight than what prevailing theories say will happen. Nor is this just a matter of political spin. It was not a cynical politician in India but an earnest American scholar who had researched affirmative action programs there who said:

The compensatory discrimination policy is not to be judged only for its instrumental qualities. It is also expressive: through it Indians tell themselves what kind of people they are and what kind of nation. These policies express a sense of connection and shared destiny.[33]

This was said about a policy which has repeatedly provoked riots in which dozens — or even hundreds — of people have been killed. The "altruistic fraternal impulse that animates compensatory policies"[34] was given much credit by this scholar, despite the age-old warning that the road to hell is paved with good intentions. India's most intolerant and violent mass movement — Shiv Sena — began as an organization seeking preferences and quotas for Maharashtrians in Bombay. The granting of those quotas only boosted Shiv Sena's standing and power. Moreover, its success in exploiting group identity led it to "defend" its constituency against an ever growing list of "enemies" — Tamils, Moslems, Christians, foreigners, among others — both politically and violently in the streets. Just as preferences and quotas tend to spread over time to new groups and new activities, so success at group identity politics tends to expand the list of grievances and "enemies" necessary to keep the movement viable and its leaders powerful.

The progression of India's Shiv Sena movement to ever wider circles of enemies and ever more expansive notions of grievances is instructive. At first, the enemy was primarily people from South India living in Bombay who were more economically successful than the indigenous Maharashtrians. However, a series of concessions on that issue only whetted the movement's appetite for more concessions on more things and for ever more grievances to keep its followers aroused and combat ready. Muslims were then targeted in a campaign climaxed by lethal riots and atrocities in 1992 and 1993. According to *The Times of India*, there were mobs "stopping vehicles and setting passengers ablaze" and "men brought bleeding to hospital who were knifed afresh," as well as "neighbours leading long-time friends to gory deaths" and women who "seen their children thrown into fires, husbands hacked, daughters molested, sons dragged away," while more than 100,000 people fled Bombay.[35] India's different groups do not have the geographical separation that facilitates civil war, as in Sri Lanka or Nigeria, but clearly the hatred and violence have been very similar.

The ever-expanding list of enemies or targets grew to include foreigners in general and those Indians who followed foreign customs, such as celebrating Valentine's Day. Shops selling Valentine cards had their windows smashed by thugs. Shiv Sena warned that it would not tolerate foreign ownership of Air India or the playing of a cricket match between India and Pakistan in Bombay. Moreover, the success of Shiv Sena has inspired other xenophobic movements in other parts of India. Attempts to appease or neutralize these movements with concessions have been largely unsuccessful and may well have contributed to their continued growth and escalating virulence.

What a movement needs for its own survival is not a set of concessions won in the past, though these may be celebrated, but an inventory of demands still outstanding, grievances still unassuaged, and "enemies" still to be dealt with. This is as true of American protest movements as of group-identity movements in India. Things have not reached the same stage of violent hostility in the United States. But neither has affirmative action existed as long in American society. Nevertheless, a very similar pattern of ever more extremist group-identity politics and grievance politics can be seen in the United States, moving in the same general direction of ever-expanding "enemies," ever-expanding demands and ever more bitter polarization.

The first demands of black civil rights movements were for equal opportunity in the plain and straightforward sense of being treated just like everyone else. Only after that goal was clearly within reach did the new demand for preferential treatment arise. Then it was decades after black protest movements began demanding and receiving preferential treatment that demands for reparations for the slavery of centuries past became a major campaign. Black protest movements' initial enemies — segregationist whites in the South — have expanded over the years to include Korean and Vietnamese shopkeepers in the ghettos, whose deaths in riots are virtually ignored by much of the media, lest they be accused of being "racist" in their reporting.

The idea that affirmative action promotes good relations among groups remains central to the defense of that policy in the United States and is implicit in the endlessly repeated word "diversity." The Bowen-Bok study of the effects of affirmative action in colleges and universities credits this program with the fact that 56 percent of white students in the institutions studied report knowing two or more black classmates "well," despite the fact that 86 percent of whites in American society at large report having black friends and 54 percent reported having five or more black friends.[36] Diversity has added nothing. On the contrary, a number of elite American colleges and universities have had reports of growing racial hostility among their students during the affirmative action era.[37]

The more plausible-sounding claim that "the cumulative structural character of inequality" means that "a regime of formal equality tends to perpetuate disparities we find intolerable"[38] likewise ignores a very large body of history about groups who began in lowly positions and then rose to levels above the level of the average member of the larger society. Jewish, Chinese, Lebanese, Indian, Japanese, German, Italian, and other immigrants have done this in countries around the world. In twentieth century America, so many individuals rose from the bottom 20 percent in income to the top 20 percent within their own lifetimes — indeed, within a decade — that the very notion of "class" becomes open to serious question in this context, when there is such rapid turnover of individuals in given income brackets.

The idea that one can automatically read the injustices of the past in the disparities of the present becomes ludicrous in light of all the minorities in numerous countries who have prospered more than the respective majority populations of those countries, without any ability to discriminate against those majorities, and often despite those majorities' continued discriminations against them. It would be very *convenient* if the present so neatly recapitulated the past, but the facts have been uncooperative. None of this denies that some groups — untouchables in India, blacks in the United States — have not only experienced large-scale and long sustained discrimination, but have also been held back by it, even if we cannot quantify how much. What the larger picture says, however, is that we cannot automatically call group preferences and quotas compensation for past discrimination nor can we credit it with reducing violence arising out of resentments about past discrimination.

Preceding chapters have shown, time and again, intergroup violence arising from majority groups that no one has discriminated against, and preferences and quotas being given such groups, whose only real problem has been their inability to compete with more skilled or more diligent minorities. Nor have either untouchables or blacks been more violent when they were most discriminated against. Poetic justice might have justified such a consequence but poetic justice does not necessarily prevail.

Often the claim is made that "benign" preferences are very different from the kind of racial discrimination found in the American South during the Jim Crow era or apartheid in white-ruled South Africa or the anti-Semitism of the Nazi era. But all group preferences are benign to those who benefit — and malign to those who pay the price. The exclusion of blacks from major league baseball before Jackie Robinson broke the color line in 1947 was undoubtedly benign to many white ballplayers, who would otherwise never have gotten out of the minor leagues if they had had to compete for jobs with such stars of the old Negro leagues as Satchel Paige and Josh Gibson. Was it "benign" that so many Aryans were able to get prestigious positions vacated by Jewish scholars and scientists who fled Nazi Germany? Even looking beyond preferential policies, most of the harms and horrors inflicted on people throughout history were inflicted so that somebody else could benefit. All were "benign" if one looks only at the effects on the beneficiaries.

EMPIRICAL EVIDENCE ON AFFIRMATIVE ACTION

The prominence of semantic issues in controversies over affirmative action policies in various countries reflects in part a shortage of empirical evidence with which to test policies and beliefs about their consequences. For example, after many years of affirmative action policies in favor of New Zealand's Maori minority, a Wellington newspaper reported in November 2000: "Extraordinarily, there appears to be little or no research into whether teaching kids the standard curriculum, but in Maori, has improved their educational outcomes." The paper adds: "Nobody knows, because nobody seems to be asking."[39] Unfortunately, such disinterest in empirical consequences is not confined to New Zealand.

In the United States, where many group preferences have sought to justify themselves as counterweights to discrimination that would otherwise prevail, such "discrimination" often turns out to be statistical "under-representation" in desirable occupations or institutions. The implicit assumption, tenaciously held, is that great statistical disparities in demographic "representation" could not occur without discrimination. This key assumption is seldom tested against data on group disparities in qualifications. For example, as of the year 2001, there were more than 16,000 Asian American students who scored above 700 on the mathematics SAT, while fewer than 700 black students scored that high — even though blacks outnumbered Asian Americans several times over.[40] Data such as these are simply passed over in utter silence — or are drowned out by strident assertions of "covert" discrimination as explanations of a dearth of blacks in institutions and occupations requiring a strong background in mathematics.

False beliefs are not small things, because they lead to false solutions. In the field of medicine, it has long been recognized that even a false cure that is wholly harmless in itself can be catastrophic in its consequences if it substitutes for a real cure for a deadly disease. Proponents of affirmative action cannot console themselves for their false assumptions on grounds that their intentions were good, because social quackery likewise substitutes for real efforts to deal with real problems that can tear a society apart. Despite an orientation of asking what "we" can do for "them," those who want to see blacks advance in fields requiring a mathematics background need to confront black students with a need to master this subject, even if that means giving up other diversions and giving up attitudes that doing academic work is "acting white."[41] This will win few friends and fewer votes. But the question is whether one is serious about results for others or simply wants to feel good about oneself.

The strongest moral case for affirmative action policies is in a country like India, where individuals are born, live, and die in the same caste. Yet that case is remarkably weak, even in India — if one judges affirmative action by its actual consequences, rather than by its ideals, rationales, or hopes. However, in India as in other countries around the world, such policies are usually *not* judged by their empirical consequences, either by most intellectuals or by most politicians.

When judged by what actually happens, what is wrong with affirmative action is even clearer in India than in the United States or in other countries, simply because of the way official statistics are collected there. American government data are collected in broad-brush categories, such as blacks, whites, and Hispanics. The parallels in India would be the four *varnas* of

the Hindu religion—Brahmins Kshatriyas, Vaisyas, and Su-
dras—but these broad idealized categories, which apply all
across India, are not the socially relevant "functional groups"
in which people actually live, interact socially, and marry in
their own communities. These latter groups are called *jatis*—
and there are thousands of them in the many communities
scattered across the vast reaches of India. The term caste has
been applied to both *varnas* and *jatis*, but statistical data are
available for the latter.[42]

The availability of official statistics broken down more finely
in India than in the United States has enormous implications.
It means that data can be discussed in much more specific
terms in India than in the broad-brush categories used in the
U.S. In India, the effects of affirmative action policies can be
traced not just to such a general category as "untouchables" or
dalits, but more specifically to Chamars in Maharashtra or
Haryana or Madhya Pradesh, as compared to other *jatis* in the
same broad category of "untouchables" in those states. That
is how we know that the more fortunate of the untouchables
or dalits receive the lion's share of the benefits or how the
"creamy layer" tends to get a disproportionate share of preferential benefits in other groups. One cannot discover from U.S.
government statistics how much of the benefits of affirmative
action go to West Indian blacks or to those blacks who are
descendants of the "free persons of color" who were freed
before the Civil War, even though other studies show that these
sub-groups have had very different histories from the history of
most other blacks.[43]

Such data as can be gleaned from a variety of private sources
in the United States suggest that the more fortunate American
blacks receive a disproportionate share of the benefits going to
blacks as a whole in the United States, just as the more fortunate
Malays tend to benefit most from affirmative action in Malaysia
or the more fortunate untouchables benefit from affirmative
action in India. But this is not so massively demonstrated statis-

tically as in India. So, while the moral case for affirmative action is stronger in India, the empirical case is weaker, because so few of the poorer untouchable groups benefit and the more fortunate "other backward classes" receive far more than all the untouchables put together. That is because these "other backward classes" are more numerous and because they are usually in a better position to take advantage of preferences and quotas, since they are more likely to have more of the complementary resources required. In the United States, there is not yet such widespread awareness as in India of how preferential programs for the less fortunate end up helping disproportionately the more fortunate, and therefore there are no comparable political or legal issues about "the creamy layer."

Neither in India nor elsewhere are affirmative action policies simply a matter of redistributing benefits. Such programs also generate major social costs which fall on the population as a whole. Losses of efficiency are among these costs, whether because less qualified persons are chosen over more qualified persons or because many highly qualified members of non-preferred groups emigrate from a society where their chances have been reduced. However, the cost of inefficiency is overshadowed by the cost of intergroup polarization, violence and loss of lives. Bloody and lethal riots over affirmative action in India are the most obvious examples, but there have also been young brahmins who have died by setting themselves on fire in protest against policies which have destroyed their prospects.

As the country which has had preferences and quotas for the less fortunate longer than any other, India presents the clearest historical picture of their consequences, as well as the clearest statistical picture. Its history is not one to encourage other countries to follow in India's footsteps, much less the footsteps of Sri Lanka.

The history of Sri Lanka is even more chilling to those who are concerned about what actually happens in the wake of affirmative action policies, as distinguished from what was expected or hoped would happen. Sri Lanka's well deserved reputation as a country with exemplary relations between its majority and minority populations in the middle of the twentieth century has become a bitter mockery in the course of a decades-long civil war, marked by hideous atrocities. Despite Sri Lanka's being a much smaller country than the United States, the number of Sri Lankans who have died in its internal strife exceeds the number of Americans killed during the long years of the Vietnam war.

The history of blacks in the United States has been virtually stood on its head by those advocating affirmative action. The empirical evidence is clear that most blacks got themselves out of poverty in the decades *preceding* the civil rights revolution of the 1960s and the beginning of affirmative action in the 1970s. Yet, the political misrepresentation of what happened — by leaders and friends of blacks — has been so pervasive that this achievement has been completely submerged in the public consciousness. Instead of gaining the respect that other groups have gained by lifting themselves out of poverty, blacks are widely seen, by friends and critics alike, as owing their advancement to government beneficence.

Within the black community itself, the possible ending of affirmative action has been portrayed as a threat to end their economic and social progress. Thus whites are resentful and blacks are fearful because of policies which have in fact done relatively little, on net balance, to help blacks in general or poor blacks in particular. Among black students in colleges and universities, those admitted under lower standards face a higher failure rate and those admitted under the same standards as other students graduate with their credentials under a cloud of suspicion because of double standards for minority students in general.

One of the most widely used defenses of group preferences and quotas is that there are precedents for them. In college admissions, for example, there have been preferences for athletes and for alumni children. Merit criteria have not been universal in other institutions either. Why then the objections to racial or ethnic preferences or preferences for women? As a strategic argument, this arbitrarily puts the burden of proof on critics of affirmative action, as if the demonstrable social costs of this program needed no justification. But of all justifications, precedent is one of the weakest. Everything that has ever been done wrong — from jay-walking to genocide — has had precedents. Any justification or criticism of affirmative action must be based on its actual consequences. If we took the argument from precedents as conclusive, then nothing could ever be corrected until there was perfection in everything else.

Verbal parallels are not enough. Hard evidence on the magnitude or empirical consequences of such things as alumni preferences is needed, but is seldom asked for or given. No one, for example, asks how far below the usual admissions standards are the alumni children who are admitted preferentially, compared to how much the standards are lowered to get the racial profile required for "diversity."

There is, however, some empirical evidence on the consequences of preferential admissions of individuals from privileged groups. When the president of the University of the Philippines had discretionary powers to admit particular students without regard to the usual academic criteria, the results were that (1) the great majority admitted this way were off-spring of "the rich and powerful," and (2) "those admitted by presidential discretion performed worse than the rest of the audience."[44] At Harvard, back during the era when more than half of all alumni sons were admitted, those special admittees were disproportionately represented among students who flunked out.[45]

Despite verbal parallels between affirmative action and preferences for the privileged, when some rich student of modest ability does not make it through an elite college, that is neither a personal nor a social tragedy, given the range of options still available to that student. But, with students from a lower income background, for whom education may be their one shot at a better life, the story is entirely different.

As for the important question of *how much* of a preference exists—that is, how far below the usual admissions standards are alumni children versus minority children admitted through racial preferences—a child of modest ability from a wealthy family is likely to have had the best education that money can buy, so his academic preparation and test scores are likely to be solid, even if not outstanding. But a minority youngster admitted to a college where the other students have composite SAT scores hundreds of points higher faces a much tougher prospect.

If the only issue in affirmative action were whether there are any other unmerited benefits, then arguments about the preferential admissions of the children of affluent alumni might make some sense. But, when the consequences of racial or ethnic quotas include creating artificial failures among the ostensible beneficiaries and polarization in the society at large, then mere verbal parallels are not enough.

MISLEADING TACTICS

One of the unquantifiable, but by no means unimportant, consequences of affirmative action has been a widespread dishonesty, taking many forms. The redesignation of individuals and groups, in order to receive the benefits of preferences and quotas intended for others, has been common in various countries. In the United States, a special dishonesty has been necessary to square group preferences and quotas with the requirement of the American constitution for equal rights among individuals. This has involved both concealment of the existence of preferential treatment and claims that such treatment is only a remedial response to existing discrimination. This adds insults to people's intelligence to the injuries they may have received, or perceived themselves as receiving, and can only add to the backlash. There is all the difference in the world between saying that you have not had an even chance in life and saying that a particular individual or institution with whom you dealt has discriminated against you.

Another widespread kind of dishonesty, in both India and the United States, is the use of hazy, unverifiable criteria to conceal group preferences in college and university admissions by automatically offsetting the better academic records of members of one group with higher "leadership" and other subjective rankings of members of other groups who would be inadmissible, in competition with others, on academic grounds. In both countries, court decisions restricting the scope or terms of group preferences in admissions to colleges and universities have been followed by efforts to put a greater emphasis on non-academic criteria in admissions. As noted in Chapter 2, the rankings of students on these non-academic criteria in India has almost invariably turned out to be higher for those with lower academic records and lower for those with higher academic records.

In the United States, nebulous factors like "leadership" or "overcoming adversity" have likewise served as automatic offsets whose validity or lack of validity is not subject to proof or disproof. State bans on affirmative action in California and Texas public universities set off a wave of creative proposals for non-objective criteria for admissions, echoing what had happened in India decades before, where the state government of Mysore "suddenly exhibited an enhanced concern for the extra-curricular accomplishments of applicants to professional colleges."[46] Nothing is easier than to come up with rationales for non-objective criteria. In India's state of Madras, for example, one supporter of such criteria argued that such criteria would "eliminate puny creatures with no personality from becoming engineers and doctors."[47]

One of the common dishonesties in the academic world is

faculty rejection of affirmative action in anonymous polls and support of it when voting publicly in faculty meetings or commenting in the media. A 1996 Roper poll, for example, found that a majority of professors, nationwide, were opposed to affirmative action in faculty hiring and to affirmative action in student admissions. Yet it is virtually impossible to find a faculty vote against these policies in American colleges and universities. Bitter fights have erupted over the issue of using secret ballots for votes on this issue, since both sides have recognized that whether the voting was secret or public could lead to opposite results.

History itself has been misrepresented as a way of strengthening the case for particular policies. Such misrepresentations of the history of the rise of blacks and women in the United States have already been noted in Chapter 6. The history of the aboriginal population in Australia has also been misrepresented in the quest for more current government benefits.[48] In country after country, deception has been an integral part of the case for affirmative action. One of the most common forms of deception is the use of rationales which bear little or no relationship to what has actually been done. No sufferings by black Americans, past or present, can justify admitting white students to an elite San Francisco public high school over better qualified Chinese American students who applied.[49] Yet, once a policy of racial quotas has been authorized, the floodgates have been opened to such things, wholly at odds with the rationales for these quotas.

Emotionally powerful and politically explosive issues often produce desperate searches for a "third way" to resolve dilemmas without confronting realities. Some even flatter themselves that this represents a more subtle and nuanced approach. But, however subtle and nuanced one's thinking may be, ultimately thinking must confront a reality where options can be few, crude, and discrete. Given the tenacity with which group preferences and quotas have persisted, and the zeal with which they have been expanded, in countries around the world, subtleties in trying to reform or reduce affirmative action can amount to little more than a verbal fig leaf over the naked continuance of the same policies as before.

ALTERNATIVES TO AFFIRMATIVE ACTION

Concern for the less fortunate is entirely different from imagining that we can do what we cannot do. Nor is the humbling admission of our inherent limitations as human beings a reason for failing to do the considerable number of things which can still be done within those limitations. In America, at least, history has demonstrated dramatically what can be done because it has already been done.

Americans need only look back to the beginning of the twentieth century to see what enormous social and economic progress has been made by some of the poorest and apparently least promising segments of the population. At the beginning of the twentieth century, only about half of the black population of the United States could read and write. Jews lived packed into slums on the lower east side of New York, with more overcrowding than in any slums in America today. As late as the First World War, the results of mass mental testing of American soldiers led a leading authority on mental tests to conclude that it was a myth that Jews were highly intelligent.[50] The situation of Chinese Americans looked so hopeless that a popular expression of the time described someone facing impossible odds as having "not a Chinaman's chance."

Not even most optimists would have predicted at that time how much all these groups would rise over the next half century—before there were preferences or quotas. Even for blacks, at the center of current controversies about affirmative action, the decline in their poverty and their rise in the professions were both more dramatic *before* the federal government created affirmative action in the 1970s. With all these American ethnic groups—and others—what happened was not a transfer of benefits from the rest of the population, but a rising *contribution* from these minorities to the growing prosperity of American society as a whole, from which both they and the larger society benefitted, as the less educated became more educated, as farm laborers and domestic servants acquired the skills and experience to take on more challenging work. This was not a zero-sum process, while redistribution is at best a zero-sum process, if it somehow manages to avoid disincentive effects and intergroup turmoil.

Why is this social process, with a proven track record, so little appreciated, or even noticed—and sometimes dismissed as a policy of "doing nothing"? Perhaps that is because, whatever its economic and social benefits, it offers few rewards to politicians, activists, and intellectuals, or to those who wish to seem morally superior by denouncing society. The heroes of these groups' rise are anonymous individuals, not public figures. Here is some history worth repeating—but only if the goal is the advancement of the less fortunate, rather than the aggrandizement of those who would be their guardians or spokesmen or elected officials.

SUMMARY AND IMPLICATIONS

The skewed pattern of beneficiaries of affirmative action programs should not only give pause as to the actual consequences of such programs, it should also call into question the very assumption on which affirmative action is based. That assumption is that an uneven distribution of income and of desirable jobs indicates discriminatory intentions toward the less fortunate, which must be counteracted by preferential policies on their behalf. But when those well-intentioned policies show the very same skewed pattern as the presumed ill intentions they are supposed to counteract, then it is hard to avoid the conclusion that something other than intentions must be involved.

Nor can behavioral and other differences among the various populations themselves be arbitrarily banished from discussion by some such pat phrases as "stereotypes" or "blaming the victim." Causation is not blame and whether they are victims or not is precisely the question.

Are the Malay majority "victims" of the Chinese minority in Malaysia, the northern Nigerian majority victims of the Ibo minority, the Sinhalese majority victims of the Tamil minority in Sri Lanka, and numerous local majorities victims of the Chettiar or Marwari minorities in various parts of India? Are the white majorities in Canada and the United States victims of Japanese minorities? Or do these minorities simply perform more successfully in the competition of the marketplace and educational institutions? The dogma that statistical disparities demonstrate discrimination assumes an equality of performance that is virtually impossible to find in the real world.

Indeed, some of the same groups that are said to be discriminated against, on the basis of statistical disparities, show the same patterns of statistical dominance over the majority population in such fields as sports and entertainment — fields in which individual talents and efforts can produce success without the kind of cultural prerequisites, such as higher education, required in many other fields. Yet no one seriously believes that Maoris can keep white New Zealanders off that country's sports teams, except by outperforming them on the field. Nor can black baseball players in the United States keep white players from hitting home runs, even though four of the top five totals of career home runs were hit by black players. Statistical disparities prove nothing about discrimination because they are common even in situations where those who are statistically dominant have no way to discriminate.

The very modest benefits of affirmative action, concentrated on those already more fortunate, with little or no benefits to those who are truly disadvantaged, have often been blamed on insufficient zeal, or even bad faith, on the part of those administering affirmative action programs. Thus the failures or inadequacies of such programs can be taken as reasons for reforms, rather than as symptoms of more fundamental misconceptions that could be reasons for ending the programs. While this argument might seem plausible to some when discussing whites administering programs for blacks in the United States, it loses even the appearance of plausibility when Malays are administering preferential programs for Malays in Malaysia or when Sinhalese have administered such programs for Sinhalese in Sri Lanka. Even in the United States, the particular officials heading civil rights agencies such as the Equal Employment Opportunity Commission have almost all been black, as have many or most administrators of affirmative action programs in private industry and in the academic world.

Despite a tendency to think of group preferences and quotas as transfers of benefits — a zero-sum process — there are in fact many ways in which these transfers can be negative-sum processes, in which what is lost by one group exceeds what is gained by another, making the society as a whole worse off. For example, when a group in which 80 percent of the students admitted to college succeed in graduating loses admissions to a goup in which only 40 percent of the students graduate, then the first group must lose 800 graduates in order for the second group to gain 400 graduates. Moreover, it has been common in various countries around the world for groups whose students have lower qualifications to specialize in easier and less remunerative fields, as well as performing less well academically.[51] Therefore the first group may lose 800 graduates, largely concentrated in mathematics, science, and engineering, while the second group gains 400 graduates largely concentrated in sociology, education, and ethnic studies.

This does not even take into account the intergroup polarization which group preferences and quotas provoke, and which can take many forms, including lethal riots, as in India, or outright civil war, as in Sri Lanka. By contrast, the gains made by less fortunate groups as a result of becoming better educated and better equipped with skills can be not only a net benefit to society as a whole, but also a source of greater respect for the group by others who see them as becoming more productive contributing members of society. In the case of blacks in the United States, much of their advancement has been of this sort, but the existence of affirmative action and of particular horror stories growing out of it, has meant that blacks' actual achievements have often been under-estimated or disregarded. Affirmative action has meant almost a moratorium on recognition of the achievements of those designated as its beneficiaries, however little tangible benefits these groups may in fact have received.

Another way in which affirmative action can be a negative-sun process is by a withdrawal of members of non-preferred groups and the loss of their contributions to the society at large. A study of preferential policies in Malaysia reports the "emigration of non-Bumiputera professionals and the outflow of Chinese capital."[52] In post-apartheid South Africa, with affirmative action for blacks, many white government workers have taken early retirement and thousands of whites have emigrated annually.[53] Those on the wrong side of preferential policies have likewise emigrated from Fiji, from Soviet Central Asia, from East Africa, and from other places where the skills and experience of these emigrants were sorely needed.

The empirical consequences of affirmative action preferences and quotas have been paid remarkably little attention — with hard data being sparse to non-existent in some countries — while controversies surrounding these policies have been discussed in terms of the vision and the rationale behind them and the counter-vision and counter-rationales of critics. Vague, emotional, confused and dishonest words, which are incidental aspects of many controversial issues, are central to discussions of affirmative action in countries around the world. Few such programs could stand on the basis of their actual empirical consequences. Nor are their moral bases any more solid.

Some groups in some countries imagine themselves entitled to preferences and quotas just because they are indigenous "sons of the soil" — even when they are in fact not indigenous, as the Sinhalese in Sri Lanka and the Malays in Malaysia are not. Yet indigenousness has acquired a moral aura, not only among those claiming such status, but among observers and scholars as well. Why an accident of history and geography should have moral implications that last for centuries is a question seldom raised, much less answered.

Even when serious moral questions surround the past or present mistreatment of groups such as the untouchables in India or blacks in the United States, the remedies proposed rapidly spread far beyond redress of the misfortunes used to justify those remedies. Not only has the internal distribution of compensatory benefits borne little relationship — or even an inverse relationship — to the degree of misfortune within the affected groups, such benefits have spread to other groups far beyond the scope of the moral rationale and far exceeding in size the intended beneficiary groups.

Innumerable principles, theories, assumptions and assertions have been used to justify affirmative action programs — some common around the world and some peculiar to particular countries or communities. What is remarkable is how seldom these notions have been tested empirically, or have even been defined clearly or examined logically, much less weighed against the large and often painful costs they entail. Despite sweeping claims made for affirmative action programs, an examination of their actual consequences makes it hard to support those claims, or even to say that these programs have been beneficial on net balance — unless one is prepared to say that any amount of social redress, however small, is worth any amount of costs and dangers, however large.

Notes

PREFACE

1. Donald R. Snodgrass, *Inequality and Economic Development in Malaysia* (Kuala Lumpur: Oxford University Press, 1980), p. 10.

CHAPTER 1: AN INTERNATIONAL PERSPECTIVE

1. See, for example, Rita Jalai and Seymour Martin Lipset, "Racial and Ethnic Conflicts: A Global Perspective," *Political Science Quarterly*, Vol. No. 4 (Winter 1992–1993), p. 603; Robert Klitgaard, *Elitism and Meritocracy in Developing Countries* (Baltimore: Johns Hopkins University Press, 1986), pp. 25, 45; Terry Martin, *The Affirmative Action Empire: Nations and Nationalism in the Soviet Union, 1923–1939* (Ithaca: Cornell University Press, 2001); Dorothy J. Solinger, "Minority Nationalities in China's Yunnan Province: Assimilation, Power, and Policy in a Socialist State," *World Politics*, Vol. 30, No. 1 (October 1977), pp. 1–23; Miriam Jordan, "Quotas for Blacks in Brazil Cause Hubbub," *Wall Street Journal*, December 27, 2001, p. A6; Priscilla Qolisaya Pauamau, "A Post-colonial Reading of Affirmative Action in Education in Fiji," *Race, Ethnicity and Education*, Vol. 4, No. 2 (2001), pp. 109–123; Matthew Hoddie, "Preferential Policies and the Blurring of Ethnic Boundaries: The Case of Aboriginal Australians in the 1980s," *Political Studies*, Vol. 50 (2002), pp. 293–312; Mohammed Waseem, "Affirmative Action Policies in Pakistan," *Ethnic Studies Report* (Sri Lanka), Vol. XV, No. 2 (July 1997), pp. 223–244; "New Zealand: Landmark Decisions," *The Economist*, November 20, 1993,

p. 93; Rainer Knopff, "The Statistical Protection of Minorities: Affirmative Action in Canada," *Minorities and the Canadian State*, edited by Neil Nevitte and Alan Kornberg (Cincinnati: Mosaic Press, 1985), pp. 87–106.

2. A. K. Vakil, *Reservation Policy and Scheduled Castes in India* (New Delhi: Ashish Publishing House, 1985), p. 127.

3. Sham Satish Chandra Misra, *Preferential Treatment in Public Employment and Equality of Opportunity* (Lucknow: Eastern Book Company, 1979), p. 83.

4. Shri Prakash, "Reservations Policy for Other Backward Classes: Problems and Perspectives," *The Politics of Backwardness: Reservation Policy in India* (New Delhi: Konark Publishers, Pvt. Ltd., 1997), pp. 44–45.

5. Gordon P. Means, "Ethnic Preference Policies in Malaysia," *Ethnic Preference and Public Policy in Developing States*, edited by Neil Nevitte and Charles H. Kennedy (Boulder: Lynne Reinner Publishers, Inc., 1986), p. 108.

6. Nancy Lubin, *Labour and Nationality in Soviet Central Asia: An Uneasy Compromise* (Princeton: Princeton University Press, 1984), p. 162.

7. David Riesman, *On Higher Education: The Academic Enterprise in an Age of Rising Student Consumerism* (San Francisco: Jossey-Bass Publishers, 1980), pp. 80–81. See also Thomas Sowell, *Black Education: Myths and Tragedies* (New York: David McKay, 1972), pp. 131–132, 140.

8. Editorial, "Reservations and the OBCs," *The Hindu* (India), April 4, 2000.

9. Executive Order No. 10,925.

10. Charles H. Kennedy, "Policies of Redistributional Preference in Pakistan," *Ethnic Preference and Public Policy in Developing States*, edited by Neil Nevitte and Charles H. Kennedy, p. 69.

11. Donald L. Horowitz, *Ethnic Groups in Conflict*, p. 242.

12. Mohammed Waseem, "Affirmative Action Policies in Pakistan," *Ethnic Studies Report* (Sri Lanka), Vol. XV, No. 2 (July 1997), pp. 226, 228–229.

13. Quoted in Alan Little and Diana Robbins, *'Loading the Law'* (London: Commission for Racial Equality, 1982), p. 6.

14. Donald L. Horowitz, *Ethnic Groups in Conflict*, p. 677.

15. Myron Weiner, "The Pursuit of Ethnic Inequalities Through Preferential Policies: A Comparative Public Policy Perspective," *From Independence to Statehood: Managing Ethnic Conflict in Five African and*

Asian States, edited by Robert B. Goldmann and A. Jeyaratnam Wilson (London: Frances Pinter, 1984), p. 64.

16. Cynthia H. Enloe, *Police, Military and Ethnicity: Foundations of State Power* (New Brunswick: Transaction Books, 1980), p. 143.

17. *Ibid.,* p. 75.

18. Ingeborg Fleischauer, "The Germans' Role in Tsarist Russia: A Reappraisal," *The Soviet Germans,* edited by Edith Rogovin Frankel, pp. 17–18.

19. Numerous documented examples can be found in just two books of mine: *Conquests and Cultures* (Basic Books, 1998), pp. 43, 124, 125, 168, 221–222; *Migrations and Cultures* (Basic Books, 1996), pp. 4, 17, 30, 31, 118, 121, 122–123, 126, 130, 135, 152, 154, 157, 158, 162, 164, 167, 176, 177, 179, 182, 193, 196, 201, 211, 212, 213, 215, 224, 226, 251, 258, 264, 265, 275, 277, 278, 289, 290, 297, 298, 300, 305, 306, 310, 313, 314, 318, 320, 323–324, 337, 342, 345, 353–354, 354–355, 355, 356, 358, 363, 366, 372–373. Extending the search for intergroup statistical disparities to the writings of others would of course increase the number of examples exponentially.

20. Bernard Grofman and Michael Migalski, "The Return of the Native: The Supply Elasticity of the American Indian Population 1960–1980," *Public Choice,* Vol. 57 (1988), p. 86.

21. Matthew Hoddie, "Preferential Policies and the Blurring of Ethnic Boundaries: The Case of Aboriginal Australians in the 1980s," *Political Studies,* vol. 50 (2002), p. 299.

22. Wolfgang Kasper, *Building Prosperity: Australia's Future as a Global Player* (St. Leonard's, NSW: The Centre for Independent Studies, 2002), p. 45.

23. Barry Sautman, "Ethnic Law and Minority Rights in China: Progress and Constraints," *Law & Policy,* Vol. 21, No. 3 (July 3, 1999), p. 294.

24. "Chinese Rush to Reclaim Minority Status," *Agence France Presse,* May 17, 1993.

25. See, for example, "Indians: In the Red," *The Economist,* February 25, 1989, pp. 25–26; Bob Zelnick, *Backfire: A Reporter Looks at Affirmative Action* (Washington, D.C.: Regner Publishing Inc., 1996), pp. 301–303.

26. Celia S. Heller, *On the Edge of Destruction: Jews of Poland Between the Two World Wars* (New York: Columbia University Press, 1987), p. 102.

27. Maria S. Muller, "The National Policy of Kenyanisation: Its Impact on a Town in Kenya," *Canadian Journal of African Studies,* Vol.

15, No. 2 (1981), p. 298; H. L. van der Laan, *The Lebanese Traders in Sierra Leone* (The Hague: Mouton & Co., 1975), pp. 141, 171.

28. "Indian Eunuchs Demand Government Job Quotas," *Agence France Presse*, October 22, 1997. See also David Orr, "Eunuchs Test Their Political Potency," *The Times* (London), February 17, 2000, downloaded from the Internet: http://www.the-times.co.uk/pages/tim/2000/02/17/timfgnasio1001.html?1123027.

29. Marc Galanter, *Competing Equalities: Law and the Backward Classes in India* (Berkeley: University of California Press, 1984), p. 64.

30. Human Rights Watch, *Broken People: Caste Violence Against India's "Untouchables"* (New York: Human Rights Watch, 1999), p. 39.

31. "Rajasthan's 'Original Backwards' Rally for Justice," *The Hindu*, May 28, 2001. (on-line)

32. "India: Mayawati Expels Three Leaders," *The Hindu*, July 22, 2001. (on-line)

33. Marc Galanter, *Competing Equalities*, p. 469.

34. Ozay Mehmet, "An Empirical Evaluation of Government Scholarship Policy in Malaysia," *Higher Education* (The Netherlands), April 1985, p. 202.

35. Chandra Richard de Silva, "Sinhala-Tamil Relations in Sri Lanka: The University Admissions Issue—The First Phase, 1971–1977," *From Independence to Statehood*, edited by Robert B. Goldmann and A. Jeyaratnam Wilson, p. 133.

36. Rep. David Dreir, " 'Disadvantaged' Contractors' Unfair Advantage," *Wall Street Journal*, February 21, 1989, p. A18.

37. Marc Galanter, *Competing Equalities*, p. 552.

38. Myron Weiner, *Sons of the Soil: Migration and Ethnic Conflict in India* (Princeton: Princeton University Press), p. 250.

39. John A. A. Ayoade, "Ethnic Management of the 1979 Nigerian Constitution," *Canadian Review of Studies in Nationalism*, Spring 1987, p. 127.

40. Donald L. Horowitz, *Ethnic Groups in Conflict*, p. 670.

41. Daniel C. Thompson, *Private Black Colleges at the Crossroads* (Westport, Connecticut: Greenwood Press, 1973), p. 88.

42. Carol S. Holzbery, *Minorities and Power in a Black Society: The Jewish Community of Jamaica* (Lanham, Maryland: The North-South Publishing Co., Inc., 1987), p. 420.

43. See, for example, William Moore, Jr., and Lonnie H. Wagstaff, *Black Educators in White Colleges* (San Francisco: Jossey-Bass Publishing Co., 1974), pp. 130–131, 198.

44. Bob Zelnick, *Backfire*, p. 113.

45. Lelah Dushkin, "Backward Class Benefits and Social Class in India, 1920–1970," *Economic and Political Weekly*, April 7, 1979, p. 666. Although the example is hypothetical, it is not out of line with what has actually occurred: "Although 18% of the places in each of the two services were reserved for Scheduled Castes, there was just one successful SC candidate, who had scored 105th on the examination." Marc Galanter, *Competing Equalities*, p. 425.

46. Barbara R. Joshi, "Whose Law, Whose Order: 'Untouchables' Social Violence and the State in India," *Asian Survey*, July 1982, pp. 680, 682.

47. A. K. Vakil, *Reservation Policy and Scheduled Castes in India*, p. 67; Ghagat Ram Goyal, *Educating Harijans* (Gurgaon, Haryana: The Academic Press, 1981), p. 21.

48. Suma Chitnis, "Positive Discrimination in India with Reference to Education," *From Independence to Statehood*, edited by Robert B. Goldmann and A. Jeyaratram Wilson, p. 37; Padma Ramkrishna Velaskar, "Inequality in Higher Education: A Study of Scheduled Caste Students in Medical Colleges of Bombay," Ph.D. Dissertation, Tata Institute of Social Sciences, Bombay, 1986, pp. 234, 236.

49. Myron Weiner and Mary Fainsod Katzenstein, *India's Preferential Policies: Migrants, The Middle Classes, and Ethnic Equality* (Chicago, University of Chicago Press, 1981), p. 54.

50. *Ibid.*, pp. 54, 55.

51. Harold Crouch, *Government and Society in Malaysia* (Ithaca: Cornell University Press, 1996), p. 186.

52. K. M. de Silva, *Sri Lanka: Ethnic Conflict, Management and Resolution* (Kandy, Sri Lanka: International Centre for Ethnic Studies, 1996), p. 21.

53. Celia Heller, *On the Edge of Destruction: Jews of Poland Between the Two World Wars* (New York: Columbia University Press, 1987), pp. 16, 17, 107, 123–128; Ezra Mendelsohn, *The Jews of East Central Europe Between the World Wars* (Bloomington: Indiana University Press, 1983), pp. 99, 105, 167, 232, 236–237.

54. Larry Diamond, "Class, Ethnicity, and the Democratic State: Nigeria, 1950–1966," *Comparative Studies in Social History*, July 1983, pp. 462, 473.

55. Donald L. Horowitz, *Ethnic Groups in Conflict*, pp. 221–226; Myron Weiner and Mary Fainsod Katzenstein, *India's Preferential Policies*, pp. 4–5, 132; Myron Weiner, "The Pursuit of Ethnic Equality Through Preferential Policies: A Comparative Public Policy Perspective," *From Independence to Statehood*, edited by Robert B. Goldmann

and A. Jeyaratram Wilson, p. 78; K. M. de Silva, "University Admissions and Ethnic Tensions in Sri Lanka," *Ibid.*, pp. 125–126; Donald V. Smiley, "French-English Relations in Canada and Consociational Democracy," *Ethnic Conflict in the Western World*, edited by Milton J. Esman (Ithaca: Cornell University Press, 1977), pp. 186–188.

56. U.S. Bureau of the Census, *Historical Statistics of the United States: Colonial Times to 1970* (Washington: Government Printing Office, 1975), p. 380.

57. Daniel P. Moynihan, "Employment, Income, and the Ordeal of the Negro Family," *Daedalus*, Fall 1965, p. 752.

58. Stephan Thernstrom and Abigail Thernstrom, *America in Black and White: One Nation, Indivisible* (New York: Simon and Schuster, 1997), p. 232.

59. *Ibid.*, p. 50.

CHAPTER 2: AFFIRMATIVE ACTION IN INDIA

1. See, for example, Lelah Dushkin, "Backward Class Benefits and Social Class in India, 1920–1970," *Economic and Political Weekly*, April 7, 1979, p. 661; Marc Galanter, *Competing Equalities: Law and the Backward Classes in India* (Berkeley: University of California Press, 1984), Chapter 2.

2. Kanti Bajpai, "Diversity, Democracy, and Devolution in India," *Government Policies and Ethnic Relations in Asia and the Pacific*, edited by Michael E. Brown and Sumit Ganguly (Cambridge, Massachusetts: MIT Press, 1997), pp. 53–54; John Echeverri-Gent, "Government and Politics," *India: A Country Study*, edited by James Heitzman and Robert L. Worden (Washington: U.S. Government Printing Office, 1996), pp. 437–438.

3. Partha S. Ghosh, "Positive Discrimination in India: A Political Analysis," *Ethnic Studies Report* (Sri Lanka), Vol. XV, No. 2 (July 1997), p. 145.

4. Partap C. Aggarwal and Mohd. Siddig Ashraf, *Equality Through Privilege: A Study of Special Privileges of Scheduled Castes in Haryana* (New Delhi: Shri Ram Centre for Industrial Relations and Human Resources, 1976), p. 4; Richard F. Nyrop et al., *Area Handbook for India* (Washington: Government Printing Office, 1975), p. 51.

5. *Keesing's Contemporary Archives*, December 8, 1978, p. 29351.

6. *Report of the Commission for Scheduled Castes and Scheduled Tribes* (April 1979–March 1980), Second Report (New Delhi, 1981), p. 297.

7. Human Rights Watch, *Broken People: Caste Violence Against India's Untouchables* (New York: Human Rights Watch, 1999).

8. "Caste and The Durban Conference," *The Hindu*, August 31, 2001.

9. Doranne Jacobson, "Social Systems," *India: A Country Study*, edited by James Heitzman and Robert L. Worden (Washington: U.S. Government Printing Office, 1996), p. 273.

10. Partha S. Ghosh, "Positive Discrimination in India: A Political Analysis," *Ethnic Studies Report* (Sri Lanka), Vol. XV, No. 2 (July 1997), p. 146.

11. Partha S. Ghosh, "Language Policy and National Integration," *Ethnic Studies Report* (Sri Lanka), Vol. XIV, No. 1 (January 1996), 144; "Still Untouchable," *The Economist* (US edition), June 16, 2001.

12. John R. Wood, "Reservations in Doubt: The Backlash against Affirmative Action in Gujarat, India," *Pacific Affairs*, Vol. 60, No. 3 (Autumn 1987), p. 413.

13. Partha S. Ghosh, "Language Policy and National Integration," *Ethnic Studies Report* (Sri Lanka), Vol. XIV, No. 1 (January 1996), pp. 159, 160.

14. Michael E. Brown and Sumit Ganguly, editors, *Government Policies and Ethnic Relations in Asia and the Pacific*, p. 54.

15. Partap C. Aggarwal and Mohd. Siddig Ashraf, *Equality Through Privilege*, p. 49. A 1981 study reported: "When asked to state if they themselves or any of their close relatives have ever suffered from ill-treatment due to their caste status, the overwhelming majority of both school (78%) and college (71%) students reply in the negative." Suma Chitnis, *A Long Way to Go*, p. 147.

16. Human Rights Watch, *Broken People*, p. 31.

17. "Reservation Policy Not Implemented in Full," *The Hindu* (India), November 18, 2001. (on-line)

18. Dennis Austin, *Democracy and Violence in India and Sri Lanka* (London: Pinter Publishers, 1994), p. 41.

19. Partap C. Aggarwal and Mohd. Siddig Ashraf, *Equality Through Privilege*, p. 31.

20. K. M. de Silva, *Managing Ethnic Tensions in Multi-Ethnic Societies: Sri Lanka, 1880–1985* (Lanham, Maryland: University Press of America, 1986), p. 39.

21. Marc Galanter, *Competing Equalities*, p. 26n.

22. Partha S. Ghosh, "Language Policy and National Integration," *Ethnic Studies Report* (Sri Lanka), Vol. XIV, No. 1 (January 1996), p. 139.

23. Kusum K. Premi, "Educational Opportunities for the Scheduled Castes: Role of Protective Discrimination in Equalisation," *Economic and Political Weekly,* November 9, 1974, p. 1907.

24. Suma Chitnis, "Positive Discrimination in India with Reference to Education," *From Independence to Statehood: Managing Ethnic Conflict in Five African and Asian States,* edited by Robert B. Goldmann and A. Jeyaratnam Wilson (London: Francis Pinter, 1984), pp. 36–37.

25. See Suma Chitnis, "Positive Discrimination in India with Reference to Education," *From Independence to Statehood,* edited by Robert B. Goldmann and A. Jeyaratnam Wilson, p. 37; Padma Ramkrishna Velaskar, "Inequality in Higher Education: A Study of Scheduled Caste Students in Medical Colleges of Bombay," Ph.D. Dissertation, Tata Institute of Social Sciences, Bombay, 1986, p. 234.

26. P. R. Velaskar, *op. cit.,* p. 236.

27. Partha S. Ghosh, "Language Policy and National Integration," *Ethnic Studies Report* (Sri Lanka), Vol. XIV, No. 1 (January 1996), p. 142.

28. P. Sunderarajan, "India: Medical Colleges, Varsities Told to Follow UGC Norms," *The Hindu,* September 14, 2001. (on-line)

29. Partha S. Ghosh, "Language Policy and National Integration," *Ethnic Studies Report* (Sri Lanka), Vol. XIV, No. 1 (January 1996), p. 158; Padma Ramkrishna Velaskar, "Inequality in Higher Education: A Study of Scheduled Caste Students in Medical Colleges of Bombay," Ph.D. dissertation, Tata Institute of Social Sciences, Bombay, 1986, pp. 253, 335, 336; Marc Galanter, *Competing Equalities,* pp. 63–64.

30. Suma Chitnis, "Measuring up to Reserved Admissions," *Reservation: Policy, Programmes and Issues,* edited by Vimal P. Shah and Binod C. Agrawal (Jaipur, India: Rawat Publications, 1986), pp. 37–42.

31. Partha S. Ghosh, "Language Policy and National Integration," *Ethnic Studies Report* (Sri Lanka), Vol. XIV, No. 1 (January 1996), p. 140.

32. Marc Galanter, *Competing Equalities,* p. 425.

33. Partha S. Ghosh, "Language Policy and National Integration," *Ethnic Studies Report* (Sri Lanka), Vol. XIV, No. 1 (January 1996), p. 142; Michael E. Brown and Sumit Ganguly, editors, *Government Policies and Ethnic Relations in Asia and the Pacific,* p. 54.

34. Partha S. Ghosh, "Language Policy and National Integration," *Ethnic Studies Report* (Sri Lanka), Vol. XIV, No. 1 (January 1996), p. 142.

35. Marc Galanter, *Competing Equalities,* pp. 64–65.

36. P. R. Velaskar, "Inequality in Higher Education," p. 263.

37. Suma Chitnis, *A Long Way To Go* . . . (New Delhi: Allied Publishers, Pvt. Ltd., 1981), p. 19.

38. *Ibid.*, p. 264.

39. *Report of the Commission for Scheduled Castes and Scheduled Tribes* (July 1978–March 1979), First Report, p. 188. See also Suma Chitnis, *A Long Way to Go* . . . , p. 16.

40. Suma Chitnis, *A Long Way To Go* . . . , p. 16.

41. *Ibid.*, pp. 16, 320.

42. Pradeep Kumar, "Reservations within Reservations," *Economic and Political Weekly*, September 15, 2001, p. 3505.

43. "UP Announces Ordinance on Quota," *The Statesman* (India), September 16, 2001 (downloaded from the Internet).

44. "Quota-Within-Quota Move Motivated," *The Hindu*, January 26, 2002 (downloaded from the Internet).

45. Marc Galanter, *Competing Equalities*, pp. 468, 469.

46. Ratna Murdia, "Issues in Positive Discrimination Policies for Disadvantaged Groups," *The Indian Journal of Social Work*, January 1983, p. 437; Suma Chitnis, "Education for Equality: Case of Scheduled Castes in Higher Education," *Economic and Political Weekly*, August 1972, p. 1676; Oliver Mendelsohn, "A Harijan Elite? The Lives of Some Untouchable Politicians," *Economic and Political Weekly*, March 22, 1986, p. 504; Suma Chitnis, *A Long Way To Go* . . . , pp. 16–18.

47. Upendra Baxi, "Legislative Reservations for Social Justice: Some Thoughts on India's Unique Experiment," *From Independence to Statehood*, edited by Robert B. Goldmann and A. Jeyaratnam Wilson, pp. 215–216. See also M. Satyanarayana and Rao and G. Srinivas Reddy, "Political Representation: National, State and Local," *Reservation Policy in India*, edited by B. A. V. Sharma and K. Madhusudhan Reddy (New Delhi: Light & Life Publishers, 1982), pp. 365–367; Pradeep Kumar, "Reservations within Reservations," *Economic and Political Weekly*, September 15, 2001.

48. B. Sivaramayya, "Affirmative Action: The Scheduled Castes and the Scheduled Tribes," International Conference on Affirmative Action, Bellagio Conference Center, Bellagio, Italy, August 16–20, 1982, p. 2.

49. Marc Galanter, *Competing Equalities*, p. 338.

50. *Ibid.*, pp. 44, 46; Michael E. Brown and Sumit Garguly, editors, *Government Policies and Ethnic Relations in Asia and the Pacific*, pp. 53, 54.

51. See, for example, Myron Weiner, *Sons of the Soil: Migration and Ethnic Conflict in India* (Princeton: Princeton University Press, 1978); Mary Fainsod Katzenstein, *Ethnicity and Equality: The Shiv Sena Party and Preferential Policies in Bombay* (Ithaca: Cornell University Press, 1979); Myron Weiner and Mary Fainsod Katzenstein, *India's Preferential Policies: Migrants, the Middle Classes and Ethnic Equality* (Chicago: University of Chicago Press, 1981).

52. Myron Weiner and Mary Fainsod Katzenstein, *India's Preferential Policies*, p. 102.

53. Myron Weiner, *Sons of the Soil*, pp. 235–243.

54. *Ibid.*, p. 250.

55. T. M. Joseph and S. N. Sangita, "Preferential Policies and 'Sons-of-the-Soil' Demands: The Indian Experience," *Ethnic Studies Report* (Sri Lanka), Vol. XVI, No. 1 (January 1998), p. 86.

56. Myron Weiner and Mary Fainsod Katzenstein, *India's Preferential Policies*, p. 68.

57. Allen W. Thrasher, "Language, Ethnicity, and Regionalism," *India: A Country Study*, edited by Louis R. Mortimer (Washington: U.S. Government Printing Office, 1996), pp. 215–216.

58. Myron Weiner, *Sons of the Soil*, pp. 225–229; Myron Weiner and Mary Fainsod Katzenstein, *India's Preferential Policies*, pp. 74–75.

59. Myron Weiner, *Sons of the Soil*, pp. 88–89; Amalendo Guha, "Colonisation of Assam: Second Phase 1840–1859," *The Indian Economic and Social History Review*, December 1961, p. 292.

60. Myron Weiner, *Sons of the Soil*, p. 78.

61. *Ibid.*, pp. 128–129.

62. *Ibid.*, pp. 92, 105.

63. *Ibid.*, pp. 103–104.

64. *Ibid.*, p. 107.

65. *Ibid.*, p. 109.

66. *Ibid.*, pp. 118–119.

67. Myron Weiner, "The Political Demography of Assam's Anti-Immigrant Movement," *Population and Development Review*, Vol. 9, No. 2 (January 1983), p. 279.

68. Mary Fainsod Katzenstein, *Ethnicity and Equality*, p. 142.

69. *Ibid.*, p. 28.

70. Myron Weiner and Mary Fainsod Katzenstein, *India's Preferential Policies*, p. 52.

71. *Ibid.*, p. 48.

72. Mary Fainsod Katzenstein, *Ethnicity and Equality*, pp. 48–49.

73. *Ibid.*, pp. 69, 106, 142.

74. "The Fire of India's Religions," *The Economist*, January 16, 1993, p. 2.

75. "Devils and Enemies," *Far Eastern Economic Review*, July 7, 1994.

76. "Demagogue of Hate," *Asiaweek*, December 22, 1995, p. 52.

77. "A Hindu Hero Feels the Heat," *Time*, International edition, Tokyo, February 24, 1997, p. 15.

78. "Bombay has Spun out of Control," *Businessweek*, October 19, 1998, p. 2.

79. "Ugly Intolerance," *The Hindu*, May 8, 2001, downloaded from the Internet.

80. "What is 'Indian'?" *The Hindu*, March 11, 2001, downloaded from the Internet.

81. Dennis Austin, *Democracy and Violence in India and Sri Lanka*, p. 43.

82. *Ibid.*, 42.

83. "Singh Faces Revolt Over Caste Scheme: The Indian Government Has Been Rocked by the Violent Response to Increased Job Quotas for Backward Castes," *The Independent* (London), September 11, 1990, p. 12.

84. The "other backward classes" alone are 52 percent of India's population, the untouchables 16 percent and tribal peoples 8 percent.

85. Marc Galanter, *Competing Equalities*, p. 64.

86. John R. Wood, "Reservations in Doubt: The Backlash against Affirmative Action in Gujarat, India," *Pacific Affairs*, Vol. 60, No. 3 (Autumn 1987), p. 408.

87. Marc Galanter, *Competing Equalities*, p. 451.

88. *Ibid.*, p. 451n.

89. A. K. Vakil, *Reservation Policy and Scheduled Castes in India* (New Delhi: Ashish Publishing House, 1985), p. 147.

90. C. L. Sharma, *Social Mobility Among Scheduled Castes* (New Delhi: M. D. Publications, 1996), pp. 105–107.

CHAPTER 3: AFFIRMATIVE ACTION IN MALAYSIA

1. Computed from *Buku Tahunan Peranghaan: Yearbook of Statistics Malaysia 2001* (Ketua Perangkawan, Malaysia: Department of Statistics, 2001), pp. 20, 28, 29.

2. Lennox A. Mills, *Southeast Asia: Illusion and Reality in Politics and Economics* (Minneapolis: University of Minnesota Press, 1964).

3. The Economist Intelligence Unit, *Malaysia, Brunei*, p. 14.

4. Computed from *Buku Perangkaan*, 28.

5. See the classic study by Victor Purcell, *The Overseas Chinese in Southeast Asia*, 2nd edition (Kuala Lumpur: Oxford University Press, 1980).

6. P. T. Bauer, *Reality and Rhetoric: Studies in the Economics of Development* (Cambridge, Massachusetts: Harvard University Press, 1984), p. 7.

7. Victor Simpao Limlingan, *Overseas Chinese in ASEAN: Business Strategies and Management Practices* (Pasig, Metro Manila, Philippines: Vita Development Corp., 1986), p. 29.

8. *Ibid.*, p. 30.

9. Donald R. Snodgrass, *Inequality and Economic Development in Malaysia* (Kuala Lumpur: Oxford University Press, 1980), p. 38.

10. D. G. E. Hall, *The History of Southeast Asia* (London: The Macmillan Company, Ltd., 1981), p. 835.

11. *Buku Perangkaan*, 42; K. S. Jomo, "Whither Malaysia's New Economic Policy?" *Pacific Affairs*, Vol. 63, No. 4 (Winter, 1990–1991), p. 475.

12. Victor Purcell, *The Chinese in Southeast Asia*, second edition, p. 283n.

13. Yuan-li Wu and Chu-hsi Wu, *Economic Development in Southeast Asia* (Stanford: Hoover Institution Press, 1980), p. 51.

14. Donald R. Snodgrass, *Inequality and Economic Development in Malaysia*, 242.

15. *Ibid.*, p. 8.

16. Mohamed Suffian bin Hashim, "Problems and Issues of Higher Education Development in Malaysia," *Development of Higher Education in Southeast Asia*, edited by Yip Yat Hoong, Table 8, pp. 63, 64.

17. Gordon P. Means, "Ethnic Preference Policies in Malaysia," *Ethnic Preference and Public Policy in Developing States*, edited by Neil Nevitte and Charles H. Kennedy (Boulder: Lynne Reinner Publishers, Inc., 1986), p. 105.

18. Michael E. Brown and Sumit Ganguly, editors, *Government Policies and Ethnic Relations in Asia and the Pacific* (Cambridge, Massachusetts: MIT Press, 1997), p. 254.

19. *Mid-Term Review of the Second Malaysia Plan, 1971–75* (Kuala Lumpur: The Government Press, 1973), pp. 76, 78.

20. Sumit Ganguly, "Ethnic Policies and Political Quiescence in Malaysia and Singapore," *Government Policies and Ethnic Relations in*

Asia and the Pacific, edited by Michael E. Brown and Sumit Ganguly, pp. 260–262.

21. *Eighth Malaysia Plan, 2001–2005* (Kuala Lumpur: Economic Planning Unit, 2001), p. 64.

22. Harold A. Crouch, *Government and Society in Malaysia* (Ithaca: Cornell University Press, 1996), pp. 37–38.

23. *Ibid.*, p. 39.

24. *Ibid.*, pp. 36–43.

25. *Ibid.*, pp. 40, 41.

26. *Ibid.*, p. 202.

27. *Ibid.*, p. 39.

28. K. S. Jomo, "Whither Malaysia's New Economic Policy," *Pacific Affairs*, Vol. 63, No. 4 (Winter, 1990–1991), pp. 469–499.

29. Bee-lan Chan Wang, "Governmental Intervention in Ethnic Stratification: Effects of the Distribution of Students Among Fields of Study," *Comparative Education Review*, February 1977, p. 110.

30. Donald R. Snodgrass, *Inequality and Economic Development in Malaysia*, pp. 249–250.

31. Firdaus Hj. Abdullah, "Affirmative Action Policy in Malaysia: To Restructure Society, to Eradicate Poverty," *Ethnic Studies Report* (Sri Lanka), Vol. XV, No. 2 (July 1997), p. 209.

32. Mohamed Suffian bin Hashim, "Problems and Issues of Higher Education Development in Malaysia," *Development of Higher Education in Southeast Asia*, edited by Yip Yat Hoong, Table 8, pp. 63, 64.

33. *Mid-Term Review of the Second Malaysia Plan, 1971–1975*, p. 85.

34. Tai Yoke Lin, "Inter-Ethnic Restructuring in Malaysia, 1970–1980: The Employment Perspective," *From Independence to Statehood: Managing Ethnic Conflict in Five African and Asian States*, edited by Robert B. Goldmann and A. Jeyaratnam Wilson (London: Frances Pitner, Ltd., 1984), p. 50.

35. *Ibid.*, p. 349.

36. *Ibid.*, p. 352.

37. *Ibid.*, p. 349.

38. Michael E. Brown and Sumit Ganguly, editors, *Government Policies and Ethnic Relations in Asia and the Pacific*, p. 259.

39. *Fourth Malaysia Plan, 1981–85* (Kuala Lumpur: National Printing Department, 1981), p. 350.

40. *Ibid.*, pp. 490–491.

41. *Ibid.*, p. 489.

42. K. S. Jomo, "Whither Malaysia's New Economic Policy," *Pacific Affairs*, Vol. 63, No. 4 (Winter, 1990–1991), p. 475.

43. Michael E. Brown and Sumit Ganguly, editors, *Government Policies and Ethnic Relations in Asia and the Pacific*, pp. 257-258.

44. In defending his change in policy, Prime Minister Mahathir said, "We can't let the efficiency and capability of our people be lower than those of other countries," *Deutsche Presse-Agentur,* June 20, 1995 on-line, which also reported "declining levels of attainment in science and technology" and that "many employers now prefer graduates with foreign degrees. At the very least, these youngsters usually have a good command in English." The *Financial Times* of London likewise reported that "a lack of skilled labour is identified by foreign investors" as "the single biggest problem in an otherwise attractive business environment" in Malaysia, and that foreign businesses were paying substantial pay increases to get and retain skilled engineers. *Financial Times,* June 19, 1996, on-line.

45. The Economist Intelligence Unit, *Malaysia, Brunei,* p. 15.

46. Ishak Shari, "Economic Growth and Income Inequality in Malaysia, 1971-1995," *Journal of Asia Pacific Economy,* Vol. 5, No. 1 (2000), p. 113.

47. *Ibid.,* pp. 119, 120.

48. Ishak Shari, "Economic Growth and Income Inequality in Malaysia, 1971-95," *Journal of Asia Pacific Economy,* Vol. 5, No. 1 (2000), 114; Edmund Terence Gomez, *Chinese Business in Malaysia: Accumulation, Accommodation and Ascendance* (Honolulu: University of Hawaii Press, 1999), p. 69.

49. Edmund Terence Gomez, *Chinese Business in Malaysia,* p. 70.

50. Harold A. Crouch, *Government and Society in Malaysia,* p. 186.

51. Mavis Puthucheary, "Public Policies Relating to Business and Land, and the Impact on Ethnic Relations in Peninsular Malaysia," *From Independence to Statehood,* edited by Robert B. Goldmann and A. Jeyaratnam Wilson, p. 163.

52. *Ibid.,* p. 164.

53. Mahathir bin Mohamad, *The Malay Dilemma* (Singapore: Asia Pacific Press, 1970), p. 44.

54. *Eighth Malaysia Plan 2001-2005* (Kuala Lumpur, Malaysia: Economic Planning Unit, 2001), p. 84.

55. *Seventh Malaysia Plan 1996-2000* (Kuala Lumpur: Economic Planning Unit, 1996), p. 86.

56. Donald R. Snodgrass, *Inequality and Economic Development in Malaysia,* p. 107.

57. Gordon P. Means, "Ethnic Preference Policies in Malaysia,"

Ethnic Preference and Public Policy in Developing States, edited by Neil Nevitte and Charles H. Kennedy, p. 105.

58. Tai Yoke Lin, "Ethnic Restructuring in Malaysia, 1979–80: The Employment Perspective," *From Independence to Statehood,* edited by Robert B. Goldmann and A. Jeyaratnam Wilson, p. 48.

59. *Ibid.,* p. 50.

60. *Fourth Malaysia Plan, 1981–1985,* p. 349.

61. Michael E. Brown and Sumit Ganguly, editors, *Government Policies and Ethnic Relations in Asia and the Pacific,* p. 234.

62. Tania Li, *Malays in Singapore: Culture, Economy, and Ideology* (Singapore: Oxford University Press, 1989), p. 115.

63. *Ibid.,* p. 134.

64. *Ibid.*

65. "Our Malays are Happier Than Yours," *The Economist,* February 3, 2001, p. 43.

66. Donald L. Horowitz, *Ethnic Groups in Conflict,* p. 670.

67. "Not One But Two New Malay Dilemmas," *Straits Times* (Singapore), August 1, 2002, downloaded from the Internet.

68. "Mahathir's Change of Heart?" *Business Week* (International editions), July 29, 2002, p. 20.

69. Government of Malaysia, *The Sixth Malaysia Plan 1991–1995* (Kuala Lumpur: National Printing Department of Malaysia, 1991), p. 3; *Seventh Malaysia Plan 1996–2000* (Kuala Lumpur: Percetakan Nasional Malaysia Berhad, 1996), p. 69.

70. Gordon P. Means, "Ethnic Preference Policies in Malaysia," *Ethnic Preference and Public Policy in Developing States,* edited by Neil Nevitte and Charles H. Kennedy, p. 114.

71. "Discriminating Policies," *Wall Street Journal,* September 11, 2000, p. A44.

72. "Race-based Awarding of Contracts Hurting Malaysia," *The Straits Times* (Singapore), January 8, 2002, p. 14 (on-line).

CHAPTER 4: AFFIRMATIVE ACTION IN SRI LANKA

1. One riot between Muslims and Hindus in 1915 was the only blemish on this record in the first half of the twentieth century.

2. K. M. de Silva, "Historical Survey," *Sri Lanka: A Survey,* edited by K. M. de Silva (Honolulu: The University Press of Hawaii, 1977), p. 84.

3. S. J. Tambiah, "Ethnic Representation in Ceylon's Higher

Administrative Service, 1870–1946," *University of Ceylon Review,* April–July 1955, pp. 127, 128.

4. *Ibid.,* p. 130.

5. K. No. O. Dharmadasa, *Language, Religion, and Ethnic Assertiveness: The Growth of Sinhalese Nationalism in Sri Lanka* (Ann Arbor: University of Michigan Press, 1992), p. 228.

6. S. J. Tambiah, "Ethnic Representation in Ceylon's Higher Administrative Services, 1870–1946," *University of Ceylon Review,* Vol. 13 (1955), p. 130.

7. W. Ivor Jennings, "Race, Religion and Economic Opportunity in the University of Ceylon," *University of Ceylon Review,* November 1944, p. 2.

8. S. J. Tambiah, "Ethnic Representation in Ceylon's Higher Administrative Service, 1870–1946," *University of Ceylon Review,* April–July 1955, pp. 125–136.

9. K. No. O. Dharmadasa, *Language, Religion, and Ethnic Assertiveness,* p. 242.

10. Chandra Richard de Silva, "Sinhala-Tamil Ethnic Rivalry: The Background," *From Independence to Statehood: Managing Ethnic Conflict in Five African and Asian States,* edited by Robert B. Goldmann and A. Jeyaratnam Wilson (London: Frances Pinter, Ltd., 1984), p. 116. See also Chandra Richard de Silva, "Sinhala-Tamil Relations and Education in Sri Lanka: University Admissions Issue — The First Phase," *Ibid.,* p. 136.

11. S. W. R. de A. Samarasinghe, "Ethnic Representation in Central Government Employment and Sinhala-Tamil Relations in Sri Lanka: 1948–81," *Ibid.,* p. 176.

12. *Ibid.,* p. 177.

13. C. Kondapi, *Indians Overseas 1838–1949* (New Delhi: Oxford University Press, 1951), p. 344.

14. H. P. Chattopadhyaya, *Indians in Sri Lanka: A Historical Study* (Calcutta: O.P.S. Publishers, Pvt., Ltd., 1979), pp. 143, 144, 146.

15. C. Kondapi, *Indians Overseas 1838–1949,* pp. 344–347.

16. Walter Schwarz, *Tamils of Sri Lanka* (London: Minority Rights Group, 1983), p. 5.

17. Robert N. Kearney, *Communalism and Language in the Politics of Ceylon* (Durham: Duke University Press, 1967), pp. 70–72.

18. Robert N. Kearney, "Sinhalese Nationalism and Social Conflict in Ceylon," *Pacific Affairs,* Summer 1964, pp. 125–128.

19. Robert N. Kearney, *Communalism and Language in the Politics of Ceylon,* pp. 80–81; William McGowan, *Only Man is Vile: The*

Tragedy of Sri Lanka (New York: Farrar, Straus and Giroux, 1992), pp. 149–58.

20. William McGowan, *Only Man is Vile*, pp. 158–161.

21. Chandra Richard de Silva, "Sinhala-Tamil Relations and Education in Sri Lanka: The University Admissions Issue—The First Phase, 1971–7," *From Independence to Statehood*, edited by Robert B. Goldmann and A. Jeyaratnam Wilson, p. 138. See also p. 127.

22. Robert N. Kearney, "Sinhalese Nationalism and Social Conflict in Ceylon," *Pacific Affairs*, Summer 1964, p. 130.

23. K. M. de Silva, "University Admissions and Ethnic Tension in Sri Lanka, 1977–82," *From Independence to Statehood*, edited by Robert B. Goldmannn and A. Jeyaratnam Wilson, p. 98.

24. Robert N. Kearney, "Sinhalese Nationalism and Social Conflict in Ceylon," *Pacific Affairs*, Summer 1964, p. 135.

25. Chandra Richard de Silva, "Sinhala-Tamil Ethnic Rivalry: The Background," *From Independence to Statehood*, edited by Robert B. Goldmann and A. Jeyaratnam Wilson, p. 121.

26. Robert N. Kearney, *Communalism and Language in the Politics of Sri Lanka*, pp. 84–86.

27. K. M. de Silva, "University Admissions and Ethnic Tension in Sri Lanka, 1977–82," *From Independence to Statehood;* edited by Robert B. Goldmann and A. Jeyaratnam Wilson, pp. 100–101.

28. Chandra Richard de Silva, "Sinhala-Tamil Relations and Education in Sri Lanka: The University Admissions Issue—the First Phase, 1971–7," *Ibid.*, pp. 128–131.

29. Walter Schwarz, *The Tamils of Sri Lanka*, p. 6.

30. S. J. Tambiah, *Sri Lanka: Ethnic Fratricide and the Dismantling of Democracy* (Delhi: Oxford University Press, 1986), pp. 20–21, 26.

31. *Ibid.*, p. 20.

32. William McGowan, *Only Man is Vile*, p. 97.

33. *Ibid.*, p. 98.

34. "Sri Lanka Confirms Report of Army Slayings," *New York Times*, August 7, 1983, Section 1, p. 5.

35. "The Unloveliness of Civil War," *The Economist*, August 18, 1984, p. 27.

36. "India and the Tamils," *The Economist*, January 19, 1985, p. 35.

37. K. M. de Silva, *Sri Lanka: Ethnic Conflict, Management and Resolution* (Kandy, Sri Lanka: International Centre for Ethnic Studies, 1996), p. 22.

38. *Ibid.*, p. 43.

39. Mervyn De Silva, "Sri Lanka rebels defy Indian force, mediation," *The Christian Science Monitor*, July 21, 1988, p. 9.

40. D. John Grove, "Restructuring the Cultural Division of Labor in Malaysia and Sri Lanka," *Comparative Political Studies*, July 1986, pp. 190–193.

41. Celia W. Dugger, "Endless War Again Laps at Sri Lankan City," *New York Times*, September 16, 2000, p. A1.

42. Chari Lata Joshi, "Try Again," *Far Eastern Economic Review*, December 20, 2001, p. 24.

43. Barbara Crossette, "The War on Terror Points a Country Toward Peace," *New York Times*, March 3, 2002, Section 4, p. 4.

44. "Tamil Rebels Yield in Talks with Sri Lanka," *New York Times*, November 4, 2002, p. A9.

CHAPTER 5: AFFIRMATIVE ACTION IN NIGERIA

1. Larry Diamond, *Class, Ethnicity and Democracy in Nigeria: The Failure of the First Republic* (Syracuse: Syracuse University Press, 1988), p. 22. These data are based on the censuses taken by colonial authorities in the decade preceding independence, rather than on the 1963 census, which was challenged and has been embroiled in controversy ever since. No subsequent census was held, due to the interethnic polarization. See *Ibid.*, Chapter 5.

2. Olatunde Bayo Lawuyi, "Ethnicity, Political Leadership and the Search for a Stable Nigerian Society," *Scandinavian Journal of Development Alternatives*, September–December 1992, p. 131.

3. William Easterly and Ross Levine, "Africa's Growth Tragedy: Policies and Ethnic Divisions," *Quarterly Journal of Economics*, November 1997, p. 1224.

4. Harold D. Nelson, *Nigeria: A Country Study* (Washington: U.S. Government Printing Office, 1982), p. 4.

5. P. T. Bauer, *West African Trade: A Study of Competition, Oligopoly and Monopoly in a Changing Economy* (Cambridge: Cambridge University Press, 1954), p. 7.

6. "The Ibo, who today play an important part in Nigerian trade, were in an almost savage state as recently as 1910." P. T. Bauer, *West African Trade: A Study of Competition, Oligopoly and Monopoly in a Changing Economy* (Cambridge: Cambridge University Press, 1954), p. 7. In earlier centuries, the Ibos were often enslaved by other tribes. Robert Reinhart, "Historical Setting," *Nigeria: A Country Study*, edited by Harold D. Nelson (Washington: Government Printing Office), p. 16.

7. Larry Diamond, *Class, Ethnicity and Democracy in Nigeria*, p. 26.

8. James S. Coleman, *Nigeria: Background to Nationalism* (Los Angeles: University of California Press, 1971), p. 142.

9. Donald L. Horowitz, *Ethnic Groups in Conflict* (Berkeley: University of California Press, 1985), pp. 448, 451.

10. Northern Nigeria, *Statistical Yearbook 1965* (Kaduna: Ministry of Economic Planning, 1965), pp. 40–41.

11. Robert Nelson and Howard Wolpe, *Nigeria: Modernization and Politics of Communalism* (East Lansing: Michigan State University, 1971), p. 127; Bernard Nkemdirim, "Social Change and the Genesis of Conflict in Nigeria," *Civilizations*, Vol. 25, Nos. 1–2 (1975), p. 94; Okwudiba Nnoli, *Ethnic Politics in Nigeria* (Enugu, Nigeria: Fourth Dimension Publishers, 1978), p. 64.

12. J. A. A. Ayoade, "The Federal Character Principle and the Search for National Integration," *Federalism and Political Restructuring in Nigeria* (Ibadan, Nigeria: Spectrum Books, 1999), p. 111.

13. Larry Diamond, *Class, Ethnicity and Democracy in Nigeria*, p. 50.

14. Kunlke Amuwo et al., *Federalism and Political Restructuring in Nigeria* (Ibadan, Nigeria: Spectrum Books, 1999), p. 53.

15. *Ibid.*, 52.

16. John A. A. Ayoade, "Ethnic Management of the 1979 Nigerian Constitution," *Canadian Review of Studies in Nationalism*, Spring 1987, p. 127.

17. Kunlke Amuwo et al., *Federalism and Political Restructuring in Nigeria*, p. 54.

18. Sarah Kenyon Lischer, "Causes of Communal War: Fear and Feasibility," *Studies in Conflict & Terrorism*, Vol. 22 (1999), p. 340.

19. Kunlke Amuwo et al., *Federalism and Political Restructuring in Nigeria*, pp. 58–59.

20. David Lamb, *The African* (New York: Random House, 1982), p. 308.

21. *Ibid.*, p. 309.

22. John A. A. Ayoade, "Ethnic Management in the 1979 Nigerian Constitution," *Canadian Review of Studies in Nationalism*, Spring 1987, p. 140.

23. Barbara Crossette, "Survey Ranks Nigeria as Most Corrupt Nation," *New York Times*, August 3, 1997, International Section, p. 3.

24. Larry Diamond, *Class, Ethnicity and Democracy in Nigeria*, p. 311; John Kraus, "Economic Adjustment and Regime Creation in Nigeria," *Current History*, May 1999, p. 234.

25. A. Bamisaiye, "Ethnic Politics as an Instrument of Unequal

Socio-Economic Development in Nigeria's First Republic," *African Notes* (Nigeria), Vol. 6, No. 2, 1970–71, p. 99.

26. Okwudiba Nnoli, "Ethnic and Regional Balancing in Nigerian Federalism," *Foundations of Nigerian Federalism: 1960–1995*, edited by J. Isawa Elaigwu and R. A. Akindele (Abuja, Nigeria: National Council on Intergovernmental Relations, 1996), p. 234.

27. *Ibid.*, p. 235.

28. *Ibid.*, pp. 235–236.

29. Kola Olugbade, "The Nigerian State and the Quest for a Stable Polity," *Comparative Politics*, April 1992, p. 299.

30. Obi Igwara, "Dominance and Difference: Rival Visions of Ethnicity in Nigeria," *Ethnic and Racial Studies*, January 2001, p. 90.

31. Sarah Kenyon Lischer, "Causes of Communal War: Fear and Feasibility," *Studies in Conflict & Terrorism*, Vol. 22 (1999), pp. 6, 340.

32. Obi Igwara, "Dominance and Difference: Rival Visions of Ethnicity in Nigeria," *Ethnic and Racial Studies*, Vol. 24, No. 1 (January 2001), p. 88.

33. Quoted in *Ibid.*, p. 87.

34. "Nigeria: Government to Set Up National Security Commission," Africa News Service, October 1, 2001.

35. "Thousands Flee Ethnic Blood-letting," *The Australian*, February 6, 2002, p. 10.

36. "Country Report: Nigeria," The Economist Intelligence Unit (London, 2002), p. 13.

37. "Country Report Nigeria," The Economist Intelligence Unit London: The Economist Intelligence Unit, 2002), p. 14.

38. Okwudiba Nnoli, *Ethnic Politics in Nigeria*, p. 245.

39. See, for example, *Ibid.*, pp. 224–227.

40. Okwudiba Nnoli, "Ethnic and Regional Balancing in Nigerian Federalism," *Foundations of Nigerian Federalism: 1960–1995*, edited by J. Isawa Elaigwu and R. A. Akindele, pp. 227–228.

41. Eghosa E. Osaghac, "Managing Multiple Minority Problems in a Divided Society," *Journal of Modern African Studies*, Vol. 36, No. 1 (1998), p. 11.

CHAPTER 6: AFFIRMATIVE ACTION IN THE UNITED STATES

1. See, for example, Peter Schmidt, "How Michigan Won Corporate Backing for Its Defense of Affirmative Action," *Chronicle of Higher Education*, November 24, 2000, pp. A21–22.

2. Steven J. Novak, "The Real Takeover of the BIA: The Prefer-

ential Hiring of Indians," *Journal of Economic History*, Vol. L, No. 3 (September 1990), pp. 639-654.

3. U.S. Bureau of the Census, *Historical Statistics of the United States: Colonial Times to 1970* (Washington, D.C.: U.S. Government Printing Office, 1975), p. 133; U.S. Bureau of the Census, "Marital Status and Living Arrangements: March 1992," *Current Population Reports*, Series P-20, No. 468 (Washington: Government Printing Office, 1993) pp. 1, 2.

4. U.S. Bureau of the Census, *Historical Statistics of the United States: Colonial Times to 1970*, p. 381.

5. Stephan Thernstrom and Abigail Thernstrom, *America in Black and White: One Nation, Indivisible* (New York: Simon & Schuster, 1997), p. 233.

6. *Ibid.*, p. 79.

7. Daniel P. Moynihan, "Employment, Income, and the Ordeal of the Negro Family," *Daedalus*, Fall 1965, p. 752.

8. Stephan Thernstrom and Abigail Thernstrom, *America in Black and White*, p. 233.

9. Jonathan J. Bean, *Big Government and Affirmative Action: The Scandalous History of the Small Business Administration* (Lexington: University of Kentucky Press, 2001), p. 79; Terry Eastland, *Ending Affirmative Action: The Case for Colorblind Justice* (New York: Basic Books, 1996), pp. 139, 177-178.

10. William G. Bowen and Derek Bok, *The Shape of the River: Long-Term Consequences of Considering Race in College and University Admissions* (Princeton: Princeton University Press, 1998), p. 11.

11. Terry Eastland, *Ending Affirmative Action*, pp. 17-18, 139.

12. Bob Zelnick, *Backfire: A Reporter's Look at Affirmative Action* (Washington: Regnery Publishing, 1996), pp. 299-300.

13. George R. La Noue, "Discrimination in Public Contracting," *Beyond the Color Line*, edited by Abigail Thernstrom and Stephan Thernstrom (Stanford: Hoover Institution Press, 2002), pp. 209-210.

14. Donald L. Bartlett and James B. Steele, "Wheel of Fortune," *Time*, December 16, 2002, p. 47.

15. U.S. Equal Employment Opportunity Commission, *Legislative History of Titles VII and XI of Civil Rights Act of 1964* (Washington: U.S. Government Printing Office, no date), p. 3006.

16. *Ibid.*, p. 3005.

17. *Ibid.*

18. The present writer conducted the first summer program to

prepare black college students for postgraduate study in economics back in 1968. This was affirmative action only in the generic sense, for the end-results were assessed by administering standardized tests that were in general use for testing others who were seeking to do postgraduate work in economics.

19. Nathan Glazer, *Affirmative Discrimination* (New York: Basic Books, 1975), p. 49.

20. U.S. Equal Employment Opportunity Commission, *Legislative History of Titles VII and XI of Civil Rights Act of 1964*, pp. 3133–3134.

21. *Ibid.*, pp. 3130, 3131.

22. *Ibid.*, pp. 3136, 3160, 3161.

23. Quoted in Hugh Davis Graham, *The Civil Rights Era: Origins and Development of National Policy 1960–1972* (New York: Oxford University Press, 1990), p. 387.

24. See, for example, Nathan Glazer, *Affirmative Discrimination: Ethnic Inequality and Public Policy* (New York: Basic Books, 1975), p. 57.

25. *United Steelworkers of America v. Weber*, 443 U.S. 193 (1979), at 207n7, 222.

26. Harry Holzer and David Neumark, "Assessing Affirmative Action," *Journal of Economic Literature*, Vol. XXXVII (September 2000), p. 487.

27. Dinesh D'Souza, *The End of Racism: Principles for a Multiracial Society* (New York: The Free Press, 1995), pp. 306–307.

28. Ron Nissimov, "Students Run into 'Top 10 Percent Law,'" *Houston Chronicle*, June 4, 2000, pp. A1 ff.

29. See, for example, Daniel Golden, "To Get Into UCLA, It Helps to Face 'Life Challenges,'" *Wall Street Journal*, July 12, 2002, pp. 1ff.

30. John B. Parrish, "Professional Womanpower as a National Resource," *Quarterly Review of Economics and Business*, February 1961, p. 58.

31. Beverly L. Johnson, "Marital and Family Characteristics of the Labor Force, March 1979," *Monthly Labor Review*, April 1980, p. 51.

32. Diana Furchtgott-Roth and Christine Stolba, *Women's Figures: An Illustrated Guide to the Economic Progress of Women in America* (Washington: American Enterprise Institute, 1999), pp. 85, 86.

33. U.S. Bureau of the Census, *Current Population Reports*, Series P-60, No. 133 (Washington, D.C.: U.S. Government Printing Office, 1982), p. 3.

34. Diana Furchtgott-Roth and Christine Stolba, *Women's Figures* (1999 edition), p. 86.

35. John B. Parrish, "Professional Womanpower as a Soviet Resource," *Quarterly Review of Economics and Business*, Autumn 1964, p. 60. See also Diana Furchtgott-Roth and Christine Stolba, *Women's Figures*, p. 57.

36. Helen S. Astin, "Career Profiles of Women Doctorates," *Academic Women on the Move*, edited by Alice S. Rossi and Anne Calderwood (New York: Russell Sage Foundation, 1973), p. 153.

37. U.S. Bureau of the Census, *Historical Statistics of the United States, Colonial Times to 1970* (Washington, D.C.: U.S. Government Printing Office, 1976), p. 49.

38. "The Economic Role of Women," *The Economic Report of the President, 1973* (Washington, D.C.: U.S. Government Printing Office, 1973), p. 103.

39. Thomas Sowell, *Affirmative Action Reconsidered* (Washington, D.C.: American Enterprise Institute, 1975), pp. 32, 33.

40. John M. McDowell, "Obsolescence of Knowledge and Career Publication Profiles: Some Evidence of Differences Among Fields in Costs of Interrupted Careers," *American Economic Review*, Vol. 72, No. 4 (September 1982), p. 761.

41. Diana Furchtgott-Roth and Christine Stolba, *Women's Figures*, p. 33.

42. See, for example, the data in Thomas Sowell, *The Vision of the Anointed: Self-Congratulation as a Basis for Social Policy* (New York: Basic Books, 1995), pp. 38–40; *idem, Civil Rights*, pp. 91–108; Chinhui Juhn, *Relative Wage Trends, Women's Work, and Family Income* (Washington: American Enterprise Institute, 1996).

43. See U.S. Bureau of the Census, *Income, Poverty, and Wealth in the United States: A Chart Book*, Current Population Reports, Series P-60, No. 179 (Washington: U.S. Government Printing Office, 1992), p. 8.

44. Diana Furchtgott-Roth and Christine Stolba, *Women's Figures*, p. 92.

45. U.S. Bureau of the Census, *Income, Poverty, and Wealth in the United States: A Chart Book*, Current Population Reports, Series P-60, No. 179 (Washington: U.S. Government Printing Office, 1992), p. 8.

46. Bob Zelnick, *Backfire*, p. 300.

47. *Ibid.*, pp. 301–302.

48. Bernard E. Anderson, *The Negro in the Public Utilities* (Philadelphia: University of Pennsylvania Press, 1970), pp. 65, 76–77, 78.

49. *Ibid.*, pp. 92, 96.

50. *Ibid.*, pp. 88, 96.

51. *Ibid.*, pp. 105–106.

52. *Ibid.*, pp. 97–99.

53. *Ibid.*, p. 195.

54. Michael R. Winston, "Through the Back Door, Academic Racism and the Negro Scholar in Historical Perspective," *Daedalus,* Vol. 100, No. 3 (Summer 1971), pp. 695, 705.

55. As late as the 1960s, I can recall being interviewed for academic appointments that would have made me the first black professor at American University in Washington and at the University of Virginia in Charlottesville — and actually being appointed as the first black professional at the U.S. Bureau of the Budget, forerunner of today's Office of Management and Budget.

56. Bob Zelnick, *Backfire,* pp. 58–60.

57. Peter Schmidt, "How Michigan Won Corporate Backing for Its Defense of Affirmative Action," *The Chronicle of Higher Education,* November 24, 2000, p. A21.

58. See, for example, Robert Klitgaard, *Choosing Elites: Selecting the "Best and the Brightest" at Top Universities and Elsewhere* (New York: Basic Books, 1985), pp. 104–115; Richard J. Herrnstein and Charles Murray, *The Bell Curve: Intelligence and Class Structure in American Life* (New York: The Free Press, 1994), pp. 280–281; Arthur R. Jensen, "Selection of Minority Students in Higher Education," University of Toledo Law Review, Spring–Summer 1970, pp. 440, 443; Donald A. Rock, "Motivation, Moderators, and Test Bias," *Ibid.,* pp. 536, 537; Ronald L. Flaugher, *Testing Practices, Minority Groups and Higher Education: A Review and Discussion of the Research* (Princeton: Educational Testing Service, 1970), p. 11; Arthur R. Jensen, *Bias in Mental Testing* (New York: The Free Press, 1980), pp. 479–490.

59. Iham Kim and Anthony R. Miles, "Why Affirmative Action Works at Michigan," *The Chronicle of Higher Education,* April 20, 2001, pp. B13–B14.

60. Mary Gibson Hundley, *The Dunbar Story (1875–1955)* (New York: Vantage Press, 1965), p. 75.

61. John H. McWhorter, *Losing the Race: Self-Sabotage in Black America* (New York: The Free Press, 2000), Chapters 3, 4. A later empirical study which seems to confirm McWhorter's thesis is John Ogbu, *Black American Students in an Affluent Suburb: A Study of Academic Disengagement* (Mahwah, NJ: Lawrence Erlbaum Associates, 2003).

62. Eric A. Hanushek, et al., "New Evidence About Brown v. Board of Education: The Complex Effects of School Racial Composition on Achievement," National Bureau of Economic Research,

Working Paper 8741 (Cambridge, Massachusetts: National Bureau of Economic Research, 2002), Abstract.

63. Ellis B. Page and Timothy Z. Keith, "The Elephant in the Classroom: Ability Grouping and the Gifted," *Intellectual Talent: Psychometric and Social Issues,* edited by Camilla Persson Benbow and David Lubinski (Baltimore: The Johns Hopkins University Press, 1996), p. 208.

64. Robert Lerner and Althea K. Nagai, *Racial Preferences in Colorado Higher Education: Racial Preferences in Undergraduate Admissions at the Public Colleges and Universities of Colorado,* (Washington: Center for Equal Opportunity, no date), p. 9.

65. Stephen Cole and Elinor Barber, *Increasing Faculty Diversity: The Occupational Choices of High-Achieving Minority Students* (Cambridge, Massachusetts: Harvard University Press, 2003), p. 169.

66. See Clyde W. Summers, "Admission Policies of Labor Unions," *Quarterly Journal of Economics,* November 1946, pp. 66-107.

67. Clyde Summers, "Preferential Admissions: An Unreal Solution to a Real Problem," *University of Toledo Law Review,* Vol. 1970, Nos. 2 & 3 (Spring/Summer 1970), p. 380.

68. *Ibid.,* p. 384.

69. John H. Bunzel, "Affirmative Action Admissions: How it "Works' at Berkeley," *The Public Interest,* Fall 1988, pp. 124, 125.

70. Arthur Hu, "Minorities Need More Support," *The Tech* (M.I.T.), March 7, 1987, p. 8.

71. Charles J. Sykes, *The Hollow Men: Politics and Corruption in Higher Education* (Washington, D.C.: Regnery Gateway, 1990), p. 47n.

72. Robin Wilson, "Article Critical of Black Students' Qualifications Rails Georgetown U. Law Center," *The Chronicle of Higher Education,* April 24, 1991, pp. A33, A35.

73. Shelby Steele, *The Content of Our Character: A New Vision of Race in America* (New York: St. Martin's Press, 1990), p. 138.

74. See my *Inside American Education: The Decline, the Deception, the Dogmas* (New York: The Free Press, 1993), pp. 155-158, 162-163.

75. See, for example, "Racism, Cynicism, Musical Chairs," *The Economist,* June 25, 1988, pp. 30 ff.

76. Thomas Sowell, *Inside American Education,* p. 144.

77. See, for example, William Moore, Jr., and Lonnie H. Wagstaff, *Black Educators in White Colleges* (San Francisco: Jossey-Bass Publishing Co., 1974), pp. 130-131, 198.

78. Thomas Sowell, *Inside American Education,* pp. 132-133.

79. Thomas Sowell, "Affirmative Action Reconsidered," *Educa-*

tion: Assumptions versus History — Collected Papers (Stanford: Hoover Institution Press, 1986), pp. 83, 85–87.

80. Robert Klitgaard, *Choosing Elites,* p. 175.

81. Stephan Thernstrom and Abigail Thernstrom, "Reflections on the Shape of the River," *UCLA Law Review,* Vol. 46, No. 5 (June 1999), p. 1610n.

82. Bob Zelnick, *Backfire,* p. 125. See also Lino A. Graglia, "Professor Loewy's 'Diversity' Defense of Racial Preference: Defining Discrimination Away," *North Carolina Law Review,* April 1999, pp. 1513–1515.

83. Robert Klitgaard, *Choosing Elites,* p. 162.

84. Stephan Thernstrom and Abigail Thernstrom, "Reflections on the Shape of the River," *UCLA Law Review,* Vol. 46, No. 5 (June 1999), pp. 1586, 1611–1612.

85. This implicitly assumes that blacks are, or should be, represented by doctors, lawyers, etc., of their own race, when there is no evidence that blacks themselves want to limit their own access to professionals in this way.

86. Jeff Jacoby, "How Affirmative Action Can Be Fatal," *San Francisco Chronicle,* August 20, 1997, p. A21. See also *Ron Joseph v. Patrick Davis,* Before the Medical Board of California, Department of Consumer Affairs, State of California, Case No. 06-97-73596, OAH No. 1997050498 (June 17, 1997).

87. Julie Marquis, "Doctor Becomes Symbol in Affirmative Action Debate," *Los Angeles Times,* September 2, 1997, pp. 1 ff; Jeff Jacoby, "How Affirmative Action Can be Fatal," *San Francisco Chronicle,* August 20, 1997, p. A21.

88. Julie Marquis, "Liposuction Doctor Has License Revoked," *Los Angeles Times,* August 26, 1998, p. A21.

89. Thomas Sowell, *Black Education: Myths and Tragedies* (New York: David McKay, 1972), pp. 92–94.

90. Merill Sheils et al., "Minority Report Card," *Newsweek,* July 12, 1976, p. 74.

91. Lani Guinier, "College Should Take 'Confirmative Action' in Admissions," *The Chronicle of Higher Education,* December 14, 2001, p. B12.

92. See, for example, the praise cited in Stephan Thernstrom and Abigail Thernstrom, "Reflections on the Shape of the River," *UCLA Law Review,* Vol. 46, No. 5 (June 1999), p. 1586, note 12.

93. *Ibid.,* p. 1589.

94. *Ibid.,* pp. 1594, 1595.

95. *Ibid.*, p. 1603.

96. William G. Bowen and Derek Bok, *The Shape of the River,* p. xxx.

97. *Ibid.*, p. 61. See also p. 259.

98. *Ibid.*, p. 21.

99. Bob Zelnick, *Backfire,* p. 132.

100. Robert Lerner and Althea K. Nagai, *Racial Preferences in Colorado Higher Education,* pp. 6, 11.

101. Robert Lerner and Althea K. Nagai, *Racial Preferences in Medical Education: Racial and Ethnic Preferences in Admissions at Five Public Medical Schools* (Washington: Center for Equal Opportunity, no date), pp. 12–35.

102. Sally Satel, "Health and Medical Care," *Beyond the Color Line: New Perspectives on Race and Ethnicity in America,* edited by Abigail Thernstrom and Stephan Thernstrom (Stanford: Hoover Institution Press, 2002), p. 143.

103. William G. Bowen and Derek Bok, *The Shape of the River,* p. 259.

104. John Perazzo, *The Myths That Divide Us: How Lies Have Poisoned American Race Relations* (Briarcliff Manor: World Studies Books, 1998), pp. 183–184.

105. Alexander W. Astin, *What Matters in College? Four Critical Years Revisited* (San Francisco: Jossey-Bass, Inc., 1993), p. 326.

106. Tany Schevitz, " 'Little Fish in a Big Pond,' " *San Francisco Chronicle,* May 6, 2001, p. A17.

107. William G. Bowen and Derek Bok, *The Shape of gthe River,* p. 259.

108. See examples in Thomas Sowell, *Inside American Education,* pp. 106–108.

109. Tamar Jacoby "Color Bind," *New Republic,* March 29, 1999, p. 25.

110. Stephan Thernstrom and Abigail Thernstrom, "Reflections on the Shape of the River," *UCLA Law Review,* Vol. 46, No. 5 (June 1999), p. 1619.

111. Jonathan Peterson, "Clinton Calls for 'National Effort' to End Racism," *Los Angeles Times,* June 15, 1997, p. 1A.

112. Timm Herdt, "4,000 Rally to Protest Proposition 209," *Ventura County Star,* October 28, 1997, p. A3.

113. George F. Will, "Jesse Jackson Has It Backward," *Washington Post,* September 7, 1997, p. C7.

114. The California State University system enrolls roughly twice

as many students on its 23 campuses as the University of California system enrolls on its eight campuses.

115. UC Office of the President, Student Academic Services, OA&SA, REG004/006 and campus reports, Aprofo23/flowfrc 9402. See also Peter Schmidt, "U. of California Ends Affirmative Action," *The Chronicle of Higher Education*, May 25, 2001, p. A24; "Sweat, Not Blood," *The Economist*, April 20, 2002, p. 30.

116. Downloaded from Internet. Web address: http://www.calstate.edu/AS/stat_reports/1996-1997/

117. *Reporting Package for the Board of Regents*, February 2001, downloaded from the Internet.

118. The College Board, *SAT Scores for Each Ethnic Group by Highest Level of Parental Education, 1994* (Princeton), p. 16.

119. See James R. Flynn, *Asian Americans: Achievement Beyond IQ* (Hillsdale, NJ: Lawrence Erlbaum Associates, 1991).

120. See, for examples of such schools, Lance T. Izumi et al., *They Have Overcome: High-Poverty, High Performing Schools in California* (San Francisco: Pacific Research Institute, 2002), p. 9; Samuel Casey Carter, *No Excuses: Lessons from 21 High-Performing, High-Poverty Schools* (Washington: The Heritage Foundation, 2000), pp. 43-44; Thomas Sowell, "Patterns of Black Excellence," *The Public Interest*, Spring 1976, pp. 26-58.

121. For comparisons of Harlem and lower east side schools, see data cited in Thomas Sowell, "Assumptions versus History in Ethnic Education," *Education: Assumptions versus History*, p. 41. For the history of the black Washington high school which scored higher on standardized tests than two of the three white high schools in 1899, see Henry S. Robinson, "The M Street School," *Records of the Columbia Historical Society of Washington, D.C.*, Vol. LI (1984), p. 122. The identity of the schools involved is established in *Report of the Board of Trustees of Public Schools of the District of Columbia to the Commissioners of the District of Columbia: 1898-1899* (Washington: Government Printing Office, 1900), pp. 7, 11.

122. See, for example, Jonathan D. Glater, "Law Firms Are Slow in Promoting Minority Lawyers to Partner Role," *New York Times*, August 7, 2001, pp. 1ff.

CHAPTER 7: THE PAST AND THE FUTURE

1. Judith Warner, "France Goes Nutty for Parity: Same Difference," *New Republic*, March 28, 2001, p. 16.

2. Charles H. Kennedy, "Policies of Redistributional Preference in Pakistan," *Ethnic Preference and Public Policy in Developing States,* edited by Neil Nevitte and Charles H. Kennedy (Boulder, Colorado: Lynne Rienner Publishers, Inc., 1986), p. 79.

3. "A Sigh is Just a Sigh," *Editor & Publisher,* April 15, 2002, p. 8.

4. Charles H. Kennedy, "Policies of Redistributional Preference in Pakistan," p. 81.

5. Myron Weiner and Mary Fainsod Katzenstein, *India's Preferential Policies: Migrants, the Middle Classes, and Ethnic Equality* (Chicago: University of Chicago Press, 1981), p. 52.

6. Edmund Terrence Gomez, *Chinese Business in Malaysia: Accumulation, Ascendance, Accommodation* (Honolulu: University of Hawaii Press, 1999), p. 71.

7. Robert Klitgaard, *Elitism and Meritocracy in Developing Countries: Selection Policies for Higher Education* (Baltimore: Johns Hopkins University Press, 1986), pp. 19, 77; The College Board, *SAT Scores for Each Ethnic Group by Highest Level of Parental Education, 1994* (Princeton), p. 16.

8. Robert Klitgaard, *Elitism and Meritocracy in Developing Countries,* p. 77, 118; Charles H. Kennedy, "Policies of Redistributional Preference in Pakistan," *Ethnic Preference and Public Policy in Developing States,* edited by Neil Nevitte and Charles H. Kennedy, p. 78; Robert Obserst, "Policies of Ethnic Preference in Sri Lanka," *Ibid.,* p. 146.

9. Otto Klineberg, *Negro Intelligence and Selective Migration* (Westport, Ct.: Greenwood Press, 1974), p. 2.

10. James R. Flynn, "IQ Gains Over Time: Toward Finding the Causes," *The Rising Curve: Long-Time Gains in IQ and Related Measures* (Washington: American Psychological Association, 1998), pp. 25–66.

11. Donald R. Snodgrass, *Inequality and Economic Development in Malaysia* (Kuala Lumpur: Oxford University Press, 1980), p. 4.

12. Amy L. Freedman, "The Effect of Government Policy and Institutions on Chinese Overseas Acculturation: The Case of Malaysia," *Modern Asian Studies,* Vol. 35, No. 2 (2001), p. 416.

13. Martin Woollacott, "Malaysia's Elite Tips Scale Too Far in its Own Favor," *The Guardian,* March 2, 1995, p. 22 (on line).

14. Sumit Ganguly, "Ethnic Policies and Political Quiescence in Malaysia and Singapore," *Government Policies and Ethnic Relations in Asia and the Pacific,* edited by Michael E. Brown and Sumit Ganguly (Cambridge, Mass.: MIT Press, 1997), p. 262.

15. "As Economy Slows, 'Subprime Lending Looks Even Riskier," *Wall Street Journal,* August 16, 2001, p. A1.

16. Compare Eric Woodrum et al., "Japanese American Behavior: Its Types, Determinants and Consequences," *Social Forces*, June 1980, pp. 1237, 1238, and Daniel O. Price, *Changing Characteristics of the Negro Population* (Washington, D.C.: U.S. Government Printing Office, 1969), p. 45.

17. Herbert Barriner, Robert W. Gardner and Michael J. Levin, *Asian and Pacific Islanders in the United States* (New York: Russell Sage Foundation, 1995), p. 235.

18. See, for example, Paulette Thomas, "Blacks Can Face a Host of Trying Conditions in Getting Mortgages," *Wall Street Journal*, November 30, 1992, p. A8.

19. Rochelle Sharpe, "Losing Ground: In Latest Recession, Only Blacks Suffered Net Employment Loss," *Wall Street Journal*, September 14, 1993, p. 14.

20. John H. Bunzel, "Affirmative-Action Admission: How it 'Works' at U.C. Berkeley," *The Public Interest*, Fall 1988, p. 122.

21. National Center for Health Statistics, *Health, United States, 1990* (Hyattsville, Maryland: U.S. Public Health Service, 1991), p. 41.

22. Compare U.S. Bureau of the Census, 1990 Census of Population, *Asians and Pacific Islanders* (1990 CP-3-05), Table 5; U.S. Bureau of the Census, 1990 Census of Population, *Social and Economic Characteristics: United States* (1990 CP-2-1), Table 6. As of the year 2000, even the omnibus category "Asian and Pacific Islanders" had median household incomes about one fourth higher than that of whites. U.S. Bureau of the Census, Current Population Reports, *Money Income in the United States: 2000* (P60-213), p. 4. However, none of these data directly confronts the issue of group discrimination, since it is individuals who are either hired or not hired, promoted or not promoted, fired or not fired. Since households differ in size from one group to another, household income data do not even provide an accurate relative ranking of groups in personal income or per capita income. For example, Hispanics have higher household incomes than blacks but lower per capita incomes, (*Ibid.*, pp. 2, 4), indicating that Hispanic households contain more people.

23. Roger Sandall, *The Culture Cult: Designer Tribalism and Other Essays* (Boulder: Westview Press, 2001), p. 128.

24. Michael Ornstein, *Ethno-Racial Inequality in the City of Toronto: An Analysis of the 1996 Census* (Toronto: City Administrator's Office, 2002), p. 97.

25. *Ibid.*, pp. 88–90.

26. *Ibid.*, p. ii.

27. Tomoko Makabe, "The Theory of the Split Labor Market: A Comparison of the Japanese Experiment in Brazil and Canada," *Social Forces*, March 1981, p. 807.

28. Michael Ornstein, *Ethno-Racial Inequality in the City of Toronto*, p. 5.

29. *Ibid.*, pp. 92, 93.

30. See, for example, Marc Galanter, *Competing Equalities: Law and the Backward Classes in India* (Berkeley: University of California Press, 1984), p. xiv; Kunlke Amuwo et al., *Federalism and Political Restructuring in Nigeria* (Ibadan, Nigeria: Spectrum Books, 1999), pp. 108, 109, 115, 124; Government of Malaysia, *The Sixth Malaysia Plan 1991–1995* (Kuala Lumpur: National Printing Department of Malaysia, 1991), p. 3; *Seventh Malaysia Plan 1996–2000* (Kuala Lumpur: Economic Planning Unit, 1996), p. 69.

31. G. Y. H. Peiris, "Poverty, Development and Inter-Group Conflict in South Asia: Covariance and Causal Connections," *Ethnic Studies Report* (Sri Lanka), Vol. XVIII, No. 1 (January 2000), p. 24.

32. Charles H. Kennedy, "Policies of Redistributional Preference in Pakistan," *Ethnic Preference and Public Policy in Developing States*, edited by Neil Nevitte and Charles H. Kennedy, p. 87.

33. Marc Galanter, *Competing Equalities*, p. 562.

34. *Ibid.*, p. 367.

35. Roger Silverman, "Devils and Enemies," *Far Eastern Economic Review*, July 7, 1994, p. 13.

36. Stephan Thernstrom and Abigail Thernstrom, "Reflections on the Shape of the River," *UCLA Law Review*, Vol. 46, No. 5 (June 1999), p. 1622. See also Terry Eastland, *Ending Affirmative Action: The Case for Colorblind Justice* (New York: Basic Books, 1996), p. 87.

37. See, for example, Eastland, Thomas Sowell, *Inside American Education: The Decline, The Deception, The Dogmas* (New York: The Free Press, 1993) pp. 132–133.

38. Marc Galanter, *Competing Equalities*, p. 367.

39. David McLoughlin, "Lessons We Could All Learn," *The Dominion* (Wellington, New Zealand), November 22, 2000, p. 13.

40. Data from the College Board.

41. See, for example, John Ogbu, *Black American Students in an Affluent Suburb: A Study of Academic Disengagement* (Mahwah, NJ: Lawrence Erlbaum Associates, 2003); John McWhorter, *Losing the Race: Self-Sabotage in Black America* (New York: The Free Press, 2001).

42. As a scholarly study has put it: "Since *varnas* are taxonomic categories rather than functional groups, attempts to enumerate

their members have been unavailing." Marc Galanter, *Competing Equalities*, p. 11n.

43. Thomas Sowell, "Three Black Histories," *Essays and Data on American Ethnic Group*, edited by Thomas Sowell (Washington: The Urban Institute, 1978), pp. 7–64.

44. Robert Klitgaard, *Elitism and Meritocracy in Developing Countries*, pp. 102, 104.

45. David Karen, "Who Gets into Harvard? Selection and Exclusion at an Elite College," Ph.D. dissertation in sociology, Harvard University, 1985, pp. 139, 158a.

46. Marc Galanter, *Competing Equalities*, p. 448.

47. *Ibid.*, p. 447.

48. Keith Windschuttle, "The Fabrication of Aboriginal History," *The New Criterion*, Vol. 20, No. 1 (September 2001), pp. 41–49.

49. See, for example, "A Hard Lesson in Diversity: Chinese Americans Fight Lowell's Admissions Policy," *San Francisco Chronicle*, June 19, 1995, pp. A1ff.

50. Carl Brigham, *A Study of American Intelligence* (Princeton: Princeton University Press, 1923), p. 190.

51. See, for example, Suma Chitnis, "Positive Discrimination in India with Reference to Education," *From Independence to Statehood: Managing Ethnic Conflict in Five African and Asian States*, edited by ed. Robert B. Goldmann and A. Jeyaratnam Wilson (London: Frances Pinter, 1984), p. 36; Nancy Lubin *Labour and Nationalism in Soviet Central Asia: An Uneasy Compromise* (Princeton: Princeton University Press, 1984), pp. 120–121; Mohamed Suffian bin Hashim, "Problems and Issues of Higher Education Development in Malaysia," *Development of Higher Education in Southeast Asia: Problems and Issues*, edited by Yip Yat Hoong (Singapore: Regional Institute of Higher Education and Development, 1973), pp. 70–71; Chandra Richard de Silva, "Sinhala-Tamil Relations and Education in Sri Lanka: The University Admissions Issue — The First Phase, 1971–7," *From Independence to Statehood*, edited by Robert B. Goldmann and A. Jeyaratnam Wilson, pp. 125–146; Sammy Smooha and Yochanan Peres, "The Dynamics of Ethnic Equality: The Case of Israel," *Studies of Israeli Society*, edited by Ernest Krausz (New Brunswick: Transaction Books, 1980), p. 173; Thomas Sowell, "Ethnicity in a Changing America," *Daedalus*, Winter 1978, pp. 231–232; Thomas Sowell, *The Economics and Politics of Race*, pp. 139–140.

52. Tai Yoke Lin, "Inter-Ethnic Restructuring in Malaysia, 1970–1980," *From Independence to Statehood*, edited by Robert B. Goldmann

and A. Jeyaratnam Wilson, p. 57. See also Gordon P. Means, "Ethnic Preference Policies in Malaysia," *Ethnic Preference and Public Policy in Developing States,* edited by Neil Nevitte and Charles H. Kennedy, p. 114.

53. Kanya Adam, "The Politics of Redress: South African Style Affirmative Action," *Journal of African Studies,* Vol. 35, No. 2 (1997), p. 232.

Index